D1456772

**Human Services
in Industry**

54
136

Human Services in Industry

Dale A. Masi
Department of Health and
Human Services and
University of Maryland

WITHDRAWN

LexingtonBooks
D.C. Heath and Company
Lexington, Massachusetts
Toronto

Tennessee Tech. Library
Cookeville, Tenn.

322003

This book was written by Dr. Dale Masi in her private capacity. No official support or endorsement by the Department of Health and Human Services is intended or should be inferred.

Library of Congress Cataloging in Publication Data

Masi, Dale A.
   Human services in industry.

   Includes index.
   1. Welfare work in industry—United States. 2. Social service—United States. I. Title.
HD7654.M36   658.3'8'0973   81-47872
ISBN 0-669-05104-7   AACR2

Copyright © 1982 by D.C. Heath and Company

All rights reserved. No part of this publication may be reproduced or transmitted in any form or by any means, electronic or mechanical, including photocopy, recording, or any information storage or retrieval system, without permission in writing from the publisher.

Published simultaneously in Canada

Printed in the United States of America

International Standard Book Number: 0-669-05104-7

Library of Congress Catalog Card Number: 81-47872

*This book is dedicated to my son,
Eric L. Masi, who has the head of
a business man and the heart of a
social worker.*

Contents

List of Figures
and Tables

Figures

Tables

Preface

In the coming decades, the industrial world will pose one of the greatest challenges to the field of human services. This challenge could represent a major shift in the delivery of social programs from the community to the work place. Not since the community mental-health-center movement has any field of practice offered such opportunities for reaching people.

Because so many people are working, the field of human services involves bringing services to the people—namely, going to where the client is. With ever-increasing numbers of women working today, the majority of our adult population is in the work place. Convenience alone becomes one of the critical elements in reaching populations in need.

Duplicating in the work place, however, the same kind of services provided in the community would be a mistake. Concentration needs to be on innovative strategies such as the use of supervisory referrals, cost-effective programs, and other dimensions that are described in chapter 4. Appropriate training for industrial social workers requires a current knowledge of alcoholism and other drug-abuse problems, the work place, unions, and organizational development, to name various new areas.

As a social worker, the author singles out this profession particularly as one that has an appropriate role in the work place. There is no doubt that other human-service providers will find that a great deal of relevance exists to their fields, and what is said about social work in this volume is seen as applicable to other similar professions.

Professionals often raise questions of values regarding this endeavor. Is not one selling out to capitalism by working for a profit-making corporation? Capitalism is the way of U.S. life. Working in a company with social-work values does not necessarily represent a value conflict. Undoubtedly for those struggling with the free-enterprise system, this may be the case. One would need to think this issue through clearly for oneself before deciding to enter this field.

Confidentiality is another value issue that is raised. If one assumes that one's employment contract spells out the terms of practice, then there is little likelihood of difficulty. Today, the Privacy Act covers all federal employees and all employers with a contract of $2,500 or more with the federal government. Very few companies are not covered in this way. The act goes a very long way toward protecting the client. For example, critical elements are accessibility of records and defining who may have access to this information. It behooves a human-service provider to spell out these prerequisites before accepting a position. In cases for which accountability is asked, statistics that do not have to breach confidentiality are most acceptable. Industry is accustomed to businesslike procedures, and the social worker must provide statistics that can show where time and effort have gone without disclosing names.

Another challenge often posed to human-service providers is how one can work for a company. Is it not like serving two clients? This is true and it is foolhardy to say it is not. Social workers, except those in private practice, are also serving two clients—the agency as well as the individual client. Industry has a goal of producing a product, usually for profit, unless it is a question of nonprofit employers. Employees who are happy and well adjusted make for productive workers. There is no contradiction when an employer is concerned with producing a product as well as with developing programs for employees who suffer from problems that affect their job performance. For instance, studies show that 10 percent of the average work force are active alcoholics, 2-3 percent are drug addicts (illegal/legal drugs), and 6-7 percent are emotionally ill. This group's work performance is only 75 percent productive. At the Department of Health and Human Services, for example, this statistic means that of 160,000 employees, 28,000 are troubled employees performing at 75 percent effort. The average salary at this department is $18,000. This sum multiplied by the number of employees, multiplied by the 25 percent loss, gives us a cost of $128 million per annum that the department is losing in worker productivity. By helping the client with his or her alcohol, drug, or mental-health problem, one is clearly helping the employee as well as the goals of the company. Previous policies of firing employees without offering professional help are certainly not preferable and help neither the employee nor the employer.

The field of industrial social work is not necessarily appropriate for all human-service workers, but for those who are comfortable in a business setting, the questions of confidentiality and other value conflicts are surmountable. The positive aspects of this field are many. Later chapters in this book describe the many possible opportunities.

It is important to define industry. Broadly speaking, it refers to any employer. The federal government is the largest employer in the United States (6 million people) and is nonprofit. There are also universities, hospitals, and other nonprofit as well as not-for-profit enterprises. Without a doubt, however, industry does represent for the most part the profit-making enterprise.

This book does not represent a study of the concept of work itself. It starts off with the assumption that work is a positive, ego-reinforcing aspect of a person's life. Of course, some work situations may be counterproductive, but for the most part the given value at the outset is that work is a positive, not a negative. As the Joint Project on Industrial Social Work Education found, schools of social work, in their social-policy and human-behavior courses, need to give attention to this concept for all social workers (see chapter 10 for discussion).

Part I examines the structure of business. It describes two of its most essential parts—namely, personnel and unions. It also shows at the same time that social workers have potential roles in industry. Chapter 1 gives a review of the history of social workers in industry. Starting from 1917, it traces the sketchy background of social workers' sporadic experience in the work place. A theory of practice has not been conceptualized until today, and this book intends to define it. Chapter 2 points out that business has been providing a host of very important human services without the benefit of social workers. Beginning with workmen's compensation and social security, the chapter describes a variety of services—some mandatory, some optional. These services are usually administered in the personnel department so this department becomes a key focal point for social workers interested in being close to the heart of company-employee programs. Chapter 3 describes the way unions have ensured that their members have access to the appropriate social services. Besides showing the role of unions, it points out opportunities for social workers to be hired within the union framework.

Part II describes particular direct services that persons with human service skills can provide. Some psychiatrists and psychologists are becoming aware of the potential in this area, and they have one tremendous advantage over social workers—they do not carry a stigma. Social workers are still seen today as being synonymous with persons' giving money away in keeping with the bleeding-heart syndrome. The stigma problem will plague social workers for a long time and will continue to be one of their greatest impediments to penetrating industry. Chapter 4 covers direct services under mental-health counseling. It also describes a model of delivery of services unique to the work place. This chapter has particular relevance for caseworkers and counsellors. Chapter 5 discusses the fastest growing specialty in the industrial area—employee-assistance programs. Because this requires casework as well as community-organization skills, this field promises the most opportunity at this writing, if the providers have the specific training in alcoholism. Chapter 6 pictures the newly emerging area of social commitment that business is displaying. Community-organization training is ideal for this field, but at this stage the field has been virtually unexplored.

Part III looks at special populations in the work place, which provide another way to enter the field. Chapter 7 pictures the large staffing presently taking place in affirmative-action areas. Who better than social workers knows how to deal with special groups such as minorities and the handicapped? Again the potential remains virtually unexplored. Administration and social planning are ideal backgrounds for people who are directing these offices. Chapter 8 illustrates a very special area, the overseas-employee population. At this time few jobs are available, but multinational companies that are expanding their operations are creating new opportunities. This chapter again is closely related to chapters 4 and 5. Chapter 9 presents the long history of the social-work services provided by the American Red Cross and the U.S. Army, Navy, and Air Force. An incredible array of services are pictured, and for the social worker who is interested (male and female) in the military, career opportunities abound [see for example, Dale A. Masi, "Social Welfare Needs—Services of the Military" (Ann Arbor, Mich.: University Microfilms, 1965)].

Part IV looks at social-work education, a field for which the picture is quite bleak and very sparsely developed. Chapter 10 explains the Industrial Task Force, which was formed by the Council on Social Work Education to study this new field. Chapter 11 presents six typical case studies, each written by a practicing social worker in industry. The author is grateful to the authors of this chapter because she feels such studies fill a beginning need for professors interested in classroom teaching. Chapter 12 stands alone as the first presentation of European practice in this area. Social workers in Europe do not have the professional status of the U.S. social worker, and their education is at a very different level. Without a doubt, however, acceptance of social workers by industry in some European countries is a goal that is far ahead of U.S. acceptance.

This book does not intend to cover all areas of practice. For example, occupational health emerges as a significant development in the work place. Everything from the work environment, physical health, and mental illness is being considered by industry. Health promotion, sometimes called mental-wellness programs, are also starting in some companies. Another area for social-work practice exists in the banking field. Increasingly, social workers are being hired as trust consultants, especially for the elderly, the widowed, and specific bank customers who need a highly specialized and important service.

Many persons should be acknowledged for their part in making this book possible. Naming any, however, would be a slight to others since so many provided editorial assistance, secretarial services, as well as background research. I do want to recognize the students whom I trained and taught as part of the industrial project. They continued to provide me with the incentive to work in the field as well as to make this book a possibility for their successors to use for classes in industrial social work or human services.

Part I
Understanding the
Industrial System

1 The History of Occupational Social Work in the United States

Because it was partly a spin-off from nineteenth-century social-work models, and partly because it was a new discipline within the art of social work, industrial social work in the twentieth century evolved in an uneven manner. Industrial social work today occupies an increasingly important position in the field from both a professional and an educational point of view. This chapter describes this evolution and provides descriptions of early examples of industrial social work.

Recent developments in the practice of social work in the work world have introduced new challenges to the profession. The growing interest in this specialized practice is reflected by the greater numbers of practitioners in business settings, the proliferation of articles documenting these experiences, and the profession's recognition of this as an area of social-work practice to be studied and incorporated into professional social-work education. As Hellenbrand and Yasser point out, it is a fertile new frontier for practice although not necessarily a new territory. They suggest calling it rediscovered territory that can now be better appreciated and explored.[1]

The following history focuses on the delivery of services. One section of the social-work profession concerns itself with issues of social-welfare policy and programs as well as legislation that affects workers, employers, and unions. The tremendous growth of legislation during the 1930s is an example of its contribution. However, policies and programs are here referred to only with regard to the basic information that the industrial social worker needs to know, such as social security entitlements. This history follows the intent of the book, that is, describing the delivery of social services in the work place, including planning management consultation and social administration as well as counseling. This author perceives many opportunities for social-work skills to be utilized by employers. Thus the history paints a background against which this new expansion will occur. The social-policy dimensions of the occupational world are important, but the purpose of this book is to cover only the service aspects of industrial social work.

Some social workers are performing social services of a contemporary origin without a previous history per se. Positions in affirmative-action offices and organizational-development departments are examples of settings that social workers are just beginning to explore. Such exploratory positions are discussed in their own right, and it is premature to try to place them in the historical context of occupational social work.

3

This history refers to functions performed by trained social workers. It does not include services performed by personnel managers, nurses, union counselors, or others who may provide social services in their assigned tasks, but who have no specialized social-work skills or training.

There is no central source for assembling the history of this field of practice. What may appear to be gaps in time are actually periods empty of development. Regrettably, some experiences were never recorded. Efforts were made to reach all the people who were part of the history and/or who contributed to its documentation, and all of them graciously consented to telephone or personal interviews. An overview of the events offers a useful perspective to students and practitioners.

History

1900-1940

One of the earliest instances of social workers performing counseling and social services for employees in a work setting occurred at the Northern States Power Company in Minneapolis, Minnesota. An in-house employee-assistance program dealing with the complex human concerns of employees and dependents has been in existence since 1917, making it probably the longest running program in the country. A social worker, Ruth Gage Thompson, who had been involved in the settlement-house movement with Jane Adams, initiated the program. At that time, Northern States Power was a small, family-owned operation whose owner had a paternalistic caring attitude toward his employees.

The Northern States Power program was unusual. It preceded the development of personnel management and services, social legislation that was later passed to ensure employees' financial security, as well as several other types of hardship protection. Before the inception of the Northern States Power program, if an employer offered any advantages for employees beyond compensation, they usually included amenities such as chapels, nurseries, safety precautions, or health care.[2] The so-called welfare secretary often hired in the early twentieth century had various duties including hiring personnel; investigating complaints; overseeing cloak rooms, dining rooms, and rest rooms; and sometimes offering help with personal problems.[3] These secretaries most often came from religious or educational backgrounds.[4] At Northern States Power, Ruth Gage Thompson's previous training and experience particularly suited her to an industry in which, because of the high risks prevalent in the early days of electrical power, crises were not uncommon.[5] However, the welfare secretary was seldom trained to help employees cope with crisis situations.

The evolution of the position of welfare secretary refined the paternalism of many businesses. The emergence of the modern industrial social worker humanized and democratized that paternalism. The role was clearly an evolutionary one emerging from the earlier untrained welfare secretary.

We do not know how many programs staffed by social workers were in existence during this time. Others probably existed in industries where an obvious need was met innovatively. The program at Northern States Power continues today, furnishing a wide range of services. It is called the Social Resource Center and is headed by a social worker with a staff of twenty professionals that provides counseling, crisis intervention, and educational presentations. Linkage and referral, self-help programs, employee-activities programs, employee solicitations for such groups as the Red Cross and the United Way, and management consultation are other services provided.

About the same time as the Northern States Power program began, another program started in New York at Macy's Department Store, which was called the Department of Social Services. Social worker Elizabeth Evans, writing about the program in 1944, nearly thirty years after its inception, saw her role as a caseworker as having three sides: (1) informational, (2) societal, and (3) psychiatric. First, she believed that she and her counterparts in other urban businesses should provide employees with comprehensive information about social agencies and the health, recreational, and educational resources of the city. Second, she thought that caseworkers should be able to recognize when conditions in an employee's living situation required assistance through loans or financial grants. Finally, she expected an industrial social worker to offer personal counseling to employees about problems or goals. She was keenly aware of the need for social work to improve upon its image in order to make a contribution to the exciting and unlimited area of industrial social work.[6]

Annelise Miro in her 1956 study[7] noted that the period of World War I initiated the employment of social workers in industrial settings in both Europe and the United States. Because so much of the male work force was fighting the war, women were employed in larger numbers than ever before. Employers were sensitive to the need to help women adjust to and integrate into the occupational setting, as well as to help them maintain their social responsibilities as mothers and care providers. Because an increasing number of the work force was female, employers often found it helpful to hire females, and in some cases trained, social workers as personnel workers or supervisors. Though no specific documentation exists in historical records as to the numbers of social workers hired, Miro states that during World War I, "throughout the industrial settings then, social workers were frequently seen though they were never clearly recognized as such."[8]

Between 1920 and 1940, few new programs in which social workers served industry seem to have been instituted. The professionally trained social worker disappeared almost completely from the industrial setting after World War I. The subject did not disappear from the minds of theoreticians, however. Mary Van Kleeck, for example, director of the industrial studies at the Russell Sage Foundation, spoke to the National Conference on Social Work several times on the topic of labor and social work. In 1934, she discussed the common goals of labor and social work. She foresaw ample legitimate opportunities for social work and labor to work together, especially during times of unemployment and the Depression, for the common goal of maintaining standards of living for both individuals and communities.[9] In 1937, prior to the formulation of any social programs in labor, Van Kleeck forewarned the social-work profession of the importance of developing a new philosophy guided by a real understanding of the mass labor movement.[10]

1940-1970

World War II again created a climate in which the needs of millions of Americans who were demanding assistance could not be ignored. Companies, unions, and often the government responded to the obvious need for emotional and financial support of employees and dependents who were uprooted, overworked, and physically or emotionally handicapped by the war. Social-work services not only helped people adjust personally to the effects of the war but also enabled them to be more productive during a time when production was a critical common goal. A sense of unity prevailed as Americans joined together for the good of the country.

The most thoroughly documented account of social work by professionally trained social workers serving wartime needs is the joint project begun in 1943 by the National Maritime Union and the United Seaman's Service.[11] In *Social Work and Social Living*, Bertha C. Reynolds recounts her experience as a professional social worker with a staff of six others in the Personal Service Department of the National Maritime Union. It was apparent to the union that social-work services were needed when, by the spring of 1943, over 5,000 members had been killed at sea. The surviving crewmen and the family members of the deceased faced pressing and often overwhelming situations. Appropriate services included assisting members and families in financial distress to procure loans, ration books, unemployment or disability insurance, locating seamen stranded in foreign ports after rescue, counseling or making a proper referral for seamen who needed hospitalization, and assisting bereaved families.

Reynolds enthusiastically described the uniqueness, thrill, and challenge of working for a group that was at the same time the sponsor and client of the program. This aspect has turned out to be true throughout the subsequent history of industrial social work. It is crucial for the social worker to understand the philosophy and organizational structure of the particular setting. Reynolds believed that:

> Professional social workers coming into this setting would find an unhampered opportunity to use their skills and at the same time a challenge (which is the essence of professional skill) to adapt to the way of life, the culture, and mores of this particular sector of a great industry.[12]

Reflecting again on her experience with seamen, she admits:

> Yes, there were real differences in approach and in thinking when a social worker moved to serve an employed group in an essential industry. The principle of relating social work to its community was unchanged, but it was a community quite different.[13]

Reynolds also offered courses to officials of other unions such as the United Electrical Workers and the Fur Workers who were assigned to welfare counseling. Professional social workers at this time were joining together with several unions throughout the United States to sponsor counseling and referral services.[14]

The federal government began employee counseling in 1942. The Civil Service Commission issued its first departmental circular on the subject as recently as 10 July 1942. This statement was a report of the Committee on Employee Counseling of the Civil Service Commission and outlined the functions of a counseling service as follows:

> To deal with any situation represented by an employee or his supervisor which affects or is likely to affect his work productivity;

> To provide information as to housing and recreational resources, educational opportunities, budgeting, social agencies, church organizations, nutrition, medical and psychiatric facilities;

> To identify the problems of individual employees which need treatment by specialists;

> To discuss with employees who seek counsel the nature of their problems and to work out with the employees solutions to their problems;

> To counsel employees regarding various problems connected with their work: living and work conditions, health, recreation, education, and other phases of self-development;

> To refer employees to local recreational agencies outside the government;

> To keep in constant touch with personnel officers and operating officials regarding recruiting standards, placement problems, and the correction of unfavorable operating conditions;

To assist in the development and presentation of orientation, induction, and staff-development programs.[15]

In 1942, Stalley predicted that: Employee counseling in the federal service . . . may be one of [the] new frontiers in social work.[16]

People holding these positions came to be known as employee-relations specialists. With the exception of Social Security headquarters in Baltimore, which continues to fill the positions with social workers, personalists of various backgrounds filled and continue to fill these countless jobs throughout the federal system. Historically, this was a major loss for the growth of social work and other professional human-service providers. Employee-relations-specialists positions should be explored by social workers as appropriate for them.

The war affected all Americans, even those not directly related to wartime industry. In 1944, the J.L. Hudson Company, a department store in Detroit, established an employee-consultation center that provided counseling services to an employee population of about 15,000. From 1944 to 1966, four MSW social workers and three assistants consulted with supervisors about troubled employees and counseled employees directly. Another of their responsibilities was the evaluation of employees' requests for financial assistance and the recommendation for usage of Hudson Foundation monies. Foundation funds remain available today to employees in financial need. The employee-consultation center was closed in 1973 when the J.L. Hudson Company merged with the Dayton Company of Minneapolis, at which time, because of the interest of the directors of the Hudson Foundation and its financial backing, a contractual agreement was established in 1974 with the United Community Service, which provides counseling, information, and referral assistance to employees, thus maintaining the services.[17]

Another rather isolated example of industrial social work appeared in 1948 at the Prudential Life Insurance home office in Newark, New Jersey. A counseling center staffed by three psychologists and a social worker offered direct counseling services to 11,000 employees and consulted with executives on ways of handling personnel problems.[18]

In 1956, Annelise Miro made one of the earliest attempts to compile a historical perspective of industrial social work in her master's thesis. In that same year, the International Conference on Social Welfare focused its attention exclusively on industrialization and social work. Social workers from all over the world discussed the various effects industrialization was having on peoples' emotional and physical well-being, on their family and community life. At the conference, the social workers proposed that "social work within industry should not limit itself to combating human and social wrongs. Social work in industry should have as its goal helping management adapt industry to the human possibilities of the worker and for the worker to adapt himself to the necessities of industry."[19]

In 1958, at the Columbia University Graduate School of Social Work Alumni Conference, Herman Stein presented a paper titled, "Is There a Place for Social Work in Industry?" Stein differentiated between social *workers* in industry and social *work* in industry. He acknowledged the presence of social workers in business settings but stated that they were in most cases performing personnel, managerial, or other functions. "The presence of social workers who are so identified and whose functions are social-work functions is virtually unknown in this country."[20] Based on the state of the art at the time, Stein remained rather pessimistic: "I do not see social work in industry as being immediately on the horizon."[21] The words of caution are consistent with the issues that have been faced as social work has moved into the business world within the past ten years. For example, Stein stressed the importance of knowing organizational as well as psychological theory. He warned that moving into a foreign setting requires a receptive attitude on the part of the social-work profession to help alleviate the sense of isolation for the social workers that appears to be inevitable. He suggested that even with certain changes in attitude and knowledge base, it would still require a hard-selling job to industry and perhaps the development of several pilot projects for analysis and demonstration.

During World War II, social-work services became available to men and women in military careers. The programs developed for military workers were originally run by the American Red Cross (A.R.C.) under a congressional mandate. Eventually, each branch of the service assumed responsibility for administering most programs although the A.R.C. continues to provide many services. The programs that developed were aimed primarily at members of the military service although they have grown to include the members' families. (These programs are discussed separately in chapter 9.)

After World War II came a time of inactivity. However, one of today's most well-established counseling programs that is staffed by social workers was initiated then. In 1959, after using the services of a part-time consulting social worker, Polaroid Corporation in Cambridge, Massachusetts, hired a full-time social worker to provide employee counseling. The department, which has gradually grown to four full-time social workers, sees its functions to be individual counseling, consultation, sensing of stresses in the environment, group facilitation, and the initiation of special programs. The department serves as a training site for graduate students in social work.[22]

Between 1964 and 1968, the National Institute of Mental Health (NIMH) and the Rehabilitative Services Administration financed a special project at Columbia University called the Industrial Social Services Center.

The center continues today to be one of the better-known programs in industrial social work. Its programs are addressed in detail in chapter 4.

1970 to the Present

During the 1970s, hundreds of employee-counseling programs were begun, and various approaches to service delivery were created. Since 1969, for example, social workers have been employed at Kennecott Copper Corporation in Salt Lake City in a program called INSIGHT. This is a twenty-four-hour-per-day counseling program for employees and their families that addresses substance abuse, and family, marital, financial, and other social and emotional problems. This program, which has become the prototype for employee-assistance programs, serves as a training site for the University of Utah Graduate School of Social Work. Employee-assistance programs are discussed in chapter 5.

CNA Financial Corporation in Chicago hired a social worker in 1973 to develop and staff an employee-counseling program as a part of the medical clinic. Industries that have long maintained that good health care is a need and a right of their employees are considering mental health to be an important aspect of overall health care and are recognizing the expertise of social work in the field.[23] Northwestern Bell Telephone Company, which employs thousands of people throughout Iowa, recognized the need for counseling services as part of its medical program. There was a high rate of incidental absenteeism at Northwestern Bell, partly because employees were taking work time to seek outside mental-health counseling and social services. Beginning with one part-time social worker in 1971, the program has grown to include five counselors, three of whom are social workers who travel throughout the state to cover several district offices. The majority of the cases are self-referred for marital and other family problems. The program aims to work directly in one-to-one relationships with employees, referring people to other agencies only if time and traveling distance are deterrents.[24] In 1975, Ford Motor Company and General Motors hired social workers as corporate coordinators of their alcohol and drug programs, which were developed under the umbrella of health counseling. As agreed in negotiations between union and management, the main focus is substance abuse although other social and emotional problems are understandably registered as concerns.[25]

Some unions have hired social workers to develop and staff social-service departments for union members and their families. This is in addition to a union counseling program that was initiated in 1941 by the AFL-CIO in which certain union members are trained to provide informal and referral counseling for other union members. This network is described in more detail in chapter 3.

A new approach to service delivery in the field of industrial social work was developed by Otto Jones, formerly with Kennecott Copper. Jones incorporated a private counseling service, Human Affairs, Inc., that contracts with companies for employee-counseling services. One of Human Affairs, Inc.'s major clients is the U.S. Steel Company, which has programs in its plants in South Chicago and Provo, Utah.[26]

The formation of the National Institute of Alcohol Abuse and Alcoholism (NIAAA) in 1970 was a significant development in the movement to serve people with alcohol problems. Within the occupational branch of NIAAA, this interest and financial support paved the way for employee-assistance programs (EAPs) in many industrial settings. The EAP model differs from the occupational-alcoholism model. The latter was initiated in the 1940s and was staffed primarily by recovering alcoholics. The EAPs have added social workers and other professionals to their staffs and solicit people with other personal and family problems besides alcohol-related ones for caseloads. Because this is such a fast-growing and highly important area within the field of industrial social work, it is amplified in chapter 5. The Boston College School of Social Work program, which pioneered in the training of social workers for the EAPs, is described in detail in the same chapter.

Interest in occupational social work virtually exploded in the 1970s, and as has so often happened during the evolution of social work, the practice area moved ahead while the educational area remained in the background. In 1975, Irl Carter authored *Industrial Social Work: Historical Parallels in Five Western Nations*, the first major documentation of the history of industrial social work.

In 1976, sensing the potential growth of industrial social work, the author of this book approached the executive director of the Council on Social Work Education and suggested a meeting be held under the council's sponsorship. The purpose would be to explore the educational implications of what was transpiring in the field. This historic meeting took place on 7 May 1976 when thirty-two practitioners, educators, representatives of organized labor and industry, as well as staff from the National Association of Social Workers came together to consider curriculum needs. Since then, the educational area has been developing at such a fast pace that a separate chapter (chapter 10) is given to the subject.

Even as this book is being written, developments are taking place so quickly that it is not possible to include them all. However, from a historical perspective, the time clearly is now for job-site social work to become established as a practice area. There is a need in the work world for the delivery of human services.

Issues

There are broad questions concerning social work's place in the world of work. As elaborated upon in this chapter, they refer to fundamental philosophical and intellectual concerns. Some specific issues in the history of social work pertain especially to the history of industrial social work and help to explain why this field has had such a rocky and slow development—for example, the emphasis by social work, at one time in its history, on the Freudian psychology; the image of social work, which unfortunately is often not seen as positive by employees or employers; and the development of the new profession of social work itself as it slowly progressed through various stages. These factors contributed to inhibiting the formulation of other areas of practice including industrial social work. In retrospect, however, perhaps this can be seen as a necessary evolution.

During the decades of the 1920s through the 1940s, while some social workers spoke of the exciting potential for social work in industrial settings, the social-work profession seemed to be focusing its attention in other directions. The Milford Conference in 1929, at which social-agency executives confronted the issue of generic practice versus specific practice, was representative of the focus at that time. Rather than venturing into new areas, the profession seemed to be focusing inward as it was defining itself.[27]

In a history of casework, Helen Harris Perlman points out an additional focus of the 1920s that tended to curb the profession's movement outward from casework:

> The 1920s brought a great flooding of light into casework from Freudian psychology. . . . There ensued a considerable period when caseworkers immersed themselves in the study of Freud's work in the effort, chiefly to understand man's motivation and irrational behaviors.[28]

Social work has struggled for years, and continues to do so today, with an image problem that has represented a conflict of interests in the eyes of business, both management and union. Friedlander writes that even during wartimes "the social worker still was considered as a person doling out largess and being a representative of a wealthy, superior class, instead of helping neighbors on a place of equality."[29] In 1944, Evans warned the social-work profession that "we have spent many years and still have not entirely succeeded in educating the public to a realization that we are not Lady Bountifuls, handing out well-filled baskets to those worthy of our care.''[30] She was well aware that the success of social work in industry depended on whether the profession could define, believe in, and sell what it had to offer. Today the image of social workers as welfare workers with bleeding hearts ready to give away tax money to undeserving clients is consistently alluded to by corporate executives. Psychologists and psychiatrists have escaped this problem and are associated by businessmen as mental-health doctors and professionals.

Hellenbrand and Yasser feel that lower-income workingpeople, their unions, and industrial management view social workers with some wariness, distrust, and at times, dislike. During the 1930s, family agencies, which were seen as representing private social services, often refused to help union workers when they were on strike. Over the years, unions thus developed a distrust of outside agencies and preferred to provide their own services to members. This preference also was an effort to maintain solidarity and organizational control.[31] In 1924, the National Conference on Social Welfare had been confronted with labor's perception of social work—that is, that "certain types of social work have indeed obstructed industrial progress by sidetracking the organization of workers through 'welfare' activities and by minimizing the evils of industrial exploitation through relief giving.''[32] In light of this background, considerable persuasion was often necessary when dealing with corporate management who tended to perceive social work as wasteful and ineffective and with unions who viewed social work with distrust. In this author's estimation, the negative image of social workers continues to be one of the major constraints to the development of industrial social work.

Leo Perlis, director of the AFL-CIO's Department of Community Services, suggests reasons why social work has had difficulty in firmly establishing itself in industry—that is, the stages for its own development as a profession. For the most part, business and corporate executives have traditionally been more concerned with production than the health and welfare of the employee. Labor focused its efforts on employees' more-concrete needs such as higher wages, shorter hours, and decent working conditions. In the midst of management and labor's lack of interest, social work was too busy trying to find itself. While diverting its energies elsewhere, most of the social-work profession apparently overlooked the fact that the two major economic forces in our industrial society, next to government itself, are labor and management and that these two forces provide a vast arena for the useful performance of social-work functions.[33]

Social-work practice developed in the social agency where the services were delivered. Since 1900, energies have been spent developing the service-delivery model, first through voluntary and then through governmental agencies. Professional private practice has become the latest model. Social workers are increasingly self-confident and better able to think of themselves as practitioners who are not necessarily tied to an agency. Frequently it is the enterprising social worker in private practice who is interested in the business community as a potential provider of services. It is more than a coincidence that private practice and industrial social work are blossoming simultaneously.

Now at the start of the 1980s, social-work education as well as practice is finally clearly moving into the industrial area. The two professional social work organizations—the National Association of Social Workers and the Council on Social Work Education—sanction efforts in this direction. Schools of social work, for example, have begun to offer courses for industrial social workers. The scatter-gun beginnings of industrial social work at the start of this century have developed into an organized movement. Never again should an individual social worker be isolated from his or her skills in the business world. The author is confident that industrial social work is here, not only to stay but also to flourish as a new practice area that can reach and serve the working man and woman.

Summary

Most of the industrial social workers in the early twentieth century were welfare secretaries, but the employee-assistance program at Northern States Power Company in Minnesota helped professionalize the field of industrial social work by providing specialized social-work services as early as 1917. World War I accelerated the progress of industrial social work because manpower shortages necessitated the rapid integration of women into the work force, and many industries helped the temporary womanpower adapt to the unfamiliar work place by providing social services. Between the wars, industrial social work made little progress at the practical level. Many industries developed programs of occupational social work during World War II when, again, sudden increases in production and changes in the population of the work force produced uniquely stressful working conditions. The National Maritime Union/United Seaman's Service Program, begun in 1943, stands out as an example of the industrial social work of that time. Since World War II, industrial social work has slowly become part of the mainstream of social work. The hiring of trained social workers by private industry has become more widespread than at any time previously. The development of the EAP model has brought about the more-frequent hiring of social workers. Social-work-education programs now more regularly offer opportunities to study industrial social work. The recent rapid growth of the private practice of social work has yielded a new population of professionals that industries can engage to provide services for their employees within the work place. Industrial social work is no longer isolated from the profession of social work as a whole.

A history of social work from the early 1900s to the present yields a number of examples of social work in industry. A review of these examples reveals how social, economic, and political conditions affected the development of industrial social work. It also becomes clear that the services provided by social work in general will influence services to be provided in the work place.

2 Personnel Departments and Employee Benefits

The first contact a prospective employee has with his or her employer is through the company's personnel department. These departments are usually responsible for overseeing the various other services companies offer employees besides simple compensation. Personnel departments administer benefit plans, some of which are voluntarily provided by companies and others of which are required by law. A social worker employed in a business or industry works for the company but serves the employees. She or he must understand employee benefits from the point of view of both employer and employee.

Social workers may have the opportunity to work in personnel departments, but they must carefully consider this possible confusion in roles. The growth of benefits packages will doubtlessly further obscure the distinction between the roles of a social worker and a personnel administrator. What is clear is that the administration and implementation of employee-benefits programs require social-work skills even if the direct personnel function of hiring and firing may not. Whether or not social workers increasingly take personnel-administration positions, the industrial social worker, hired to work directly with the employees of a company, must understand the personnel department and the various employee benefits in order to function effectively.

This chapter presents a factual overview of the development of personnel departments and the evolution of a variety of benefits now commonly provided to workers.

In 1929, benefits cost the average employer 3 percent of total wages and salaries. In 1949 the cost was 16 percent, and in the 1970s it rose to nearly 30 percent. Businesses have continued to meet the rising costs of benefits because they recognize that benefits attract and help to keep well-qualified workers. The occupational social worker should comprehend the basic character of benefits because, along with job description, salary, and advancement, the benefits are of primary importance to the workers who are the clients of the industrial social worker.

The nature of employee benefits varies considerably from business to business. To obtain specific information, the industrial human-service worker can consult many sources such as government publications on social security and unemployment insurance and books and periodicals on personnel management, labor relations, and social-welfare programs. The colleagues of an industrial social worker provide another source of specific information. These colleagues work alongside the social worker when administering health-insurance and medical-benefits programs, labor-relations programs, and programs for special populations.

History of the Development of
Personnel Departments

Quite simply stated, the growth of unions and the aftereffects of World Wars I and II were the most significant factors that influenced the growth of personnel management and employee benefits. However, the origin of the management and benefits systems probably goes back to the beginning of industrialization and the development of the employer-employee relationship.[1] Employers saw benefits as a way to assure themselves of a labor force. Unions were responding to the need to protect individuals from potential on-the-job risks as well as to insure the growth and stability of their organizations. Many early endeavors were short lived and sporadic. However, the combined effects of the growth of unions, the U.S. response to wartime conditions, and the great Depression considerably strengthened employee-benefits programs in the early 1920s and again in the 1930s.

The growth of unions had a significant impact on the evolution of personnel administration and thereby on employee benefits. Beginning in the mid-nineteenth century, the number of trade unions increased substantially. They gained strength by consolidating into the American Federation of Labor (AFL) in 1886. As a means of stemming the union tide, but also in response to the need to maintain contact with increasing numbers of employees, organizations frequently hired social, or welfare, secretaries. As detailed in chapter 1, these secretaries helped workers with concerns related to working conditions as well as medical care, housing, educational facilities, and recreational activities.[2] In effect, unions were demanding and receiving increased benefits, and management in nonunion industrial shops was improving benefits in order to keep workers satisfied and unions out.

World War I magnified these developments. The war created a tremendous demand for workers because industries needed additional workers while the armed services were simultaneously drafting a large percentage of the labor force. This forced the United States and other countries to focus attention on the possibilities of more-efficient utilization of workers.[3] This population increase among the work force temporarily enlarged the scope of benefits programs.

Then the Depression of the 1930s called the entire employment system of the United States into question. The 25 percent unemployment rate within the labor force created widespread concern about the structure of an economy that could permit such a devastatingly high unemployment rate. In response to demands that workers be protected against such economic insecurity as a matter of public policy, the U.S. government authorized studies of all aspects of employment practices. The passage of the Social Security Act in 1935 was one result of these studies. The act introduced three main programs: (1) social insurance and old-age and unemployment benefits, (2) public categorical assistance, and (3) health and welfare services.[4]

The wage freezes instituted during World War II had the greatest impact on social programs in business and industry. Unions could not negotiate for higher wages so they concentrated on improved benefits. William Glueck, writing in 1974, made the following summary:

> The majority of the benefits and services programs offered in work organizations today are primarily the product of the past thirty years. It is true that before World War II employers offered a few pensions and services because they had the employees' welfare at heart, or to keep out the union. But most programs began in earnest during the war when wages were regulated.[5]

Now, whether an industry is a plant with 10,000 employees whose personnel decisions are made by its corporate headquarters or a small, family-owned factory that employs 100 people or less, an industry has a legal mandate to offer certain benefits to its employees. Benefits and services beyond those required are frequently offered to employees and vary according to the size and nature of the industry. One trend to watch for in personnel benefits and services is the development of employee-counseling programs and affirmative action programs. (The term *industry* as used here includes hospitals, schools, social-service agencies, and other nonprofit organizations as well as factories and businesses.)

Mandated Benefit Plans

Unemployment Insurance

Unemployment insurance, like other social-welfare programs, developed with the passage of the Social Security Act in 1935. Some states had earlier instituted a similar form of insurance (Wisconsin was first in 1932), but the Social Security Act originated national unemployment insurance. A special provision of the act offered considerable impetus for rapid adoption of the unemployment insurance laws. This impetus took the form of a federal tax on payrolls, 90 percent of which would be returned to states if they passed acceptable unemployment compensation programs. By 1937, all states plus the District of Columbia had complied.[6] Since then, Alaska, Hawaii, Guam, Puerto Rico, and the Virgin Islands have implemented programs.

The unemployment insurance system established under the Social Security Act is a federal/state system. Some federal guidelines exist within which individual states have been free to develop the particular program that seems best adapted to prevailing conditions. For specific details about a particular state's program, there are local divisions of employment-security offices throughout the United States.

Eligibility for unemployment insurance depends on the number of weeks of previous employment and the amount of wages paid. These two variables determine the amount of the benefit payments and the number of weeks during which payment continues. In most states, the weekly benefit rate equals approximately one-half the average weekly wage in the preceding fifty-two weeks, but it may not exceed a specified maximum amount. In Massachusetts, for example, that maximum is $115 per week. The amount of the weekly benefit varies from state to state and usually lags far behind increases in the cost of living. The number of weeks that the benefit can be paid is usually twenty-six weeks. During times of high unemployment, because of special federal supplementary legislation, states may extend benefits to thirty-nine weeks. Additional thirteen-week extensions have been granted due to exceptional circumstances such as the 1978 blizzard in Massachusetts.[7]

To be entitled to insurance benefits, an employee must also be entirely out of work or working less than full time; some limited part-time earnings do not interfere with entitlement. An employee is usually eligible for benefits only if she or he has been laid off, not fired. If an employer disputes an employee's claim for unemployment benefits, appeal procedures exist to settle the disagreement.

In addition to meeting these criteria, an employee must be ready and able to work full time in regular or other suitable work and be unable to find employment. Factors such as travel expenses, distance to job, prior earnings rate, and degree of risk involved to the health, safety, or morals of the person are considered when determining what is suitable employment.[8] Assessment of a person's intellectual, physical, and emotional capacities may be difficult and lends itself to disagreement between the unemployed person, the unemployment office, and/or the employer.

The Social Security Act has been amended over the years so that it now covers almost every group of employees. Self-employed workers remain the one group not covered, except in California where the self-employed can elect to contribute to self-coverage. Most states now provide unemployment insurance coverage for domestic workers, agricultural workers, and employees of nonprofit organizations. Federal employees are covered by an unemployment program closely resembling state programs.[9] Members of the armed forces and railroad workers each have unemployment insurance under separate programs. Elected officials, independent contractors working abroad, and people who are not U.S. citizens are excluded from the provisions of the Social Security Act.

In all but three states—Alabama, Alaska, and New Jersey—the entire cost of the program is paid by the employer in the form of state and federal taxes. An employer's contribution rate is based on the extent to which the company has contributed to the unemployment roll. The standard tax rate is 2.7 percent of the first $6,000 of taxable wages per employee.[10] Those employers who have paid out the most unemployment have higher rates, sometimes as high as 5 or 6 percent. This movable rate scale acts as an incentive to employers to stabilize employment policies and to discourage employee layoffs.

Most people experience some disorientation as a result of unexpected unemployment. A few suffer strong feelings of identity loss. Some workers who apply for unemployment insurance benefits may need specific assistance with the complex application procedures; others may need support during a time of strike or layoff. Some employers may expect industrial social workers to assist in the assessment of incidents surrounding job termination and the employee's capabilities and limitations. The sensitive and well-informed industrial social worker will be able to serve both employers and employees with competence.

Workmen's Compensation

Similar to unemployment insurance, workmen's compensation has some features common in all states, but each state also has its own laws that include details that vary greatly and change frequently. All states require the compensation of workers whose death or total or partial disability results from his or her employment. In almost all states, the maximum weekly benefit for disability equals at least two-thirds of the worker's gross weekly wage. About half the states have increased the benefit from two-thirds wage to full wage.[11] Some states pay an additional amount for dependents. Most states have a maximum payment. In Massachusetts, for example, the maximum is $150 per week including payments of $6 per week per dependent. After receiving the maximum amount, if the disability persists, the worker has a hearing to request permanent-disability status. No statutory limit exists in any state as to time or dollar amount for medical care or physical-rehabilitation services for any work-related impairment. Benefits to survivors in case of an employee's death vary from state to state, some of which pay a lump sum, others a weekly benefit. The amounts of these benefits may be contingent on the number and age of dependents. Most states do have a maximum payment in the event of death. For example, Massachusetts pays a maximum of $16,000 over a period of no more than 40 weeks. In Maryland, survivors categorized as fully dependent on the deceased worker may receive benefits totaling a maximum of $45,000 over a period of no more than 186 weeks.

An application for workmen's compensation is usually initiated by the employee who reports the accident to his or her employer. The latter must file a written report of the accident within forty-eight hours to the Division of Industrial Accidents (State of Massaschusetts). There is usually a one-week waiting period prior to the first payment.

A variety of injuries and illnesses are covered by workmen's compensation. Regardless of who is at fault, an employee injured while on the job receives workmen's compensation. All states provide full coverage for work-related diseases such as asbestosis, silicosis, and chronic bronchitis. Compensation in weekly amounts plus additional lump sums are allowed for loss or disfigurement of certain body parts and loss of bodily functions such as vision and hearing. Decrease in hearing due to noise levels in working places is declared a reimbursable job-related disability in many cases. Given substantial evidence to relate the condition to the job, workers can receive compensation for heart attacks, chronic lower-back pain, ulcers, hernias, and other conditions related to stress and on-the-job wear and tear. Should an employee develop a neurosis due to a physical loss, such a condition is considered a reimbursable disability. A disabling psychiatric condition that can be linked to job stress is more difficult to prove, but it is a condition that merits compensation. In Newton, Massachusetts, a policeman received disability retirement in 1979 after a psychiatrist diagnosed that his anxiety was causally related to a series of particularly stressful incidents that had occurred in the course of duty.[12] Berkeley Rice describes several major lawsuits that are now in litigation concerning executive stress including one by a widow suing her former spouse's employer because of his suicide.[13]

Since the World Health Organization and the American Medical Association have recently defined alcoholism as a disease, the question has been raised as to its compensability when it results in a disabling condition. The navy has classified it a noncompensable disease. The air force and army still classify alcoholism as a condition rather than a disease because the potential cost in disability claims to the services could be unmanageable. This stance is presently being challenged and should be followed in case of changes. As an illustration, a former employee, claiming his alcoholism was caused by participation at parties and other entertainment required of Ford Executives, brought suit against the Ford Motor Company, but he lost the suit.

Workmen's compensation is not charged directly to the workers. Employers pay the expense of either a private-insurance or state-operated plan. These plans offer reductions in rates based on a company's safety record.[14] The reduced rate acts as an incentive to companies to encourage programs and policies that foster employee safety. Also, because of the difference in risk involved between working in a machine shop and an office, employers purchase workmen's compensation at various rates.

It is important to remember that no federal guidelines regulate the workmen's compensation programs of individual states. There is a consensus on some standards, but considerable variation exists. The regional office of any state department of labor provides specific information about workmen's compensation in its area. A social worker may also find an expert on workmen's compensation in the person of the specialist many companies employ to administer special programs for handicapped workers. The function of these specialists is further detailed in chapter 7.

Social Security

At present, social security is subject to change under proposed legislation by the Reagan administration. The following picture, however, describes the prevailing system.

Working Americans are guaranteed some assistance when they retire (after the required number of quarters) or if they become permanently disabled. Unlike workmen's compensation and unemployment insurance, which are funded entirely by the employer, the cost of social security is shared equally by the employer and the employee.

By passing the Social Security Act in 1935, the U.S. government recognized publicly and financially its citizens' fears of economic insecurity. Since 1935, many changes have been made to provide improved protection for workers and their families. Initially, social security covered only the worker upon retirement at age sixty-five. In 1939, the provisions of the act were changed to pay survivors when the worker died as well as certain dependents when the worker retired.

Originally, social security benefits covered only workers in industry and commerce. In the 1950s, coverage was extended to include most other workers including self-employed people, state and local employees, household and farm employees, members of the armed forces, and members of the clergy.[15] Federal government employees are covered by a different pension plan.

By 1965, social-security-disability benefits were made available to a covered worker at any age and to disabled widows, widowers, and in some cases, divorced wives at age fifty or over. A person is considered disabled if she or he cannot work because of a severe physical or mental impairment that has lasted, or is expected to last, for at least twelve months or that may end in death. There is a waiting period of five months before benefits can begin. Once payments begin, they continue as long as the person is disabled. The Social Security Administration has information regarding additional benefits for dependent children and parents of survivors and other special programs.

To receive social-security-retirement benefits, a worker must have been employed for a certain number of years. The Social Security Administration determines eligibility by examining a worker's work and earnings records. Most workers who have been employed for a minimum of ten years have sufficient credits to receive benefits. However, young workers who become disabled may not have enough. Having sufficient credits may make a worker eligible for social security, but the credits alone do not determine the amount. The specific amount depends on the worker's average earnings covered by social security, which is calculated by the Social Security Administration.

Social-security-retirement and -disability benefits are paid regardless of income received from other sources, although a retiree who continues to work may not exceed a certain amount of earnings and receive social security benefits simultaneously. After age 70, however, earnings are unlimited. Benefits are not subject to federal income tax. For some retiring workers, social security payments may be the only source of income. The following facts imply that it is increasingly difficult for a retiree and his or her family to live solely on social-security-retirement or -disability benefits. In June 1978, the *average* monthly check for a retired worker without dependents was $254; it was $433 for a couple. A cost-of-living increase raised these benefit payments in 1979 to $283 and $482 respectively—hardly appreciable during current inflation. Even a retiree who received the *maximum* benefit payable to those aged sixty-five and older received just $489.70 in 1978 and $553.70 in 1979.[16] Table 2-1 shows additional examples of various types of social security payments effective June 1978.

Voluntary Benefit Plans

Since social security is compulsory for most workingpeople, it is a primary source of income for retired employees. However, many Americans supplement it with savings, investments, or part-time work since social security provides a meager income. In addition, private pensions provide additional retirement income for many Americans.

As Glueck defines it, "a pension is a fixed amount [not wages] paid by a former employer or his representative at regular intervals to a person or that person's surviving dependents for past services performed."[17] Since private pensions are voluntary, not all employers provide the option, and even when available, some employees choose not to join. Glueck also quotes

Table 2-1
Examples of Monthly Social Security Payments (Effective June 1978)
(dollars)

Benefits	Average Yearly Earnings after 1950 Covered by Social Security							
	$923 or less	$3,000	$4,000	$5,000	$6,000	$8,000	$10,000[a]
Retired worker at 65	121.80	251.80	296.20	343.50	388.20	482.60	534.70
Worker under 65 and disabled	121.80	251.80	296.20	343.50	388.20	482.60	534.70
Retired worker at 62	97.50	201.50	237.00	274.80	310.60	386.10	427.80
Wife or husband at 65	60.90	125.90	148.10	171.80	194.10	241.30	267.40
Wife or husband at 62	45.70	94.50	111.10	128.90	145.60	181.00	200.60
Wife under 65 with one child in her care	61.00	133.20	210.00	290.40	324.00	362.00	401.00
Widow or widower at 65 if worker never received reduced benefits	121.80	251.80	296.20	343.50	388.20	482.60	534.70
Widow or widower at 60 if sole survivor	87.10	180.10	211.80	245.70	277.60	345.10	382.40
Widow or widower at 50 and disabled if sole survivor	61.00	126.00	148.20	171.90	194.10	241.40	267.50
Widow or widower with one child in care	182.80	377.80	444.40	515.40	582.40	724.00	802.20
Maximum family payment	182.80	384.90	506.20	633.80	712.10	844.50	935.70

[a]Maximum earnings covered by social security were lower in past years and must be included in figuring average earnings. This average determines payment amount. Because of this, amounts shown in the last column usually will not be payable until future years. The maximum retirement benefit usually payable to a worker who is 65 in 1978 was $489.70.

from a study by Bailey and Schuenk (1972) in which they found that unionized employees in large firms, and who had high incomes tended to participate in private pensions plans. Beir (1971) learned that 72 percent of unionized employees are covered by private pensions, while 44 percent of nonunionized employees have pensions.[18]

Some employers pay the entire cost of the employee pension. Employees themselves support their own pensions in some industries with a regular contribution while they are working. In other cases, employee and employer share the cost of the pension. Frequently, under the terms of these last two contributory plans, employees have the option of increasing their share. Essentially, however, the benefit formula is based on salary and number of years of performance. The end result usually yields a monthly benefit that, including social security, is approximately 50 percent of the individual's projected salary during the last year of employment.[19]

In response to an expressed concern about guaranteeing employee-pension payment and rights, the Employee Retirement Income Security Act, sometimes referred to as the Pension Reform Law was passed in 1974 as Public Law 93-406. ERISA, as it is commonly known, provides certain protections and guarantees for payment of private-pension benefits by setting certain minimum standards for pension plans. ERISA includes guidelines for employee participation, vesting rights, funding, reporting, and disclosure. It established a Pension Benefit Guaranty Corporation within the Labor Department that provides insurance to workers who are covered by private-pension plans. ERISA's standards apply to all private plans except for church, church-related, or public-employee plans. ERISA was enacted to protect employees who invest in pensions that dissolve when companies go out of business.[20]

The safeguards provided by ERISA are important and address some critical issues regarding employee's rights. However, since the time of its enactment, some people have been concerned that the amount of money and paperwork involved in meeting ERISA's standards might force smaller companies to abandon their pension programs and discourage new companies from initiating such programs. The provisions and procedures of ERISA are doubtless here to stay, but perhaps amendments can simplify the act so those who administer it can handle its requirements without the services of a lawyer.

Other Insurances

Life Insurance

Many employers provide, at no cost to the employee, a life insurance policy that provides either a lump-sum payment, a guaranteed income, or some combination of both to an employee's family in the event of his or her death. Coverage is provided through a group plan that does not require the employee to have a physical examination. Premiums are based on the characteristics and risk factors of the group at a particular work place.

Medical Insurance

Medical insurance is one of the most costly, most preferred, and most diverse of all employee benefits. Some employers fully finance this benefit but in most cases the employee shares the cost. Because of the diversity and intricacies of health insurance plans, many people are ignorant of what their coverage does and does not provide or how to secure payment. Plans vary—for example, some have high options where an employee pays more and where higher coverage is provided. Some employers offer their employees a variety of plans from which to choose. Medical insurance is fairly individual depending upon the employee, the employer, and the plan chosen. Both individual employees as well as social workers in community agencies often turn to social workers in a company for guidance and interpretation regarding insurance and other benefits.

The recent evolution of the health maintenance organizations (HMO) has offered an alternative to commercial health insurance coverage. As defined by Congress, "an HMO is an organized health-care-delivery system which provides a wide range of comprehensive health-care services to a voluntarily enrolled population in exchange for a fixed and prepaid periodic payment."[21] In 1973, Congress passed the HMO Act that requires employers of at least twenty-five persons to offer the option of an HMO health plan along with a traditional health-benefits plan if an HMO plan is available nearby. Employers are not expected to rewrite their existing contracts but to make the adjustment when an existing contract is renewed or when a new contract is offered.[22]

Disability Insurance

Many employers purchase insurance for employees that provides income protection for short- or long-term, physical or psychiatric illness, or permanent disability. Some states require that employers provide short-term disability, which usually extends from sixteen to twenty-six weeks. Long-term disability begins after a waiting period, often three to six months, during which time the person is covered by paid sick leave or short-term disability. Benefits may be payable for life or until age sixty-five when retirement benefits become available. Typically, employees are guaranteed a specified monthly income such as half pay. The actual amount paid by the disability insurance plan is often tied to the benefits received from other sources such as workmen's compensation and social security.[23] Neither workmen's compensation nor social security disability, however, are contingent upon amounts received from other sources. Therefore, it is possible for an employee to receive disability payments from as many as three sources if she or he suffers from a work-related disease or injury, has endured the five-month waiting period for social security, and was covered by a private disability plan.

Other Benefits and Services Provided by Industry

As each company is unique, so too is the package of fringe benefits offered an employee by that company. The following are examples of the variety of benefits that may be offered. It is not so much a comprehensive listing as it is a picture of the possibilities that presently exist and that may be available in the work setting:

> Educational programs, ranging from in-service training to reimbursement for tuition for job-related courses, are provided by many employers.

> Financial services such as credit unions, savings plans, and other investment plans are offered by larger companies.

> Social and recreational programs including intramural athletic teams and group-rate ticket purchases to plays and concerts are offered to employees by many companies. Tours at discount prices are a recent addition to many employee-service programs.

> Counseling services for employees and families with respect to problems regarding work, marriage, family, finances, substance abuse, and other concerns are becoming more prevalent. Examples of employee-assistance programs, mental-health, and social-services programs in industries are discussed in more detail in following chapters.

> Added benefits are often closely related to the nature of the work setting itself. For example, family members of a university faculty may attend classes at that school and receive free or discounted tuition. Hospitals frequently write off the balance of hospital bills incurred by their employees after receiving some payment from the employees' insurance plans. Department stores and manufacturers often give their employees discounts on the purchase of merchandise.

Although fringe-benefits packages have increased to the points already described, there is a continuous push for further expansion. High interest exists today, especially in unionized businesses and industries, in obtaining dental and legal services for employees, either through insurance or direct offering by an employer.

Issues

For many Americans, employment has become a form of investment in the future as well as an occupation for the present. The increasing financial security offered by many jobs frequently rules out career changes for workers. The cost of increasing benefits can sometimes force a profit-minded management to slow the pace of salary increases. It is important for good labor/management relations to maintain a careful balance among the incentives offered to workers. The occupational social worker also must understand the possible frustrations and conflicts of employers and employees alike as they negotiate their mutual, if imperfect, futures.

Furthermore, benefits are not distributed equitably. Employees with higher positions in the corporate structure usually receive additional benefits. Benefits such as automobiles, expense accounts, and extra vacations are distributed by position rather than democratically to all employees. Moreover, many such benefits are attached to terms of employment so that the privileged worker need not pay income tax on them. Perhaps the most generous benefits of this sort are stock options and profit sharing. These benefits allow the employee to become part owner of the company. However, too often this possibility is reserved for the top echelon of management.

Another major area of inequity in benefits is between the full-time and the part-time workers. The latter have often been excluded from receiving most fringe benefits. Unfortunately, since most part-time workers have been women, employers regarded benefits for them as unnecessary because women traditionally have had other means of support—that is, husbands. Now that the women's movement has highlighted issues such as this, dramatic changes have taken place in company policies for part-time workers. Now, the half-time worker is sometimes accorded a portion of benefits.

Although benefits should be considered necessary unto themselves, they may be used by an employer in place of an adequate salary. The Department of Defense, for example, traditionally practiced this philosophy. With a we-take-care-of-our-own approach, services were provided from birth (with a comprehensive world-wide medical system) to death (with a system of cemeteries throughout the United States). Often, however, salaries were kept at a low point; Congress argued that the services and benefits made up for this fact. Congress recently has raised military salaries, and now career military workers receive salaries in fair competition with civilians.

Finally, the resemblance of many employee-benefits packages to social- or human-resources programs is unmistakable. Because of this resemblance, a trained social worker may be particularly well suited to employment in the personnel department of a business or industry. However, the functions of the personnel administrator may always remain necessarily different from those of a social worker.

One of the highest placed social workers in industry, who is a personnel manager for a large industrial concern, told this author that his social-work skills are being used to help him perform a personnel job, not a social-work job. He feels that his client is different from the client of a regular social worker because his job in personnel requires him to screen employees for management potential and to administer benefit programs. However, he thinks that, because of his social-work training, he is better able to work with people. For example, he feels that on the one hand he has tried to be sensitive enough so that persons rejected for jobs walk out of the company with dignity. On the other hand, several social workers employed in a personnel department in a hospital have told this author that they thought they were acting as social workers. Questions such as who the client is—the company or employee—obviously come to mind in this discussion. Trends in personnel programs seem to indicate that these roles may become more blurred, and separating the personalist from the social worker in some programs may be increasingly difficult to do.

Summary

Modern employee-benefits programs and contemporary personnel-management departments matured partly because the developing trade unions favorably influenced the social consciousness of industry. When 25 percent of the population was unemployed during the Depression of the 1930s, the U.S. government instituted policies to prevent future unemployment insecurity. Since then, businesses and industries have provided both mandatory and voluntary employee benefits administered by their personnel departments or officers. Industrial social workers need an overview of the various kinds of benefits in order to efficiently serve both employers and employees. The Social Security Act of 1935 initiated regular payments to full-time workers who become unemployed through no fault of their own. In addition to insurance against unemployment, workers are insured against death or disability that results from their employment. Workers and their survivors and dependents are also guaranteed a form of pension upon retirement. Almost all employers pay compulsory taxes to support the unemployment insurance and workmen's compensation programs. Employers and employees share the tax that supports social-security-retirement benefits. To supplement these mandatory employee-benefits systems, many employers voluntarily provide additional benefits to their employees. For example, some employers give their workers all or part of a private pension. Others offer life insurance, medical or disability insurance, and sometimes health care. Frequently employees voluntarily share the cost of these benefits. Recently, employee benefits have expanded and often include educational, social, and recreational programs and counseling and financial services. While most employees are guaranteed benefits under the mandatory provisions of the Social Security Act, voluntary employee benefits are still offered on a somewhat unequal basis. The social worker's training suits him or her to understand and facilitate employee-benefits programs. As these programs continue to expand, social workers may find their services to be in increasing demand by personnel offices. At the present time the author is employed in the office of the Assistant Secretary for Personnel (ASPER) at the Department of Health and Human Services and considers the post a fully appropriate place for a social worker.

3 Unions

Unions deliver social services in the work setting through union counselors and, less often, social workers. This chapter describes both areas. For the social worker to be employed by the company itself or by the union directly is a critical decision.

The trade union is best understood when perceived as an economic organization. Its primary responsibility by definition is to improve wages, hours, and the working conditions of its members. However, the union operates in an adversary atmosphere in which the increased wages it seeks for the worker represent costs to the employer unless, of course, it is balanced by increased productivity.

More than one hundred national and international unions exist in the United States today. Although a few represent professionals such as teachers, most are comprised of blue-collar workers and those in the service trades. Union members are viewed customarily as the working class by virtue of their occupation and education. These working-class trade unions, out of self interest, often adopt more-liberal views on many social-welfare issues.

Originally, organized labor viewed the social-welfare community (and they were correct) as a middle-class-charity movement. However, in the 1930s, philanthropic organizations and employers could not meet the needs caused by massive unemployment from the Depression. So it was in that decade that social workers began to align themselves with trade unions, thereby strengthening the bond between trade unions and the social-welfare community. The years during World War II saw even greater involvement between the two. Social-service programs were developed by a number of unions for their members. By the end of the war, organized labor and the social-welfare community were mutually committed to maintaining a closer, if somewhat strained, relationship with one another.

Today, there is indeed a place in trade unions for the social worker, even though much of the stigma and many suspicions held earlier still remain. The stigma and suspicions are associated with the fact that social workers were originally associated by unions as being the handmaidens of management. Trade unions continue to view the professional practice of social work as isolated from both the world of work and the workers as a target population.

This chapter briefly describes the history of unions in relation to social-welfare programs. It then explores specific social-service programs within the unions, especially the community-services department of the AFL-CIO. The newest development of human-service programs with alcohol and drugs is also presented. The United Automobile, Aerospace, and Agricultural Implement Workers of America (UAW) and its involvement in social services are then described. Finally, the role of social workers and unions is discussed.

A Brief History

Trade unions from the beginning have been concerned with social-welfare issues. The involvement of organized labor in the formulation of social policy and the delivery of social services can be viewed as a response to its own history. The current social-welfare practices and policies of labor have evolved because of industries' failure to meet the personal and family needs of its employees.

Most commonly, the Society of Printers is identified as the first labor organization in the United States. Established in 1794, its purpose was to provide its members general aid and death benefits. This idea began to catch on, and in succeeding years numerous other craft unions developed benevolent societies. This theme of the trade union as a mutual-aid, self-help group has been a pervasive thread in the movement ever since.

The 1830s were marked by a new development—namely, the organization of workingmen parties that were formed to achieve social goals such as free universal education, a shorter working day, and relief from debtor's prison.[1] The first national labor union was founded in 1869—the Knights of Labor. Earlier, the Molly Maguires had been the underground movement of the labor unions. The Knights of Labor presented a broad-base coalition of workmen, farmers, shopkeepers, as well as professionals. As a reform movement it sought industrial health insurance, government ownership of railroads, prohibition of child labor, inheritance tax, income tax, and many other political goals. Because of the emphasis on government implementation of the social-welfare programs and not on labor-party formation, demise came early.

A more-substantial trade union started to develop with the founding of the AFL in 1886. Interpreting the earlier history of trade unions as a failure of socialist efforts, Samuel Gompers, the long-term AFL leader, called for safe and sane business unionism:

The groundwork principle of America's labor movement has been to recognize that the first things must come first. The primary essential in our mission has been the protection of the wage worker: to increase his wages; to cut hours off the long workday which was killing him; to improve the safety and the sanitary conditions of the workshops; to free him from the tyrannies, petty or otherwise, which served to make his experience a slavery.[2]

The benefits to which Gompers felt all workers should be entitled were to be achieved mainly through what has come to be known as collective bargaining, the act of labor and management's sitting down and negotiating an issue.

In 1935, disputes between the craft unions and the industrial unions of six AFL unions caused the former to be expelled from the AFL and to form the Congress of Industrial Organizations (CIO). This committee's goal was to organize the nonunion members and to promote industrial organization.

When World War II came, U.S. laborers were put to work as never before. The CIO flourished, but the AFL flourished even more because of the government construction boom. In 1955, the AFL and the CIO suffered a loss of power due to the Taft-Hartley Act (the outlawing of the closed shop), which was passed in 1947. It took nine years for the AFL and the CIO to merge to become the AFL-CIO. As of 1959, it did not include bakers or laundry workers. The teamsters were included in the merger but were later expelled because of racketeering. This merger, however, did not create organizational unity or the expanded unionization of U.S. workers that it was expected to do. In 1968, the UAW withdrew from the AFL-CIO. At this point, then, there was the major federation—the AFL-CIO—and, outside of it, two major unions—the UAW and the teamsters. Just recently the UAW and the AFL-CIO have become reaffiliated.

Women in Unions

In 1952, women made up 32 percent of the labor force, 15 percent of whom were unionized. From a total of 184 international and national trade unions listed in the directory of the U.S. Department of Labor for 1958, only 4.7 percent of all union officials were women. By 1968 the proportion had fallen to 4.6 percent.[3] By 1980, women made up over 40 percent of the labor force, and still only 15 percent were unionized. Although there are more female unionists than before, and although they are in more-different trades than before, the labor unions are still managed by men. In fact, of the 3.6 million female unionists in 1971, only a handful were actually making policy.

The National Coalition of Labor Union Women (CLUW) is an organization of male and female unionists, united by their special concerns for female workers. It is not a union but an organization made up of individuals and chapters. It has thousands of members and signifies a new major force in the union movement.

Delivery of Human Services

The issues confronting labor unions, while certainly including improved working conditions, go beyond wages and hours. The promotion of human values is inherent in unionism and collective bargaining in the work place. Unions are increasingly concerned with community services so that human values will continue to be enhanced by governing authorities.

The union contract does not cover most personal problems that workers face. Even those agreements that provide fringe benefits, such as insurance and coverage for health care, do not deal with the real and often tragic family needs of employees in the interrelated worlds of the home and the work place. Yet those human problems often affect production and labor/management relations.[4]

Many issues are included under the broad umbrella of human services. Mental and physical health, preventive medicine, alcohol abuse, drug abuse, and family adjustments are but a few of these. Unions provide a majority of these human services. For example, the AFL-CIO community-services program offers a referral system for financial, marital, legal, and alcohol- and drug-abuse counseling.

AFL-CIO Community-Services Program

The AFL-CIO established the Department of Community Services to meet the health and welfare needs of union members and their families: "As the union member is first and foremost a citizen of his community, so the objective of the trade-union movement is inseparably tied to the welfare of the community."[5]

This community-service program attempts to accomplish four main goals: (1) to acquaint members with the social services available and to serve as a link between the worker with the problem and a source of community help, (2) to develop a better understanding of social problems and the need for additional services through education, (3) to train union members for active participation in their community, and (4) to devise methods for making full use of community health and welfare agencies.

The community-services program operates a countrywide social-service-referral network utilizing the manpower of paraprofessionally trained volunteer union members to carry out the objectives mentioned. These volunteers represent office workers, skilled craftsmen, production-line personnel, and business agents. All volunteers are encouraged to lend a hand as responsible community members to provide assistance to fellow workers where needed. This union counseling program is coordinated by a large staff of full-time people. The program offers counseling and referral for a large variety of problems such as crimes and delinquency, alcoholism, drug abuse, mental illness, housing and rent control, consumer activities, Medicare, Medicaid, cancer detection, and problems of the elderly.

Approximately thirty-four years ago, the organized-labor movement entered into an arrangement with a number of national and local voluntary agencies, principally the Community Chests, now the United Way of America. In return for the unions' raising funds by payroll-deduction, the United Way organizations, both national and local, would include labor representatives on their policymaking boards and committees as well as full-time labor representatives on their staffs—all to be selected by the AFL-CIO through their local central labor bodies. The current memorandum of understanding negotiated between the AFL-CIO Department of Community Services and the United Way of America contains, among others, the following seven provisions:

1. *Representation on board.* All AFL-CIO representatives being considered for membership on the United Way of America board of governors and other committees will be nominated by the AFL-CIO.
2. *Executive committee.* The AFL-CIO will be represented on the executive committee of the United Way by two members.
3. *Officers.* AFL-CIO will be represented in officer positions of the United Way.
4. *Professional staff.* The director of the United Way Labor Participation Department will be nominated by AFL-CIO, subject to the approval of the United Way. There will be at least six full-time AFL-CIO community services representatives on the staff of the United Way in addition to the director. From this group, there will be at least one full-time AFL-CIO representative assigned to each of the initial four United Way regional offices. Additional AFL-CIO community services representatives will be assigned to other regional offices as they develop.
5. *Labor giving.* The United Way and the AFL-CIO Community Services Department will cooperate to encourage communities to conduct annual education and service promotion including, among other things, voluntary participation of workers in fund-raising drives for the United Way through payroll deduction. Every effort should be made for employees to understand what they are being asked to support on an annual basis. Both parties should engage in a continuing review of employee fund-raising methods.
6. *Collective bargaining.* The United Way believes that voluntary community health and welfare agencies including United Way of America should respect the right of their employees to join organizations or their own choosing for collective-bargaining and grievance purposes, if that is their desire. They should not stand in the way of the employee's desire to organize.

7. *Union label.* The United Way agrees to continue to use and exhibit the union label in all its printed materials, and it further agrees to purchase, whenever available, only union-made goods and services.[6]

As a result of this arrangement and similar arrangements with other agencies including the American Red Cross, the National Council on Alcoholism, the Boy Scouts of America, and the National Council on Crime and Delinquency, the organizational machinery of Community Services consists of 350 full-time staff people. They work through the community-services committees of local AFL-CIO central labor bodies and with independent unions such as the UAW, teamsters, and United Mine Workers in hundreds of industrial communities across the country. They constitute the first, largest, and only national delivery system of social services in the U.S. labor movement.[7]

Union Counseling

The primary purpose of the union counselor is help meet the human needs of the employee. By providing valuable information to the troubled person and by sympathetic referral, the counselor encourages the employee to take advantage of help-giving services and facilities provided by the community. The union counselors are not social workers—that is, they do not counsel, give advice, or provide material assistance. Their one function is to make a referral—to guide the worker to the right social agency and to follow through to insure service.

Through a period of eight to ten weekly sessions of two to three hours each, the union member learns to help. During these sessions, AFL-CIO members meet with representatives of the community's social agencies and other professionals to discuss specific health and welfare services. "During the course, recent firsthand information shapes the way in which referrals are made and helps guide union counselors in requesting services per se (and in requesting changes through federal, state, and city legislative apparatus)."[8]

When the course is completed, utilization of the counselors is of extreme importance. All union-counselor programs, like all services, vary from community to community. Frequent announcements at local meetings and in union papers have been found to be essential to the continuance of the program, and it must be used to be appreciated. The community services of the local labor body plan regular monthly or bimonthly meetings of graduate counselors. These meetings keep counselors informed of new developments in community health and welfare activities.

Union counselors not only act as referral agents, but they also organize blood-donor drives, sit on various community-advisory bodies, help in administering disaster relief, and support fund-raising efforts such as the UWA.

United Labor Agency

In a bold new effort to bring social services to the worker, Leo Perlis proposed the united-labor-agency concept. The first was established in Camden, New Jersey, in 1946 and the second one in Denver, Colorado, more than twenty-five years later. UWA welcomed the United Labor Agency.[9]

The United Labor Agency, Inc., is the principal health and social-service agency of organized labor in the worker's community. It is a local community agency, legitimized as an Internal Revenue Service 501-C-3 (tax-exempt, nonprofit) organization. It is difficult to evaluate because of its uniqueness. It is registered as a charity by states and cities and operates under the corporate authority of an elected board of trustees and the policy control of the local central labor council.[10]

The national AFL-CIO presently charters 739 local central labor councils, fifty state labor councils, and one in Puerto Rico to carry out its purposes and objectives, including the AFL-CIO Community Services Program. Through these councils labor agencies are developed.[11] These agencies show a significant expansion of labor into human services. Current programs include information and referral services, life-sustaining-devices programs, consumer-complaint bureaus, union-counselor programs, manpower and supportive-services programs, exoffender-remotivation projects, senior citizen programs, vocational-exploration programs, housing-referral programs, as well as art and humanities projects. What the role of social workers in labor agencies will be is still unclear. It is evident that the functions of labor agencies are social workers' business. How the staff training and expertise will be developed is an important question for the unions as well as for the social-work profession.

The Human Contract

A recent development in the delivery of human services at the work place is the human contract that takes interest in the workers' health, welfare, and living conditions. It is becoming, through necessity and collective bargaining, a separate entity of the union contract, which basically addresses wages, hours, and working conditions.

The human contract is (1) a policy for union-management cooperation to help meet the family and personal needs of the company employee-union member beyond the plant gates; (2) a program of information counseling, referral, and follow-through; (3) a process with a union-management committee in the work place—trained union counselors handle problems on health, welfare, and living conditions under the human contract as counterparts to shop stewards who handle grievances on wages, hours, and working conditions under the union contract.[12]

The nature of personal and family problems encompasses a wide range from financial and marital problems and health abuses and addictions to consumer education and crime prevention. Any one of these problems could be the cause of great personal anguish that in turn would affect productivity and morale. Therefore, it is important for both labor and management to get involved together in developing a sense of joint responsibility.

The question is how to handle problems of a personal nature for the worker. The answer, according to the union, is not in hiring a social worker, someone outside the membership, but developing instead a "variety of community services, both public and voluntary, ready and willing to provide information, train counselors, follow through on referrals, and devise programs of prevention, treatment, and recovery."[13] This was true historically, but it is not necessarily true now.[14]

The human contract, when perfected, must be designed to deal with five major categories:

1. Financial—for example, public assistance, supplementary income, and debts;
2. Family—for example, marital, in-laws, and child/parent;
3. Health—for example, alcoholism, mental health, drug abuse, and hypertension;
4. Consumer—for example, housing, rentals, and fraud;
5. Miscellaneous—for example, legal aid, recreation, education, and crime prevention.

> The union contract does not cover it all, . . . but it can be made to cover more—by extension and supplementation—through the human contract. . . . [T]he front line of ethical conduct and civilized behavior in our business society is neither the executive suite nor the marketplace . . . [but] the collective-bargaining table.[15]

Alcoholism/Drug Abuse

Chapter 5 presents the occupational-alcoholism field in general; this discussion centers on the combined work of labor and management in this area. Management and labor are increasingly viewing alcoholism as a human problem that demands greater attention. Both labor and management are also concerned by recently published statistics that estimate that over $9 billion is lost annually in productivity because of work-related alcohol misuse. As this concern grows, labor contracts or memoranda of understanding will contain stronger stipulations governing the discharge of workers for alcohol-related offenses and detailing their rights. In addition, contracts will provide for varied amounts of medical coverage for alcoholism treatment, reflecting both labor's concern for the job security of alcoholic employees and management's concern for minimizing the loss of experienced manpower.[16]

In recent guidelines published by the National Council on Alcoholism, it is clearly stated that when the worker is suffering from alcoholism, or when the problem is alcohol related, the worker should then be referred to appropriate alcoholism treatment in community-approved facilities or resources. However, if the worker is not suffering from alcoholism, or if the problem is not alcohol related, the problems should then be handled under the appropriate provisions of the existing contractual agreement.[17] The primary objective of a joint labor/management alcoholism-recovery program is to provide effective assistance and treatment to those individuals suffering from the disease of alcoholism.

It has been shown through long-established union-management recovery programs that when the disease concept is accepted and when alcoholism is diagnosed and treated as a disease, the results are gratifying. Joint recovery programs are also effective because, in any alcoholism-recovery program, the goals of both union and management are identical in wanting to assist the individual to arrest the disease and to be restored to full health and back on the work force. In dealing with such an objective, both union and management can work together to achieve this common goal. This joint effort thus lessens the ability of the alcoholic to manipulate his problem into a controversy between management and union representatives. This does not happen when both parties are working together.

The union-management approach is designed to step up efforts to eliminate alcoholism, educate the workers as to the dangers of alcoholism, identify alcoholics in need of treatment, establish a referral system, encourage health insurance carriers to endorse the medically approved treatment of alcoholics, and work with professionals in the community for better-coordinated treatment programs.

The union-management committee's intensive cooperation in the community, in addition to joint cooperation at the plant level, can be a great step forward in helping workers and their families to live happier lives, thereby making the community a better place in which to live and work.

AFL-CIO Takes a Stand

The AFL-CIO took a policy stand on the issues of alcoholism, drug abuse, and other personal problems. Enclosed are two resolutions, one from the November 1979 Constitutional Convention and one from the executive council meeting in February 1980. These statements affirm the AFL-CIO's policy encouraging their affiliates to establish joint union-management programming. The AFL-CIO traditionally does not interfere in the internal affairs of affiliates, particularly in their collective-bargaining arrangements, so each national and international union will determine for itself how to negotiate the human contract.

> WHEREAS, alcoholism, drug abuse, health, and personal problems are seriously affecting the jobs of many members of our unions, and

> WHEREAS, negotiated union-management programs have proven to be the most effective method of bringing the many community services to our people who are afflicted with alcohol- and drug-abuse problems; therefore, be it

> RESOLVED: that the 13th Constitutional Convention of the AFL-CIO go on record, supporting such negotiated union-management programs and ask all local and international staff to negotiate such programs in their agreements.[18]

Many workers face personal and family problems which affect their lives, their jobs, and the lives of their fellow citizens.

Through the AFL-CIO Community Services program, thousands of union counselors have been trained, and thousands of health and welfare agencies have been enlisted to help provide information and referral services as well as counseling and care to many workers and their families both on and off the job.

In recent years, a number of corporations have taken an interest in providing such services for their employees unilaterally. Too many of these corporate programs have as their top priority the encouragement of worker loyalty to management. This is the wrong approach for the wrong reason.

Workers should be helped to meet their human needs because they are human beings in need of help. In the organized work place, the most effective delivery system of social services is under joint union-management auspices and in cooperation with community health and welfare agencies, both public and voluntary.

The AFL-CIO, therefore, commends the union counseling program which has proven so useful for many years and condemns the establishment of in-plant social-service programs for any purpose except to meet human needs.

We reaffirm our commitment to fulfill the human contract by providing human services and encourage our affiliates to consider establishment of more such programs through collective-bargaining relationships.[19]

The UAW

In 1968, the UAW, under Walter Reuther's leadership, withdrew from the AFL-CIO. The services the UAW provides for its members originated, in many instances, with Reuther. The UAW has a community-services department located in Detroit, Michigan, responsible through their regional director for such programs as the joint labor/management alcohol and drug abuse recovery program. The UAW provides materials and information to start local social-service programs in local unions and community-action-program councils.

It is up to each local union to implement the alcohol- and drug-abuse-recovery program. The major automobile manufacturers usually pay for these programs; therefore the cost is included in the union contract. In other industries, the cost is dependent upon the individual contract and situation.[20]

No particular policy has been developed as yet by the UAW concerning other social services, but there is a policy developed by the International UAW in regard to alcohol- and drug-abuse-recovery programs. However, the local unions of the UAW may launch other social-service programs for their members. For example, in 1978, a legal-services plan was initiated in the Chrysler Corporation for hourly Chrysler workers and retirees. There are now ten offices under this plan staffed by a full-time attorney and many offices with part-time attorneys. This plan provides all reasonable necessary services including court representation for most cases at no cost to the employee. The plan pays for the cost of litigation and the cost of appeal where appropriate. For the preparation of legal documents such as wills, trusts, leases, contracts, real-estate-sale and real-estate-purchase agreements, the plan will provide the necessary legal services at no cost but will not include court representation.

The International UAW also has three family-education centers, and the UAW Constitution mandates local unions to establish education committees. The education department of the International UAW, supported by a percentage of dues money, has the largest union education staff in the U.S. labor movement.[21]

The Role of Social Workers in Unions

"The work environment is a crucial focus of adult life. It is the source of the means of economic survival, life satisfactions, and inevitably, of stresses."[22] Unfortunately, the people who own and run the country's productive facilities have traditionally cared more about production and productivity than the health and welfare of the workers.

In World War II, when wages were stabilized, the fringe-benefit program began to take shape. These benefits included medical care, hospitalization, sick leave, and pensions, to be followed by mental-health coverage, legal aid, and other benefits. Management saw fit to supply staff doctors and nurses, but because they were management employees they sometimes did not develop the workers' confidence and were frequently mistrusted by union members.

Despite indifference or opposition by management, unions, and much of the work force itself, there were instances between the world wars in which industrial social workers were employed by unions. The Burley Tobacco Growers' Association, for example, was reported to be employing three trained social workers in 1924.[23] The Ford Motor Company during the years of 1920 to 1941 provided social services in a beginning effort.[24] Henry Ford had offered each of his workers $2.50 a day, payable only if the man led a clean and constructive life. Ford created the Sociological Section of the company to investigate. If the workers were not clean and constructive, it was the task of the Sociological Section to educate them. The Sociological Section also taught English and provided basic education. Eventually the section offered financial assistance, then conducted interracial negotiations, and finally, after 1940, performed what was more recognizable as industrial social work. Most of its staff was untrained, but a few trained social workers were hired after World War II. The section was terminated in 1948.

As previously explained in chapter 1, the best example of industrial social work in a union receiving its greatest stimulation from wartime conditions is one referred to frequently in accounts of industrial social work—that is, the joint project, begun in 1943, of the National Maritime Union and the United Seaman's Service.[25] In the spring of 1943, more than five thousand of the union's members had been killed at sea when their ships were attacked by planes or submarines. Some sailors who had survived as many as five sinkings continued to sail. It had become apparent in 1942 that seamen and their families faced urgent and frequently overwhelming problems. At first, one elderly seaman with a desk and a secretary served the union members.[26] In the fall of 1942, the United Seaman's Service provided (with the help of federal funds) industrial social work with offices located in the Union Hall. The United Seaman's Service provided caseworkers who had master-of-social-work degrees and were acceptable to the union because they belonged to the Social Services Employees' Union. The project was a success, but it was terminated when mobilization ended.

After World War II, social workers were busy debating the finer points of group work and casework and in discussing private initiative versus governmental responsibility. They failed to see the work place as a most important channel for the application of their knowledge. This is not to say there were not some isolated examples of social workers' being hired by unions. The Painters' Union in New York and the International Longshoremen Association (ILA) in Honolulu as late as the 1950s and 1960s were such cases.

A more-recent example of social workers in unions is the case of the Amalgamated Clothing Workers and Textile Workers Union (ACTWU). Representing 500,000 ACTWU members, the Social Services Department and local social-services committees provide services to members and their families, retired members, and union staff. The program planning and technical assistance reaches all levels of union staff and leadership general offices, vice-presidents and managers, local leaders and servicing representatives.[28]

Many of the services offered to the members are group-educational or -counseling programs, assistance to members with personal or job problems, consultation to the union in external and internal policies, training programs for union personnel, and so on. The program developed to meet the original concerns and goals—that is, the educational and service needs of membership and broad participation and support from all levels of the union. The program worked so well that the response exceeds present national staff limits. A main function of the social worker is to train or give guidance to the union counselor when needed. Union counseling is a unilaterally sponsored referral program conducted entirely by union professionals without formal recognition by management.

Summary

The organized work place is a particularly sensitive place for the social worker. No strong allegiance can be shown to either the employer or the worker. The social worker must be responsible to a joint union-management committee. The sole responsibility of the social worker is to help the client solve, in confidence, his personal and family problems. "It is in the problem and implementation of the human contract in the work place that social workers can play a most important role in fulfilling their functions as caseworkers, group workers, and community organizers and contribute to the development of social policy in industry and the community."[27] Knowledge of company problems, union problems, the subtleties and nuances of labor/management relationships, and the grievance procedure of the collective-bargaining agreement is essential in order for a social worker to function in the work place. It will be a great accomplishment when specially trained social workers "are employed in thousands of plants, mines, mills, stores, and offices across the country to help labor and management implement the human contract for the benefit of the working people and their families."[29]

Part II
Services to be Provided

4 Counseling

At a recent General Mills American Family Forum in Washington, D.C., Dr. Herbert Pardes, director of the NIMH, stated that it has been found that 15 percent of the population at any given time needs mental-health services.[1] Potentially, at least one-fifth of all employees are or will be victims, to some degree, of mental disorder, deterioration, or deficiency.[2] There is a profound need for mental-health services for this working population. Companies are beginning to decide that these services can be delivered within the working environment. This location is ideal because many deterrents to employees' getting help (cost, transportation, time off) would be eliminated.

Occupational mental health is defined in several ways. First, it is concerned with the mentally ill worker whose symptoms affect his functioning on the job. Second, it is concerned with thought, feeling, and behavior, both healthy and unhealthy, as it is seen in the work place. This definition takes into account factors in the work environment that support mentally healthy behavior as well as those that contribute to the development of unhealthy behavior.[3]

This chapter presents the incidence of mental illness in the work place and argues that the work place is an appropriate setting for the treatment of emotional problems. It then describes a model for treatment that is both unique and relative to the work place.

Four specific areas of counseling are explored: mental health, occupational stress, sexual harassment, and retirement. Vocational counseling is not discussed as it is really job counseling in which jobs are matched to the employee. This requires knowledge and skills of a different type than mental-health professionals have.

Several companies have already developed counseling programs within the work place, and a brief description of these programs is given. Several approaches to counseling programs exist, depending on the types of needs the company employees have, and examples within the chapter show the various applications.

Finally, the issues involved in the development of a new model of service delivery are discussed. Because this is a new setting for the delivery of social services, the foundation for service delivery has to be laid. Controversial issues involving social workers are discussed to enable the social workers to understand the unique role that they will hold in an industrial setting as a supplier of mental-health-care services.

Prevalence of Mental Illness in the Work Place

Estimates indicate that over 94.7 million Americans are employed.[4] The average workingperson spends one-third of his or her day at the work place and in reality, most people spend more time at work than they do awake at home. Work plays an extremely important role in the lives of people. Freud identified two significant hallmarks of adult functioning—the abilities to love and to work.[5] Work meets several needs in people's lives, including economic survival, life satisfaction, and a sense of reality. Work gives a sense of personal identity.[6] It is also a place to socialize and make friends. Increasingly, work is being seen by our society as a positive and important aspect of people's lives. In the past, our society has emphasized family life and leisure time, and social workers have traditionally ignored the therapeutic value of work.

However, work can also lead to stress that can eventually lead to emotional illness. Because work is finally being seen as a vital activity for the majority of people, there is a growing need to have mental-health care available in the work place. Several findings indicate such a need:

1. Up to 10 percent of employees are or will be victims of some degree of mental disorder, excluding alcoholism.
2. The cost of mental illness of employees through poor performance is estimated to be in excess of $14.2 billion annually.[7]
3. a. Rosen et al. report that of 3,165 patients, age 20-64, seen in the cooperating industrial dispensaries, 153 (4.8 percent) were considered by the dispensary physician to have an emotional, psychiatric, mental, or personality disorder.
    b. Of every 100 men, 5.3 percent had emotional problems. Of every 100 women, 4.1 percent had emotional problems.
    c. In terms of marital status, these problems were particularly high among separated and divorced persons (10.3 percent) and lower among both the single (4.4 percent) and married (4.8 percent).
    d. Frequencies of reported emotional problems were higher in census tracts of high socioeconomic ranking (6.8 percent compared to 4.1-5 percent for other socioeconomic areas).[8]
4. In an experimental investigation by Gordon, performed in a large chemical plant, the following findings were established:
    a. Seven percent of the plant staff were seen in psychiatric consultation as the result of referrals by plant physicians, supervisors, or employees themselves.
    b. This group accounted for a large majority of the absenteeism by employees.

c. They had, as a group, a greater percentage of the major and sub-major accidents than the rest of the plant. They caused an excessive proportion of personnel problems. They frequented the dispensary more. They took up more time of physicians, nurses, supervisors, and shop stewards than other employees.

d. Early in employment, they had set a pattern of poor productivity that had been maintained over the years.

e. Records show that many efforts were extended to help these people—for example, disability wages had been paid numerous times and medical attention had been spent—but it was not unusual to find forty to fifty days lost for disability per year.

f. This study showed that these individuals could not be described as having commonality by age, sex, or personality. Their commonality was failure to work productively.

g. The presenting symptoms were usually those common to an anxiety state.[9]

In his article, "Obstacles to Treatment for Blue-Collar Workers," Dr. Bertram Brown, the former director of the NIMH, reports that emotionally troubled auto workers do not use psychiatrists and mental-health centers even though the cost of the treatment is covered by the union's insurance. Instead they rely on themselves or family and friends. The implication is that merely providing health insurance coverage does not invariably lead to improved mental health.[10]

In a survey done in Michigan, it was discovered that only 13 percent of the UAW members knew about the mental-health coverage and that a full 46 percent did not know if they had coverage or not. Only 1 percent were using the benefits. The majority of workers thought the family doctor was an appropriate source of help for mentally ill workers.[11]

In this study as well as others, the stigma of being labeled as mentally ill contributed to the lack of use of services. In a study by Carvel Taylor of the five-hundred employees she saw in the work setting, it was found that none of these employees had ever seen an outside psychiatrist, psychologist, or social worker. The employees trusted social workers in the work place because they were employed by the organization.[12]

The researchers recommended that ways be found to increase access to the services of mental-health professionals. What better way to do this than to have the services provided at the work setting. The visibility of the program is increased, transportation is not a problem, and the hours are appropriate for the employee.[13]

Weiner, Akabas, and Sommer performed a demonstration project in the garment industry in New York. Their project provides interesting and surprising findings. Their impression that mentally ill individuals can work was proved by the findings of this study. Even men and women with severe emotional problems were found to be able to function on the job. The group of employees studied was found to have mainly neurotic disorders. The surprise came when 35 percent of the patient pool was found to be psychotic since it is believed that psychotic people are unable to work. However, most of the patients observed continued to work throughout the demonstration. The ability of these emotionally ill employees to continue working is one of the significant findings of the study—it suggests that a job may be within the capabilities of an emotionally ill person.[14] This is further evidence that emotionally ill people are indeed a part of today's working force and that the work place is an appropriate setting for meeting their needs.

In a study conducted by Conley, Conwell, and Arrid to measure the cost of mental illness, it was found that mental illness constitutes our nation's costliest health problem.[15] There are costs to the employer as well as the employee. The greatest material cost is the decrease in productive activity. Loss of output is caused by absenteeism, longer and more-frequent spells of unemployment, withdrawal from the labor force, and inefficiency on the job caused by the mental illness. The employee becomes chronically dissatisfied with his or her job. Failure to achieve the goals that intelligence, training, and experience merit causes discomfort. Job tensions intensify psychological disorder. Intangible losses leave victims insecure, bewildered, and frustrated with low self-esteem, and they sometimes lead to premature death and suicide.[16]

Mental illness has additional costs to the employer. It can manifest itself by physical illness that causes unnecessarily high labor turnover and disability retirement. It can cause substandard production. Poor employee morale, strife, and excessive labor trouble may develop.[17]

McMurray claims that the worst crime committed against employees is that the employer refers the mentally ill for so-called counseling to a lay counselor—that is, a supervisor, a company physician with no psychiatric training, the clergy, or personnel staff members. These people, however, are not qualified mental-health professionals.[18]

A need for mental-health services has been established, but the question still remains as to whether the work place is the appropriate vehicle for delivery of the services to the working population. The following conclusions were reached by Weiner, Akabas, and Sommer after exploring the question: Why should there be a mental-health program in an industrial setting?:

At any given time, a portion of the labor force is experiencing difficulty maintaining employment because of emotional problems. The number of employees who can remain in the work place on the job can be increased by having mental-health professionals located in the hub of the network of the work place.

In order for the counseling service to begin a counseling program in the work place and to be accepted and trusted by the employees and employers in the work place, there will have to be a change in the service delivery and the clinical technology employed.

They conclude that the work setting can have positive implications for both the recovery and prevention of mental illness for employees. Since limitations exist in availability and access to community mental-health care for employed individuals, the working place is a strategic location for service delivery. Mental-health programs in industry can help individuals maintain a productive role. The success of these services delivered at the work place location is dependent on the changes the social worker makes in his or her service delivery.[19]

The traditional role of the social worker cannot be generalized to the industrial setting. A new model of service delivery must be established. Austin and Jackson, in their paper "Occupational Mental Health and the Human Services" also agree that the social worker in the work place requires a comprehensive view of the worker as a client with the focus on job satisfaction, occupational health, and the mental-health services offered by labor unions. Implications arise here for both intervention and program planning.[20]

This new field of industrial mental health has implications for the role the occupational psychiatrist will play. The psychiatrist will need not only the knowledge of mental illnesses as diagnostically defined but also the knowledge of the influence of the industrial environment on these illnesses. A greater emphasis will be placed on preventive mental health. The psychiatrist will play an important role in developing the policies and procedures of corporations in order to foster healthy employees.[21]

A New Model of Service Delivery

In order to establish the role of the human-services provider in the work place, the author has developed a new model to mental-health service delivery. Social workers should incorporate seven aspects into their practice as described in the following paragraphs.

1. The supervisor plays an important role in situations in which job performance is being affected. The social worker is the contact between the supervisor and the employee as well as the contact and continuity between the supervisor and the outside therapist, if there is one. The social worker in the work setting is able to consult with the supervisor and involve the supervisor in the treatment plan, if appropriate. Often, however, the supervisor is so emotionally involved that she or he is unable to be objective about the employee's performance. Supervisors often blame themselves or feel

responsible for the poor performance of the employee. Conversely, a supervisor may be so frustrated that he or she is very angry. This involvement is analogous to the spouse's role when the partner is having difficulty functioning. This behavior can be a barrier to the supervisor-employee relationship. In addition to being the counselor for the employee, the social worker acts as a counsel for the supervisor as well, helping the supervisor see that the employee is accountable for performance and that the social workers role is to diagnose and refer. If the employee is seen by a therapist in the community, the social worker acts as a counsel for the supervisor as well, helping the supervisor see that the employee is accountable for performance and that it is the social worker's role to diagnose and refer. Often a community therapist will not communicate with the work place because of mistrust. This is often due to concern over confidentiality and how the information might be used against an employee. The supervisor who equally mistrusts the mental-health profession would not initiate contact either. The social worker in the work place can provide the connection that can interpret to each person involved what is occurring and thus help the employee receive treatment while functioning on the job. This supportive role has been found to be very important. Some employees may need years of therapy but can continue functioning if an objective, supportive social worker is in the work place who understands the work situation.

2. The social worker also must develop skills to help the employee look at his or her problems in a broader perspective. The social worker is in the work place and is able to listen, move around within the organization, know how the organization operates, and experience the problems employees have.[22] These give the social worker the ability to view the problem as the employee sees it, also as the supervisor may see it, as well as relating the problem in the work context, making it relevant for the employee.

3. The type of visits to the occupational social worker will be different than the community visits because the employee has greater access to the social worker. Even though there may be regular appointments, the social worker and client are in the same world—the work place. They can run into each other in the cafeteria and other places. More important, the social worker is physically close by and can be available for brief assistance when necessary. Rather than only carefully structured meetings, the work place allows for informal, brief, and even chance encounters between worker and client.

4. The social worker in the work place is there for crisis therapy. Any immediate situation can be handled on the spot by a social worker who is in-house, which is reassuring for employees as well as management.

5. The availability of counseling for women is another aspect. Many working women have children and families, and that can make keeping appointments in the community in the evening or on weekends very difficult.

The social worker hired by the industry lends availability and access to mental-health services for women who work.

6. Another important aspect of service delivery is the sanction the employees receive from the employer to seek help if needed. The organization should have concern toward those with a mental-health problem and hopefully show a willingness to help by providing counsellors. The management transfers that trust to the social worker. When the program gains a reputation of caring and listening, along with respect for confidentiality, self-referrals will begin.

7. The social worker should use the concept of community and apply it to the work place in understanding the environment of the employee. She or he should view the roles, values, relationships, and patterns of interaction to see how they differ from the geographic community.[23] She or he should study the organization and the systems of authority and communication present. The social worker must maintain visibility within the industry. A uniqueness exists in the industrial setting that the social worker needs to recognize. This uniqueness stems from the facts that the work community is composed of workers, that the community goal is production, that the community power is held by the institutional representatives of management and labor, and that the community culture is mirrored by the ethnic backgrounds of the employees.[24]

Social-Work Services

Weiner, Akabas, and Sommer present five areas in which the social worker can provide service in the industrial setting: casefinding, diagnostic process, referrals, treatment, and follow-up.[25]

The nature of the presenting problem is different from any other kind of social-work practice. The problem as seen by the employer or supervisor arises from work-related areas such as absenteeism, inaccurate reports, tardiness, and the inability to cooperate with peers or to communicate problems with the supervisor.[26] For self-referrals, the employee might know that she or he is having marital or financial difficulties that are affecting performance at work. Some fear they may be fired and know that until personal problems are handled, work is affected. For the industrial social worker, effective functioning on the job is an important treatment goal. The focus is on helping the employee stay employed if the employee wishes. The method or intervention might be to help the employee with personal problems, but the goal still remains to maintain adequate job performance. The social worker looks at the intrapsychic makeup of the individual only as it applies to his functional ability.[27] The purpose is to help the individual adjust to the working world. If the social worker can keep people functioning on the job, then social workers are making progress toward good mental health.

Industrial social workers fit perfectly with the psychosocial framework of traditional social-work practice since the main emphasis is on the central role of the environment in influencing human behavior. The emphasis on social-work values meshes with the industrial-social-work concept. In fact, social work is uniquely suited to the industrial setting because it upholds the professional commitment to enhancing social functioning—that is, helping the individual to have maximal functioning at work, in the family, and in society.

Mental-health counseling can be seen in three dimensions. First, the social worker can assist the individual. The person could have neurotic or psychotic characteristics that need to be diagnosed and treated. The second dimension involves outside-the-individual, or social, problems. Such problems could be marital, battering, incest, child abuse, rape, or problems of sexual preference. The third dimension involves conditions that affect the individual's temporary well-being. These could be the need for legal counseling or financial assistance. In a study by Human Affairs, Inc., a national social-work corporation that offers contracting services to corporations, the problems identified fall into the following categories:

Social (marital, personal, parent/child), 37 percent;

Mental-health, 14 percent;

Legal, 9 percent;

Alcohol-related, 9 percent;

Job-related, 8 percent;

Financial, 6 percent;

Health, 14 percent;

Other, 2 percent.

Financial problems increasingly have been found to affect mental health.[28]

A specialized intake form will have to be developed to handle this unique setting of service delivery. An intake instrument should address the worker's work history, worker's support system, and goals of treatment as they relate to the impact of the employee's problem on job performance.

Most of the cases the social worker will serve will be short term and crisis oriented in nature. The remaining cases will require more-intensive contact with clinicians and will be referred elsewhere for help.

The unique ingredient in this treatment approach is the use of the industrial network in the treatment process. Not only will there be links with supervisors but also the union will be involved. Representatives of the industrial work place can make significant contributions.

Stress Counseling

One area of counseling that would involve the industrial social worker is stress counseling. When stress is surfacing as poor job performance, counseling in the work place should occur. By definition, stress is a reaction by the body to a stimulus that is unpleasant.[30] Not everything in life is pleasant so some stress is natural and inevitable. Donald Norfolk, in his book *Executive Stress,* says that stress at manageable levels can be positively beneficial to health. He states that stress actually helps to prolong life. This fact is noticeable, for instance, among U.S. presidents who live longer on an average than vice-presidents and longer still than candidates who run but fail to win the presidency.[31]

In medical terms, stress is the behavior an individual exhibits when she or he can no longer meet the demands of his or her environment.[32] The body responds to stress as if it were going into battle. Blood is pumped faster, breathing is sped up, and adrenalin is released into the bloodstream. When an individual gets out of balance, disease is the most acceptable form of retreat. The cost of stress has been estimated at $10-20 billion—a figure higher than the gross revenue of any but the three largest industrial corporations.[33]

People commonly think that stress only affects executives, particularly those at high levels of management who make important decisions, but researchers have found that occupational stress affects blue-collar workers as well.[34] They suffer from stress because either their job is too simplistic and routine or it is so difficult and fast paced that they cannot keep up. Recently, the lack of autonomy in a job has been seen as a real stress producer. For example, it accounts for why secretaries are found to be in the second-highest category of stress-related occupations.

Rogers, in a study performed in Canada, discovered that workload was perceived to be the highest individual cause of stress in Canadian organizations. Decision making also was a high precipitator for managers. He found that no relationship exists between stress and the manager's age, education, or type of organization. This implies that the ability to cope with stress is related to variables such as social environment, personality configuration, and extraorganizational stress-producing variables such as marriage and finances. The basic problem is in identifying the precipitators of the stress. Ways in which the organization and management can reduce the stress of employees are, for example, providing company sports, insisting on regular vacations, and establishing a company counseling service.[35]

Thomas Holmes and Richard Rahe, psychiatrists at the University of Washington Medical School have developed a life-crisis scale (see table 4-1). A life crisis is defined as the accumulation of at least 150 points in a twelve-month period. For the twenty-four months following a life crisis, the body is at risk. This life scale certainly provides us with information for reflection.[36]

Table 4-1
The Social Readjustment Rating Scale

Life Event	Mean Value	Life Event	Mean Value
1. Death of spouse	100	23. Son or daughter leaving home	29
2. Divorce	73	24. Trouble with in-laws	29
3. Marital separation	65	25. Outstanding personal achievement	28
4. Jail term	63	26. Spouse begins or stops work	26
5. Death of close family member	63	27. Begin or end school	26
6. Personal injury or illness	53	28. Change in living conditions	25
7. Marriage	50	29. Revision of personal habits	24
8. Fired at work	47	30. Trouble with boss	23
9. Marital reconciliation	45	31. Change in work hours or conditons	20
10. Retirement	45	32. Change in residence	20
11. Change in health of family member	45	33. Change in schools	20
12. Pregnancy	40	34. Change in recreation	19
13. Sex difficulties	39	35. Change in church activities	19
14. Gain of new family member	39	36. Change in social activities	18
15. Business readjustment	39	37. Mortgage or loan less than $10,000	17
16. Change in financial state	38	38. Change in sleeping habits	16
17. Death of close friend	37	39. Change in number of family get-togethers	15
18. Change to different line of work	36	40. Change in eating habits	15
19. Change in number of arguments with spouse	35	41. Vacation	13
20. Mortgage of $10,000	31	42. Christmas	12
21. Foreclosure of mortgage or loan	30	43. Minor violations of the law	11
22. Change in responsibilities at work	29		

Source: T.H. Holmes and R.H. Rahe, "The Social Readjustment Rating Scale," *Journal of Psychosomatic Research* 11-23-218, 1967.

The federal government's National Institute for Occupational Safety and Health has rated 140 occupations by the pressure they produce. The twelve jobs with most stress are as follows:

1. Laborer,
2. Secretary,
3. Inspector,
4. Clinical lab technician,
5. Office manager,
6. Foreman,
7. Manager/administrator,

8. Waitress/waiter,
9. Machine operator,
10. Farm owner,
11. Miner,
12. Painter.

Other high-stress jobs include (in alphabetical order) bank teller, clergyman, computer programmer, dental assistant, electrician, fireman, guard/watchman, hairdresser, health aide, health technician, machinist, meat cutter, mechanic, musician, nurse's aide, plumber, policeman, practical nurse, public-relations person, railroad switchman, registered nurse, sales manager, sales representative, social worker, structural metalworker, teacher's aide, telephone operator, warehouse worker.

A special population vulnerable to stress is women. Women often have a dual role—holding down a job and running a family—and they are frequently single parents.

Dr. Beric Wright, in his book *Executive Ease and Disease,* has presented the following findings:

1. Seniors and successful top managers in large corporations have longer lives than less-successful managers.
2. Cardiovascular disease—coronary thrombosis and raised blood pressure—are the biggest problems.
3. One-third of all businessmen will die before reaching the age sixty-five.
4. Thin people live longer than fat people.
5. Overtired, overworked, stressed people are more coronary prone.
6. Mental illness is likely to occur at times of stress and/or instability.[37]

As previously stated, clerical workers are highly prone to stress. In a study done by Dr. Suzanne Haynes, an epidemiologist with the National Heart, Lung and Blood Institute, reports that workingwomen as a total do not have a higher rate of heart disease than housewives but that women in sales and clinical occupations do. This group has twice the rate of coronary diseases than other women. This group represents 35 percent of all workingwomen, or 18 million women. Haynes also found that the women with the greatest risk were clerical workers with blue-collar husbands and three or more children. Executives let out their stress on their secretaries. The secretaries then have to deal with increased pressure at work.

A valid question to ask would be: What are the environmental pressures that relate to stress? First, successful job matching cuts down on stress. Not only is successful job matching extremely important, so is the working environment and the nature of the job itself. Second, some employees must deal with dominating managers. Third, many jobs hold role ambiguity.

Fourth, delegation of job responsibilities affects the amount of stress—that is, it is important to match authority and responsibility. Fifth, a boring job can lead to frustration. Sixth, the employee must get enough sleep to maintain appropriate job performance.[38]

Several suggestions have been presented by researchers as to how to reduce or control stress. Getting plenty of exercise and using moderation in habits are important.[39] Exercise has several beneficial results. For example, it reduces the level of anxiety, is a way of letting off steam, builds up stamina, counteracts the biochemical effects of stress, and reduces the risk of psychological illness.[40]

Employees are also getting involved and doing something about stress. For example, one day a month, the Irwin Union Bank of Columbus, Indiana, has a psychiatrist visit to discuss with the employees the stresses and strains involved with their job. In the intensive-care unit at the University of California Medical Center in San Diego, the nurses conduct a so-called wake to talk about their grief after the death of a patient. Also, in the California Security Pacific Bank, the executives and managers are trained to observe the initial signs of stress in employees.

There has been a major breakthrough in receiving a pension for stress. On 26 July 1979, in a two-to-zero vote, the Newton Retirement Board granted accidental-disability retirement to a nine-year veteran of the Newton (Massachusetts) Police Department. James L. Guaragna, age thirty-five, had had specific work experiences that left him psychologically unable to perform his duties as a police officer. A series of stressful work-related incidents occurred between 1970-1971, incidents that included four or five assaults while making arrests and one attempt to run over him. His case was based on the phobic neurosis he had developed as evidenced by his looking around constantly for the people who had assaulted him. His psychiatrist stated that the stress was job related.[41]

Stress is an inherent part of modern organizational life and must be recognized and dealt with. The industrial social worker can play an important role in counseling the employees who manifest stress by having heart attacks, high blood pressure, peptic ulcers, and insomnia. The social worker needs to be aware of the factors that come into play in the unique treatment setting of the work place.

One corporation that is handling stress by counseling is the Mead Corporation. Mead has seminars on stress management, and their purpose is to promote positive mental- and physical-health practices. Early identification of symptoms is encouraged. The themes of the seminars are the productive use of stress and maximizing the use of one's personal energies with physical fitness, relaxation, and effective cognitive practices.[42]

At the recent General Mills American Family Forum, Dr. Leonard Moss, a psychiatrist in private practice, a consulting psychiatrist to the

Mobil Oil Corporation, and author of *Management Stress,* described his model of occupational-stress reduction. He finds that stress comes from many sources—work, social, personal, cultural, and family. The individual handles this stress by support systems, individual characteristics, and social-support systems. He defines support systems as preparation, training, orientation, colleagues, and friends. Individual characteristics are summarized as coping capacity, previous job experience, health history, and demographic background.[43]

Social supports are spouse, boss, friend, medical doctor, and others. All these sources have consequences for health versus illness and how well the individual adjusts and is able to function on the job. Moss's premise is that the higher the pressures, both job and life, the stronger the social supports must be for the individual to perform adequately at his or her job.[44]

Social workers have many alternatives to handling the stress of employees. The first thing they can do is to educate the employees about stress and be an advocate of exercise and good eating habits. Consultation with the supervisor regarding job duties and how they relate to the employee's stress is in order. Social workers can develop skills in biofeedback, cognitive-reappraisal techniques, and relaxation responses. A preventive role also exists for social workers—namely, conducting educational programs and running stress-reduction clinics.

Sexual Harassment

Sexual harassment on the job is quite widespread and is an area in which the social worker can play an important role. In a recent testimony on sexual harassment in Washington, D.C. (October 1979), it was reported that almost every woman surveyed in a wide variety of government departments had experienced some type of behavior from male bosses and/or supervisors that constituted sexual harassment.[45]

Sexual harassment involves a spectrum of behaviors. The OPM defines sexual harassment as "deliberate or repeated unsolicited verbal comments, gestures, or physical contact of a sexual nature which are unwelcome."[46] Anytime a man uses the power of his influence to bargain for sexual favors, he is sexually harassing his female employees. The behavior may be blatant or subtle. Because of this strong influence, the woman who refuses such advances has to pay a high cost—that is, risking losing her job. Women in this position of sexual harassment often feel discouraged and that they have no recourse. Women thus tend to remain silent because their work represents economic well-being.

This subject is gaining increased attention. The HHS is setting an outstanding example in this area. It has developed and circulated a policy statement, completed a video tape on the subject, and has contracted for a training session on sexual harassment to be held for the Federal Women's Program Staff. The latter are the people assigned responsibility in the federal work force to insure women's concern are given appropriate attention. ITT has taken the lead in the private sector by also developing a policy. Literature is very scarce and much of it refers to court cases, which are on the increase. Mental-health workers should provide psychological relief to the harassed as the lawyers strive for financial reimbursement.

The social worker in the work place could be very helpful in both supplying information and lending support. Women's groups could be started to provide women with an outlet for frustration and also help with sexual-harassment problems. This area is most appropriately treated in the work place because two employees are affected—the harassed and the harasser.

Retirement Counseling

Retirement is a phase in everyone's life. A job provides an individual with self-identity. When one is no longer employed, this void has to be filled. Changes occur in one's self-definition as well as one's self-esteem and these changes have to be handled.

Our society and cultural values make growing old a very difficult process. The elderly are not provided with aspirations, goals, and meaningful reward as they have been in the previous stages of life. Economic independence, prestige, and social importance are sometimes taken away. Old age is viewed in our society as the least desirable age.[47] We have a negative viewpoint of growing old as opposed to other cultures such as the Oriental in which the elderly are revered and honored.

Preretirement is a vital part of counseling. For approximately forty years an individual identifies himself or herself strictly by occupation. One becomes one's occupation. Upon retirement, the person must find a personal identity by humanitarian standards. At this point introspection begins, and a person begins to assess self-worth and accomplishments. If the sense of worth came solely or largely from work, then there will be severe loss of self-esteem.[48] Preparing an individual for this introspection is critical.

In 1979, Congress passed an important bill—HR5383. This bill raised the mandatory retirement age in the private sector to seventy, and it eliminated mandatory retirement in the federal sector. This bill was based on the facts that mandatory retirement tied to age is arbitrary and that chronological age is not a good indicator of the ability to perform a job.[49]

The social worker can help the employee make the transition from employment to retirement as smoothly as possible. Factors directly related to unsuccessful transition are the lack of information, of orientation, and of planning. Preretirement discussion groups are an excellent vehicle in giving the employee in transition an opportunity to share with others in the same life situation similar and unique thoughts, questions, and difficulties that result from the retirement process.[50]

A research report written by Roger O'Meara concludes that retirement can bring:

Financial,	Alcoholism,
Housing,	Marital,
Legal,	Loneliness,
Loss of prestige,	Loss of identity,
Second career,	Failing health,
Lack of purpose,	Fear of death.[51]

Social workers in industry should make the preretirement program highly visible. Research has indicated that preretirers are an ignored group unless their difficulties become so unbearable that they are obvious to others around them. Retirement planning can cover areas such as social security, profitsharing, income readjustment, geographical relocations, and requests for extensions. Financial planning is very important in the process.

More and more companies are developing programs for retirement counseling. Both seminars and individual interviews are used. The preretirement discussion group, based on a situation-transition group, is a small discussion-education group employing the use of trained facilitators for the purpose of helping individuals who have similar stressful life situations. This group informs the preretirers about the event of retirement and provides a supportive social and emotional atmosphere in which the preretirers can interact. Uncertainties arising from the unfamiliarity of retirement are discussed. Loss of status, identification, productivity, and friendships with fellow employees are the central themes.[52]

It has been found that pathology can be caused by having too much free time. The social worker can provide alternatives to the time that was previously spent working. Interests and hobbies can be developed. The retirement phase is very important. More people are living longer and as a result spending many more years in retirement than previously. Demographic changes will affect mortality, and in the year 2010 the elderly who are now 19 percent of the population will then be 21 percent, and by 2030 three out of every ten (30 percent) will be sixty-two and over.[53]

The federal government has mandated that within two years of potential retirement, the federal employer must sit down with the employee and discuss issues regarding retirement. These major items involve money and insurance. The employer must discuss the length of service by the employee, the computation of annuity related to length of service, and the health and life insurance status. The employer must also answer any other questions raised by the employee.[54] The OPM has also suggested it would be appropriate to prepare employees in the following areas—medical, psychological, social security, and costs of living in different areas of the country.

Thus, the social worker can play an important role in the preretirement process. He or she needs the skills of group facilitation and also needs to be aware of the aging process and the needs and feelings of the retirement-age group. A knowledge of available resources is another requisite for effective retirement counseling.

Corporate Counseling Programs

Many corporations have already established counseling programs for their employees. Different types of programs have been developed according to the employee's needs. They vary in structure as well as location and number of services offered. The following sections provide several examples of programs currently in operation.

Polaroid Corporation. The Polaroid Corporation, which designs, manufactures, markets, and distributes cameras and photographic equipment, began its counseling department in 1948 with one social worker as a consultant. It now has four counselors, all with graduate degrees in social work. The counseling department at Polaroid developed because of its concern for people and its desire to further the well-being of both the individual and the company. It pursues two main objectives:

1. To assist its members in solving problems that tend to lend imbalance to individual well-being and restrict the ability to function and develop and to assist the corporation in locating human and organizational stresses and handling the conflict;
2. To address the environment in which the individual operates and where crises occur.

The functions of Polaroid's counseling program are

Individual counseling,	Group facilitation,
Consultation,	Special programs,
Sensing stresses in the environment,	Research.[55]

U.S. Steel South Works Counseling Center. This industry began a program in a plant in South Chicago that employes 12,000 people. This program is staffed by three professional social workers. The types of services offered are

A range of counseling from common-sense advice to social treatment based on the task-centered casework model;

Linkage service with appropriate community resources;

Emergency services.

The program was founded on the assumptions that social workers know the resource network in the community and that people need these services. This industry feels that the program is successful and owes the success to the fact that the counseling service advertises its services broadly and actively. The staff stresses that it will help anyone with any kind of problem, which has lowered the threshold of resistance.[56]

Citibank. Citibank is the second-largest commercial bank in the world. It employs approximately 23,000 people in the United States and 26,000 overseas. The program began in 1971 and provides a wide range of services. The counseling is short term and crisis oriented. The problems range from depression to preretirement planning, but most of them involve financial difficulties. Citibank's program has a clinical psychologist, general counselors, and a psychiatric consultant who comes in two hours weekly.

Citibank has a unique approach to handling financial difficulties. Whenever employees receive notice of garnishment, they are invited to see a counselor. If the employee is willing to accept assistance, the counselor will discuss with the legal collector alternatives other than garnishment. In 85 percent of these cases, the counselors have found ways other than garnishment to solve the financial situation.

Citibank also includes services for its deaf employees. A sign-language interpreter is hired at the organization's expense whenever a deaf employee asks for counseling. The staff advisory service also sponsors a meeting once a week for the deaf employees to make their needs and concerns known.[57]

General Mills. General Mills employs 10,000 employees who work directly under the parent company, 2,000 of whom are located at corporate head-quarters in Minneapolis, Minnesota. Two years after an alcoholism program was begun, Corporate Medical Director James L. Craig, M.D., realized that alcoholism was only one problem. He recommended a program be implemented that included mental-health counseling. This service is on contract

with the Metropolitan Clinic of Counseling. The types of services offered
are twenty-four-hour crisis intervention; a free intitial visit; psychotherapy
and counseling for personal, marital, interpersonal, and other problems;
and follow-up visits at no charge. The counselor visits the company one
afternoon per week to conduct the clinic.

In 1977, the counseling program assisted 190 employees' one-half of
them were self-referred and the other half were referred by the medical
department.[58]

**The Industrial Counseling Program of Family Counseling of Greater New
Haven.** Family Counseling of Greater New Haven, one of the country's
oldest family agencies, provides counseling and social services to the New
Haven business and industrial community on a contractual basis. The staffing consists of one senior staff person who does public relations, administration, and coordination and one first-year MSW candidate. The services offered are

Assistance with personal or interpersonal problems in work site or community;

Training program for management or supervisory personnel;

Consultation to the medical department.[59]

Social Security Administration. This program serves approximately 21,000
clerical, technical, and professional employees in the Baltimore area and an
additional 1,500 employees living in Washington, D.C. This counseling service is the first management-sponsored program and was established in 1944.
It was for many years the only federal-agency program. Its services include
professional counseling and referral services for employees with work-related
problems, emotional problems, alcohol and drug problems and advisory services for supervisors of employees with work-related problems that affect
their functioning at work. It is utilized by supervisors and managers as well as
line workers. Their use of this service has helped to qualify the services as objective and confidential. The program staff is composed of fourteen professionals. There are eight social workers (six with MSW, two with BS) and six
staff with MA degrees in psychology/education.[60] It is the longest running industrial social-work program in the United States.

Issues

Several issues have arisen in regard to the role of the social worker as
mental-health worker in the work place. The first issue, for example, is one

that is frequently brought up in social-work practice—the issue of confidentiality. Where does this confidentiality begin and end? Are the records part of the corporation's property? Are the records seen only by the social worker? Specific issues related to these records are policies regarding the following:

What should go into a care record?

What kind of forms should be utilized?

Who has access to records?

How will cases be coded?

When are records destroyed?

How is ancillary staff such as secretaries and students trained?

Where are records kept?

Confidentiality has particular significance in the work place because it can endanger the livelihood of the individual if it is breached.

Another issue involves who the social worker represents. For example, when the employer, employee, and the union's interests are not coordinated, then those agent is the social worker? Clearly then the social worker serves the employee, but there are times when the professional role must be clearly stated to management as well as to the union.

In-house versus out-of-house social workers are another issue. There are both positive and negatives aspects to each. In-house is defined as a program physically located in the company. Out-of-house is a program physically located away from the company. Most programs are located in-house.

Another question is: Who performed the services? There are two possibilities to the delivery of services. The services can be delivered by a professional who is a contractor or by a professional who is employed by the organization. This is a decision that should be considered by the organization in designing the program.

Both the in-house-program and the out-of-house-program staffs can be contracted out or employed by the corporation, thus forming four models for the delivery of services. The location and who the employer is depend on the specific needs of the employees of the corporation.

Reisman, Scribner, and Reiff found, on the one hand, that mental-health services were underutilized by workers in the lower socioeconomic group primarily because of high costs and because many services were inaccessible to transportation and office hours were restricted.[61] In-house social workers would eliminate these problems. On the other hand, mental-health services provided by management arouses some worker suspicion; trust issues can develop, but in-house social workers have the advantage of spotting problems that occur right in the work place. The social worker that is located in-house is better able to handle the stigma that workers find is associated with being labeled mentally ill because they can handle the concern in the work place itself.

Training for industrial social workers is another issue of concern. Social-work education needs to identify the uniqueness of the industrial setting and adopt appropriate training for the skills that will be needed. The model proposed in this chapter lays a strong foundation for training for the social worker in the work place.

Industrial social work and mental-health service is becoming a reality. Social workers will have to be trained if they are to be effective in the work place, and this should be a positive force in the prevention of mental illness.

Summary

The majority of Americans is employed. It is a good possibility that at least 10 percent of these people will at some time need mental-health services. This chapter has explored the need for mental-health services and has offered the option of having service delivery in the work place. A new model of service delivery was discussed with special emphasis on the uniqueness of the work setting as opposed to the traditional arena of service delivery in the community. Special areas of counseling were developed by the author with a description of the role that the social worker can play in the industrial setting. Different corporate programs were presented. Finally, special issues of concern in laying a groundwork for new service delivery were explored.

5 Occupational-Alcoholism/Employee-Assistance Counseling Programs

By passing the Federal Comprehensive Alcohol Abuse and Alcoholism Prevention, Treatment, and Rehabilitation Act (the Hughes Act) in 1970, the ninety-first Congress established several substantial mechanisms to help alleviate a large social problem in the United States—alcoholism and its relationship to the work force. The act provided, first, for the creation of the NIAAA, separate from the NIMH, thus separating alcohol from mental health; it permitted the evolution of an entirely new approach to the treatment of alcoholism. Second, the law established within the NIAAA an occupational branch mandated to originate programs related to alcoholism in the work place. Third, the act required that all federal agencies, both military and civilian, have alcohol programs for their employees.

The social-work profession continues to feel the impact of the Hughes Act because practitioners with an MSW are well-qualified candidates to staff occupational-alcoholism/employee-assistance programs (OA/EAPs) if they receive the necessary training in the special field of alcoholism. OA/EAPs are developing more extensively and rapidly than the other sorts of programs where social workers might also serve (for example, affirmative-action programs, mental-health-counseling programs, and programs promoting corporate social responsibility).

OA/EAPs are expected to increase in number and importance in the future. The NIAAA plans to make OA/EAPs available to 50 percent of the work force by 1984. HHS began, in 1979, under the author's direction, to develop an OA/EAP for its employees that would subsequently be available as a model for other agencies. It is situated in the office of the secretary, and the director reports directly to the assistant secretary for personnel. The HHS plan is included in appendix A as an example of a comprehensive approach that could be used by a large agency or company to implement an EAP. Private industry is expected to reflect this progress.

This chapter discusses the history, concepts, and philosophy of OA/EAPs. It describes their essential ingredients and specifically discusses a variety of OA/EAPs administered by the author. The latter programs have been managed by Boston College and funded by the NIAAA. The Boston College OA/EAPs constitute a descriptive introduction to this area of practice for the student of social work.

Concepts and Philosophy of EAPs

Contrary to popular belief, most active alcoholics are employed. Consequently, OA/EAPs are designed to help the problem drinker in the work place, which will also reduce the costs of poor work performance absenteeism. Instead of training supervisors to look for symptoms of alcoholism, OA/EAPs focus primarily on workers' job performance and attendance. Although not all people who have problems with job performance suffer from alcoholism, the NIAA estimates that more than 50 percent do. Moreover, the National Council on Alcoholism (NCA) estimates that approximately one out of every ten to thirteen employees—8 to 10 percent of the labor force—has a problem with alcohol and that costs to the economy vary from $8 billion to $15 billion a year. Absenteeism alone accounts for two-thirds of these costs.[2]

Figure 5-1 describes the progression alcoholism from its early to its middle and late states. The figure summarizes the various behaviors manifested by the alcoholic from the drinking to relieve tension that occurs in the early stages of addiction to the impaired thinking that can result in the late stage. Figure 5-2 demonstrates the progression of the deteriorating job performance of the alcoholic that parallels the stages of disease. Together, the two charts provide a clear picture of the relationship between the disease and the work place.

Because it is a progressive disease, alcoholism often takes ten to fifteen years before reaching its middle stages when it begins to affect job performance. Frequently, an employee in the middle stages of alcoholism is a valued worker and more often than not occupies a position of responsibility in a supervisory, middlemanagement, or top-executive category. Therefore, treatment of these employees becomes a matter of substantial importance to a company. Stanford Research Institute, in a study on alcoholism in industry, estimates that, by treating workers with a drinking problem, industry saves about $6,000 per year per worker.[3]

More important than the costs of alcoholism, however, is the fact that the highest rates of recovery from the disease occur in programs in offices and factories, not in clinics or hospitals. Such success is attributable to certain variables. First, attempts to detect and treat alcoholism are most successful during the middle stage of the disease. Second, job status and income may mean more to many alcoholics than has been realized previously. According to the NCA, the average alcoholic will give up his or her family five years before she or he gives up a job.[4] Other reasons for the need to treat alcoholic workers in the work place are discussed in the following paragraphs.

1. The primary behavioral mechanism of the alcoholic is denial. The alcoholic will not voluntarily seek help and will continue to deny and cover

ADDICTION (READ DOWN)

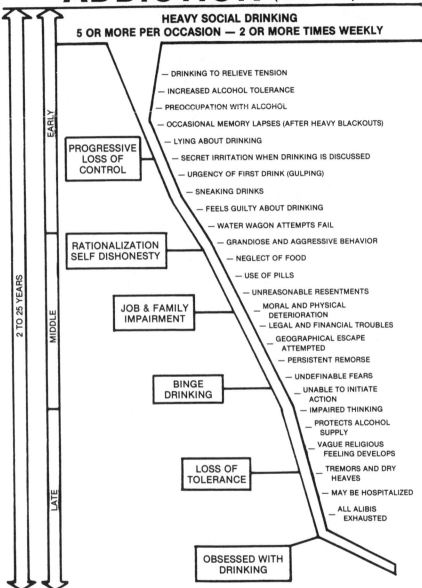

HEAVY SOCIAL DRINKING
5 OR MORE PER OCCASION — 2 OR MORE TIMES WEEKLY

— DRINKING TO RELIEVE TENSION

— INCREASED ALCOHOL TOLERANCE

— PREOCCUPATION WITH ALCOHOL

— OCCASIONAL MEMORY LAPSES (AFTER HEAVY BLACKOUTS)

— LYING ABOUT DRINKING

PROGRESSIVE LOSS OF CONTROL — SECRET IRRITATION WHEN DRINKING IS DISCUSSED

— URGENCY OF FIRST DRINK (GULPING)

— SNEAKING DRINKS

— FEELS GUILTY ABOUT DRINKING

— WATER WAGON ATTEMPTS FAIL

— GRANDIOSE AND AGGRESSIVE BEHAVIOR

RATIONALIZATION SELF DISHONESTY — NEGLECT OF FOOD

— USE OF PILLS

— UNREASONABLE RESENTMENTS

JOB & FAMILY IMPAIRMENT — MORAL AND PHYSICAL DETERIORATION

— LEGAL AND FINANCIAL TROUBLES

— GEOGRAPHICAL ESCAPE ATTEMPTED

— PERSISTENT REMORSE

— UNDEFINABLE FEARS

BINGE DRINKING — UNABLE TO INITIATE ACTION

— IMPAIRED THINKING

— PROTECTS ALCOHOL SUPPLY

— VAGUE RELIGIOUS FEELING DEVELOPS

LOSS OF TOLERANCE — TREMORS AND DRY HEAVES

— MAY BE HOSPITALIZED

— ALL ALIBIS EXHAUSTED

OBSESSED WITH DRINKING

EARLY / MIDDLE / LATE

2 TO 25 YEARS

Source: M.M. Glatt, The Alcoholic & the Help He Needs, 2nd Edition (Lancaster, England: M&P Co. Ltd., 1972).

Figure 5-1. The Progressive Disease of Alcoholism

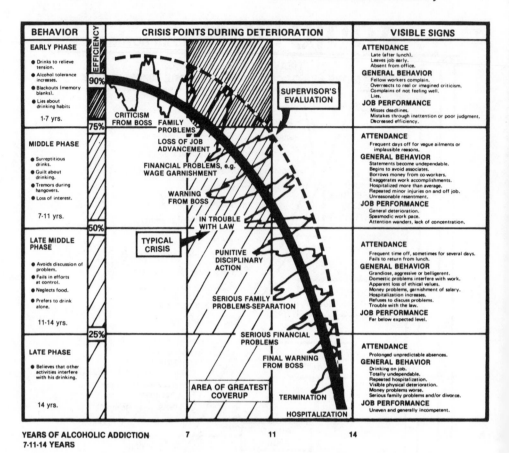

<figure>
| BEHAVIOR | EFFICIENCY | CRISIS POINTS DURING DETERIORATION | VISIBLE SIGNS |
</figure>

Source: Dayle F. Lindly and Robert T. Dorris, "Am I Drinking Too Much?" (Santa Monica, Calif.: Council on Alcoholism and Related Disorders,) 1967.

Figure 5-2. How an Alcoholic Employee Behaves

up the problem. The alcoholic needs to be confronted with the facts about his or her behavior. The crisis often precipitated by such confrontation may enhance the individual's motivation to do something about the drinking, thereby increasing responsiveness to treatment efforts. Rather than having to "hit bottom," as Alcoholics Anonymous (AA) calls the late stage of alcoholism, an employee confronted by a supervisor at work may be provided the chance to obtain treatment before dismissal results.

2. The relationship between the employer and employee provides a legitimate reason for confrontation and intervention when deteriorating job performance is documented since the employee is contracted to perform a specific job. If a worker is not performing to capacity, then the employer has a right to take action. An employer who provides the services of an OA/EAP for his or her workers is taking action in a humane rather than an adverse way.

3. Steady employment often becomes the basis for the denial of problem drinking. Supervisors and others at work are in the important position of perceiving the problem and contributing to its solution since families are often pressured by the stigmas of alcoholism and may be unable to deal with the problem. Management at the work place can help eradicate the stigma, however, by requiring that the employee obtain help rather than waiting until dismissal becomes the only answer.[5]

Roman recently described the following assumptions for implementing OA/EAPs:

> Identification by a supervisor of an employee who exhibits poor job performance is the most clear-cut mechanism for identifying an individual with an underlying drinking problem.

> Alcoholism should be regarded as a medical problem in the work place and should be treated as such.

> Regular disciplinary procedures for poor performance should be suspended while an employee with an identified drinking problem conscientiously seeks assistance.

> An employee's return to adequate job performance should be the criterion for judging a successful outcome of treatment.[6]

In addition, expanding OA/EAPs have developed outreach strategies for families as often as possible. Because insurance coverage usually includes family members, programs have been prepared to assist members of an employee's family who also have drinking problems if they seek the assistance. In addition, OA/EAPs also treat employees whose family member is an active alcoholic. Employees who fall into this category also show problems with job performance. A husband at work may be preoccupied about an alcoholic wife at home with the children. As alcoholism increases among senior citizens, adult children can become preoccupied at work worrying about their parents. Current case loads reflect that these employees now often seek help.

The people just described are often referred to as the other victims of alcoholism. At the congressional hearings on family members of alcoholics held in 1977, Josie Coutoure, executive director of the Other Victims of Alcoholism, estimated that four persons are directly affected by every alcoholic. These other victims frequently use mental-health facilities, as well as the services of physicians, to try to cope with the stress of living with an active alcoholic. Table 5-1 shows the parallel between the problems of the alcoholics and the problems of their families. The NIAAA recently studied the us of HMOs by other victims. The study showed a significant drop in their use of medical and psychiatric services after the alcoholic family member had received treatment.[7]

In 1979, OA/EAPs with the Boston College project have included an intensive alcoholic history on all incoming clients and have kept separate statistics for the other-victims category. Through this means many of these other victims surface. Frequently, these people seek help for non-alcohol-related problems such as marital problems, and they blame themselves for causing problems in the relationship. Skillful interviewing and sensitivity to alcohol problems by staff often uncover a spouse who has a long history of alcohol abuse. The other victim often denies the reality of the disease, however, and this denial can be as strong as that of the alcoholic. Because of the growing awareness of the needs of other victims, Congress proposed in 1978 that a considerable portion of the NIAAA's budget be allocated for their treatment. However, the proposal did not pass.

Several treatment facilities in England and Germany visited by the author in June 1978 had separate treatment facilities for other victims. These clients are treated whether or not the alcoholic comes for treatment. The fact that other victims are entering treatment more often and that more interest is being shown in their behalf clearly indicates that the disease affects more people than may ever have been originally estimated.

Historical Development

In the 1940s, Consolidated Edison, Kemper Insurance, Eastman Kodak, and the Dupont Corporation started some of the earliest programs to treat alcoholism. Most programs originated in the companies' medical departments. Before the implementation of these efforts, dismissal usually resulted if an employee's alcoholism became intolerable on the job. Despite the demonstrated effectiveness of these programs, however, with recovery rates as high as 60 to 70 percent, new ones did not immediately proliferate. In 1959, there were only 50 programs in major corporations in the United States. In 1971, the number grew to 300; in 1973, it was 600; and today approximatley 2,250 such programs exist.[8]

In 1972, in his first Caravan Survey (a study of *Fortune 500* company executives), Roman ascertained that 25 percent of the companies surveyed had some type of program to identify and provide assistance to employees with drinking problems.[9] Of this group, 51 percent reported that the program enjoyed strong support from top management, 39 percent indicated moderate support, and 10 percent indicated no support. By 1976, in the updated Caravan Survey, Roman reported that the level of management support in those companies with programs had changed significantly for the better—that is, 66 percent of the executives reported strong support, 31 percent indicated moderate support, and only 3 percent reported no support.[10]

As previously stated, the single factor that gave impetus to the concern for alcohol problems was the passage of the Hughes Act.[11] It mandated the following two key provisions that further developed OA/EAPs:

1. The NIAAA established an occupational branch tht granted $50,000 to each state to fund two occupational-program consultants. The responsibility of these consultants is to develop OA/EAPs in the private and public sectors. Most states maintained these positions even after the funding was exhausted, and some such as California and New York fund more than a dozen consultants. The occupational branch also funds demonstration projects. Notable models have been the OA/EAP of the Airline Pilots Association, the University of Missouri grant for faculty and staff, the AFL-CIO project in Appalachia, and most recently, the efforts in organized baseball to reach employees with drinking problems.

2. Section 201 of the Hughes Act mandated the Civil Service Commission to establish an office, now called the OPM to develop and maintain, in cooperation with the secretary of NEW (now HHS) and other federal agencies, appropriate prevention, treatment, and rehabilitation programs for alcohol abuse and alcoholism among federal employees. Letter number 792-4 of the *Federal Personnel Manual* dated 7 July 1971 required agencies to establish EAPs. The Department of Defense and each of the military services have also mandated such programs for military and civilian employees. In addition, these programs are included as line items in the departments' budgets.

A secondary factor that has helped keep the problem of alcohol abuse as a high priority in government agencies has been the work, since 1976, of the Federal Interagency Committee on Alcoholism. During the author's chairmanship of the Work Group on Federal Internal Programs (a subgroup of the Inter-Agency Committee), ten recommendations, including one calling for an executive order to implement OA/EAPs for all federal workers, place steady pressure on the federal agencies to initiate and develop good programs.

Since 1971, the federal government's interest in alcoholism has included other action by legislation. In 1973, for example, Congress passed the Rehabilitation Act. Section 504 guarantees the rights of handicapped people; since the attorney general defined alcoholism and drug addiction as a handicap, the law gave further impetus to OA/EAPs. In 1976, Attorney General Bell stated that as long as an employee is qualified to hold a position, she or he cannot be carelessly removed from the position. Good faith

Table 5-1
Effects of Alcoholism on the Alcoholic and the Family

Alcoholic Behavior	Family Reactions
Drinking episodes fairly infrequent.	
Attempts to Deny Problem	
Shame;	Feelings of embarrassment, humiliation;
Discussion of drinking episode;	Discussion of drinking episode;
Promises;	
Making-up;	Making up, ideal role playing
Ideal role playing;	false hope;
Recurrent drinking.	
	Disappointment, hurt, confusion;
	Advice seeking from relatives and friends;
	Trial and error.
Attempts to Eliminate the Problem	
	Social isolation;
	Loss of perspective;
	Drinking becomes focus of anxiety;
	Drinking blamed for all problems;
	Feelings they are different;
	Attempts to cover up;
Resentments;	Resentments;
Lack of communication;	Lack of communication;
	Loss of self-worth, feelings of failure;
Periods of sobriety;	Guilt, false hope, temporary gain in self-worth euphoria;
Recurrent drinking;	Efforts to control obsession with drinking;
	Concentration on short-term goals;
	Attempts to maintain illusion of happy home;
	Self-pity;
	Protection of children;
	Dependence on children for emotional support;
Pleasant interactions with children;.	Anger and anxiety;
	Jealousy of children's affection for alcoholic;
	Attempts to involve children in trying to control alcoholic;
	Loss of creativeness.
Disorganization	
	Hopelessness;
Nondrinking periods;	Skepticism;
	Tension;
Recurrent drinking;	
	Nagging, silent treatment;
	Children torn in loyalties, confused, terrified;
Inconsistent behavior;	
	Behavior problems in children;
	Violence - relief, then shame;
Unreasonable demands;	
	Compulsive behavior;
	Fear of insanity;
	Avoidance of sex.
Loss of job, violence.	

Alcoholic Behavior	Family Reactions
Outside help sought	
	Guilt, loss of self-respect and self-confidence; Chaos; Fear; Inability to make decisions and follow through.
Attempts to reorganize in spite of problems	
	Crisis occurs that requires action (wife returns to work, possible separation, and so on); Wife becomes manager, discipliner, decision maker, controller, assumes husband and father roles; Alcoholic is ignored; Reorganization of priorities, with children first;
Attempts to undermine discipline; Desperate attempts to regain children's affection;	Pity for alcoholic; Children ignore alcoholic; Children's acceptance of drinking as permanent;
Open expression resentments against children; Abuse; Feelings of isolation; Attempts to enter circle of warmth or smash it;	Outside activities increase.
Increase in money problems, violence, accidents, illness, bizarre behavior Attempts to stop drinking; Repeated drinking.	Hope is rekindled; Hope is destroyed; Social agencies frequently consulted; Al-Anon—increase in stability and self-worth; No attempts to cover up drinking.

Efforts to Escape

Difficulties to overcome: Where to go, money, avoidance of further violence; Attempts at sobriety and resultant feelings of guilt; Threats of violence or suicide; Children's criticism for staying or leaving; Relatives withdrawal of support; Relatives antagonism toward alcoholic and resultant defensiveness; Conflicting advice of help.	*Decision to separate or divorce due to:* Near catastrophies; Accumulated problems; Practical difficulties; Damage to children.
Before decision to separate can be made, wife must: Resolve conflicts about self and husband; Give up hope for marriage; Find self-confidence to face unknown future;	Accept failure of marriage; Get rid of feelings of responsibility for the alcoholic; Be able to plan for long-term future.

Developed by Louise Mehrman for South Oaks Hospital 01975 Amityville, NY 11701 Unpublished.

is expected of companies with OA/EAPs. Affirmative-action departments charged with monitoring compliance with the mandates of the Rehabilitation Act are now working closely with OA/EAPs. In 1978, Congress proposed the Hathaway Amendment that called for all federal contractors with contracts of $2,500 or more to have an OA/EAP for employees. Although the amendment did not pass, it had a fair amount of support and may be proposed again.

Ingredients of a Program

Nine specific components are essential to an effective OA/EAP. Since OA/EAPs deal with subjects of critical importance to employees, such as job performance, referral by supervisor, union involvement, and confidentiality, all OA/EAPs should include the following aspects:

1. Written company policy must state that the company views alcoholism as a disease. In addition, the procedures for dealing with alcohol abuse in the work setting must be explained within this policy. An outline of the policy usually includes a company's basic philosophy and explains the company's willingness to assist employees. The policy specifies the availablity of time off for hospitalization and includes a description of coverage by medical insurance. It also explains the role of the supervisor as the central reference point of the program.
2. During the stages of the drafting of this policy by unionized industries, both labor and management must be involved, and both must support the policy. In the written document, the union's role should be defined along with the rights of the employee and the function of the union steward.
3. A companywide educational program must be established so that employees are aware of the company's policy.
4. Training for supervisors must be furnished, including program descriptions and an explanation of the company policy or law in the case of federal employees. During training, role playing of the confrontation interview is common. The films, *The Dryden File* and *Alcohol and the Working Woman* are especially useful for training.
5. The OA/EAP must provide access to a professional person who is capable of interviewing troubled employees as well as diagnosing and referring them appropriately.
6. The program must supply resources for treatment that will work cooperativley with referrals.
7. Each program must develop procedures for compiling records, making reviews, and performing follow-ups.

8. Every OA/EAP must describe and enforce a policy of confidentiality.
9. A program of self-evaluation should be implemented by each OA/EAP.

Models for OA/EAPs

Different administrative approaches to programs exist, each with a variety of ramifications. Companies usually follow traditional formats and do not experiment with their own setting. Not all companies require the same administrative approach. Some descriptive examples follow.

In-House Programs. The majority of OA/EAPs are in-house programs administered under the company's auspices by a coordinator with a counseling staff. The programs are housed in either the medical or personnel department. The New England Telephone Company program is an example of an in-house program located in the medical department; the HHS program is an example of a program housed in the personnel department.

Most in-house programs do the intake interview then refer employees to a treatment program. A few, however, have in-house counseling. As long as a professional such as a social worker is employed by an in-house program, ongoing counseling can be effective in the work place. Programs with ongoing counseling also make referrals for certain cases in need of long-term psychotherapy. The Polaroid Corporation, for example, provides counseling in the work place.

Contracts. If a company does not want to establish its own program, it can enter into a contract with a university, a human-service provider, or a hospital to provide the program either on the company premises or off. For example, Boston College has a contract with the John F. Kennedy (JFK) Federal Center in Boston to provide OA/EAPs for employees of thirty federal agencies. On-site counseling takes a place in the building itself, and office space is provided by the contractor. Human Affairs, Inc. is an example of an outside contractor that usually provides services off-site.

Pros and cons exist to both approaches, which require serious thought before selecting a model. Companies particularly sensitive about confidentiality may find outside contracting to be more effective.

Consortiums. Over 70 percent of Americans work for small companies (fewer than 1,000 employees). Yet each small company cannot be expected to support its own OA/EAP staff. Thus, a cooperative approach is needed and can be useful in promoting OA/EAPs. Two of the programs affiliated with Boston College are consortiums (Taunton-Brockton and the JFK Regional Center). They are described in further detail later in this chapter.

Nonprofit Employers. Nonprofit employers make up a substantial portion of possible work places. For example, educational institutions are the second-largest category of employers in Massachusetts. Hospitals and social agencies are also employers of large numbers of people. OA/EAPs are developing slowly in hospitals. In the fall of 1977, a group of five social-planning students was placed in a block-field arrangement for four months under the supervision of the author. These students developed a plan for an OA/EAP for eight of the Harvard teaching hospitals and schools. Universities have usually moved faster than hospitals in establishing OA/EAPs. For example, the University of Missouri annually hosts a national conference of university OA/EAP administrators. The fourth conference was held during the summer of 1979, and more than forty university representatives have attended each year. Rutgers and the Massachusetts Institute of Technology both have OA/EAPs directed by full-time people who have MSWs. Social agencies, the third type of nonprofit enterprise, are ironically lagging behind the other two in developing programs, but no doubt they will soon start developing such services for employees.

Labor Unions. Labor unions have various methods of implementing and administering OA/EAPs. Unions may administer the program directly, or they may cooperate with management in running the program through the joint endeavor of unions and management.[12] Unions usually support a company's OA/EAP, even if the support is only tacit.

Leo Perlis, director of the AFL-CIO Community Services, points out that the AFL-CIO, which represents 14.5 million workers and is associated with 110 national and international unions and more than 60,000 locals, supports the establishment of OA/EAPs in plants to deal with employees who experience problem drinking. Perlis indicates that the following ingredients comprise a cooperative relationship between unions and management during the operation of an OA/EAP: establish a joint committee on alcoholism, which will serve to consider alcoholism an illness to be treated and which requires attitudinal changes on the job, in negotiations, in availability of services both at the job site and in the community, in job security and seniority, and in all company polices and procedures.[13]

Occupational Alcohol and Drug Training Program

Started seven years ago by the Graduate School of Social Work and directed by the author, the Boston College program was the only NIAAA-funded endeavor that trained social workers to work in OA/EAPs. It is thus the project that demonstrated the methodology of training for this specialized work. Funding for the Boston College program came from companies as well as the college. An average of sixteen students participated in the program each year. Their participation served as a portion of their graduate-course work for MSW. Half the students were studying casework; the other half studied community organization/social planning (CO/SP). Their training qualified them to be either program coordinators/administrators or counselors in companies.

The CO/SP intern provided the following services to the company:

Development of a company policy;

Formation of information and referral services;

Training of supervisors;

Staffing of advisory committees;

Education efforts;

Public relations;

Administrate offices that write monthly reports, host visitors, and so on.

The counseling intern provides the following services:

Information and referral of industrial clients;

Ongoing counseling with priority given to problems of job performance, alcoholism, drug addiction, and other victims of alcoholism or addiction, emotions, and behavior;

Liaison with treatment facilities;

Maintaining statistical records of all clients;

Contributing to supervisory training sessions.

Professional social-work training requires an internship. Since OA/EAPs constitute a new branch of social work, companies do not already employ social workers who could be used as supervisors for such internships. A college or university that already has operational programs thus becomes the logical training ground. In order to thoroughly train student social workers, the Boston College program selected a variety of industrial sites and utilized several different approaches. Tables 5-2 and 5-3 show one form of the effectiveness of these programs, and brief descriptions of them follow.

Table 5-2
Number of Cases Handled by EAPs, 1975-1979

Type	JFK Federal	Hanscom[a]	NET	Boston College[b]	Taunton/Brockton	Polaroid[c]	Total
Alcohol/Drug	70	96	92	36	74	3	371
Work/career related	39	21	32	6	15	0	113
Financial/legal housing	20	21	26	21	63	0	151
Mental/physical health	64	54	79	23	85	4	309
Family/marital	60	64	100	20	115	4	363
Other victims[d]	4	NA	3	NA	19	3	29
Other	3	2	2	4	1	0	12
Total	260	258	334	110	372	14	1,638

[a]Boston College withdrew from the Hanscom program in 1978, consequently case figures cover the period 1975-1978.

[b]Boston College in 1978 hired a social worker to perform casework duties. Case figures cover period 1975-1978.

[c]Polaroid figures include only 1978—1979 with an intern.

[d]Other victims category added in 1978 signifies family members or other individual (supervisor) who are directly affected by behavior of the alcoholics.

Table 5-3
Type of Problem and Sex, per Site, May 1978-May 1979

Type of Problem	JFK Federal		NET		Taunton/ Brockton		Polaroid[a]		Total	
	Men	Women	Men	Women	Men	Women	Men	Women	Men	Women
Alcohol/drug	24	5	12	3	17	6	3	2	56	16
Other victims[b]	3	1	0	4	0	14	1	0	4	19
Family/marital	4	1	4	1	13	19	2	2	23	23
Mental health	11	12	11	2	12	18	1	3	25	35
Legal/financial	3	4	1	0	6	8	0	0	10	12
Total	45	23	28	10	48	65	7	7	128	105

[a]Polaroid joined the program in September 1978.
[b]Other victims category added in May 1978.

New England Telephone Company

Although the company has 28,000 employees throughout seven states, the program concentrated on specific offices in the downtown-Boston area. Within the company, the EAP was located in the medical department. New England Telephone had had an occupational-alcoholism program, staffed by three recovering alcoholics, for almost ten years, but the director of the medical department sought to expand the program using the employee-assistance model. He wanted the program to include female as well as management-level employees. After three years, the program was so effective that the company hired one of the Boston College graduates. Thus, the training site at New England Telephone has become autonomous; eventually, all internships in its EAP will be supervised by social-work employees of the company.

Boston College Faculty/Staff
Assistance Program

Since Boston College acts as a vanguard for OA/EAPs, the college itself was almost obliged to offer a program for its own employees. Boston College administrators supported this concept and selected an advisory committee of faculty and staff. The committee first surveyed the faculty to ascertain whether the latter felt need for or interest in an OA/EAP. Forty percent of the faculty, an unexpectedly high amount, returned their questionnaires. They supported the idea of an EAP and listed what they considered to be their five greatest problems. The most frequently stated were financial, mental health, marital and family, physical health, and alcohol and drug abuse.

The EAP began and, after two years, the college hired a part-time MSW to provide ongoing counseling on campus. Because faculty used the services of the program, the administration chose to have a graduate MSW provide the counseling rather than a graduate student. The graduate student in community organization provided the outreach and coordination.

JFK Federal Center

The JFK Federal Center includes thirty federal agencies throughout New England. An occupational-health consultant, employed by the Civil Service Commission (now OPM), serves as coordinator of the OA/EAPs for each agency and acts as liaison between the agencies and the Boston College project director. The Government Accounting Office (GAO) cited the JFK program as a model consortium in its 1977 report on federal programs. The JFK program is the largest consortium, and one of the oldest, in the country; its influence has been nationwide. This site has hired a full-time MSW and a Boston College graduate and is also autonomous.

Taunton EAP, Inc.

This EAP, also a consortium, was formed because of the needs of ten small companies, including Rand McNally, Reed and Barton Silver, a local hospital, a utility company, and a bank, all located in Taunton, Massachusetts, a city fifty miles south of Boston. In 1974, these companies joined forces to form their program under the coordination of the executive director from the Chamber of Commerce. First, the Boston College project director met with the presidents of the various companies and described OA/EAPs. Each company signed up for the program and appointed a personnel director as the agent for the company. The personnel directors in turn formed the advisory committee for the program. The staff of the Boston College project worked particularly closely with this committee. Program coordinators went into each company to train supervisors and to run educational program. The caseworkers to whom employees are referred work in the local hospital, and all clients are counseled there.

The Brockton Consortium

This consortium was formed by a group of companies from a city near Taunton, and these companies sought to join the Taunton group. Representatives from these companies along with members of Taunton EAP, Inc., now compose the Taunton-Brockton Consortium. The program is housed in the local Catholic Charities office, and this social agency is one of the participating members. Another graduate of the program was hired by the consortium to work full time making them fully autonomous.

Polaroid

As already described, Polaroid has had a long history in industrial social work. When one of their social workers was given special responsibility to assist alcoholic employees, the company placed under the social worker's supervision one of the Boston College trainees.

Hanscom Air Force Base

For five years, the Boston College training project had contracted with the Electronics Systems Division of Hanscom Air Force Base at Bedford, Massachusetts, to provide an EAP for its civilian employees who were eligible to receive services. The EAP operated in its own facility and worked closely with the five unions as well as the youth center and the medical dispensary.

Second-year CO/SP students were required to develop a plan for the implementation of an alcoholism program. Students worked as a group in a block placement. The following are two plans that were developed, which were supervised by a faculty member:

1. *Harvard-Affiliated Hospitals.* Five second-year community-organization students in the Boston College project spent a semester working full time to develop a major EAP for eight of the Harvard teaching hospitals and schools.
2. *Boston College Plan for Responsible Drinking among Students.* The administration of the college became increasingly concerned with what it considered to be a high amount of irresponsible drinking among its students. In 1978, the college developed a cooperative arrangement with a planning team from the School of Social Work's project and student and administrative representatives from the college in order to devise a system to reduce such drinking. Boston College believed that since there is a program for faculty, there should be a similar program available to students.

Issues

Any new field brings with it controversy and questions. Treating problem drinkers in the work place is no exception, and some controversy surrounds OA/EAPs and their approaches. Unions and management have joined forces to help treat employees for alcoholism rather than to fire them. Both unions and management also believe that constructive confrontation with an employee is often preferable to merely carrying him or her on the job.

The author believes that several issues regarding OA/EAPs face workers and need to be addressed immediately. If these issues are not resolved, the development of programs will continue without the involvement or input that can be provided by professionals, particularly social workers. These issues include the following:

1. *Need for research and evaluation.* Many of the concepts now used in OA/EAPs should be rigorously tested. New models need to be developed,

such as the new approach for women in OA/EAPs designed by the author.[14] Too often companies use only models designed for someone else's employees rather than developing a specific program of their own. In addition, there is an insufficient allowance of time and money for evaluation of programs now in operation. Systems that measure the cost-effectiveness and cost benefit of OA/EAPs should be researched and the results incorporated into actual practice.

2. *Role of professional versus nonprofessional.* Traditionally, the recovering alcoholic has staffed OA/EAPs. Slowly, social workers, educational counselors, and psychologists are moving into these positions. There is much misunderstanding on both sides, and some resolution concerning roles will have to take place because the two groups tend to have different viewpoints and to misunderstand each other. Perhaps a reconciliation will occur soon since the Association for Labor Management Administrators and Consultants on Alcoholism (ALMACA), which is the national organization for people who staff OA/EAPs, recently appointed a social worker as its executive director.

3. *Confidentiality.* Troubled people are naturally distrustful. They feel it as a threat to their job and future promotions when companies suggest they participate in such programs. OA/EAPs must perfect confidentiality. All staff members who handle material connected with OA/EAPs should be trained in the ethics of confidentiality and the fundamentals of the Privacy Act. Furthermore, inspectors and evaluators of OA/EAPs must not seek access to files at the expense of client confidentiality.

4. *Lack of executive participation.* Too often, OA/EAPs are created by management for the blue-collar worker, by the senior military officer for the young soldier, or by faculty members for students. On the one hand, OA/EAPs should serve all employees equally so that the program never seems to be a witch hunt. On the other hand, it is actually more of a risk for employees in management to admit to having problems that require assistance. Blue-collar workers have union support and grievance procedures that people who work in executive positions do not have. Some companies have adopted a policy of referring executives and management employees directly to an outside program without requiring them to pass through the OA/EAP. More strategies such as this must be developed so that OA/EAPs can work effectively for all employees.

5. *Social-work image.* A social worker employed by a private business may find his or her worst problem concerns how the employer presumes the social worker regards money. Many businessmen believe that social workers wish to spend money impulsively on benefits and services without giving consideration to conserving company funds. Businessmen might prefer to have OA/EAPs administered by someone with a master's degree in business administration (MBA). Employers presume that people with that profes-

sional degree understand the exigencies of money making. To eradicate this image, social workers as well as other human-service providers must reveal to the world of private industry that they too know how to be cost-effective. Also, while still in training, social workers should take business courses. A social worker with some academic training in business will be able to compete more successfully with MBAs for positions in OA/EAPs.

6. *Training.* The author thinks that training is the single most important need in the field of occupational-alcoholism counseling. OA/EAPs will be continually called into question as long as the staff does not have appropraite education and credentials, particularly about alcoholism itself. Social workers should have training in the different approaches to treating alcoholism and should understand why alcoholism should be viewed as a family disease that is not responsive to traditional psychotherapy. Graduate schools of social work must recruit and train personnel specifically for positions as coordinators and counselors, and schools of social work must develop courses about the work place that cover topics such as industrial relations and personnel management.

The growing frequency of the establishment of OA/EAPs means that a large, new population of workers who may need help will have that help available to them. Carvel Taylor, for example, a social worker who directs the OA/EAP at CNA Insurance Company, said that in her first year she saw five hundred employees who had never been to a psychiatrist, psychologist, or social worker.

Summary

Most alcoholics are employed, but frequently their progressive illness costs them and their employers time and money. Because the highest rates of arresting the disease of alcoholism occur in work places rather than hospitals, OA/EAPs have become vital to the successful treatment of alcoholism. Conscientious participation in such a program can aid a problem drinker and his or her family. The treatment of alcoholism in the work place has grown considerably in the last forty years; 2,250 OA/EAPs exist today. The federal government has supported OA/EAPs since 1970 with legislation. For example, the Hughes Act and its amendments and the Rehabilitation Act of 1973 have meant that OA/EAPs are becoming more available to employees of the federal government. Some of the components every OA/EAP must contain are a view of alcoholism as a disease, the availability of professional counseling, educational and referral resources, and strict confidentiality. OA/EAPs may be structured to occur in work places themselves or elsewhere, depending on the size and description of the company that initiates such a program. The Boston College Occupational Alcoholism and Drug Training Program was the demonstration model of training programs that prepares social workers to work in OA/EAPs. Some of the issues regarding OA/EAPs that still require resolution are the need for research and evaluation, the role of professionalism, the necessity for confidentiality, the lack of executive participation, the image of social work that many businessmen have, and the need for controlled training for social workers who work in OA/EAPs.

6 Corporate Social Responsibility

Corporate social responsibility (CSR) is another aspect of business in which social workers may function. The purpose of this chapter is to define what CSR means as well as to trace its development. Multinational corporations are also defined and discussed in relation to CSR. Philosophical issues are presented. Aspects of CSR programs such as a code of ethics and a social audit are defined and discussed. Various functions of a CSR program are presented, including consumer relations, environmental programs, and corporate giving, and the role of social workers in this area is then briefly presented.

The chapter shows to the student of human services yet another area in which they can work in the business world. It is one of the main areas in which social change can be effected and the business community utilized to affect the social environment as well as the community in which it operates. Because of the level within a company in which these programs operate, as well as the knowledge needed, an MSW should be accompanied by an MBA. Most CSR officers today have an MBA. Business is going to its own schools to provide the necessary courses to cover training for these programs. In effect, social-work curriculums, especially those geared toward social policy and community relations, may well complement this training. However, it is natural for business to look to its own educational institutions for their staffs and unrealistic to expect companies to hire social workers for these positions. However, with the two degrees, the social worker would then have superior training and certainly be a good candidate. The numbers of these programs are growing throughout the country.

Philosophical Background

CSR signifies a relationship between business and society. It includes deciding how business is to function and establishing priorities and considers the larger community as a factor in arranging those priorities.

In his book *The Future of The Multinationals*, J. Miller defines Friedman's theory that people have social responsibilities but that the responsibility of business is to provide its customers with safe and useful products at reasonable cost as established in the free market. To do otherwise is to subvert our free society.[1] This is today's application of Adam Smith's concept of laissez faire.

This philosophy was countered in the EXXON Background Series on social responsibility, which maintains that laissez faire allowed free-reign results in excesses, which in turn results in government regulations, unions labor laws, and special-interest groups.[2]

The opposite extreme view of the relation of business and society is to see business as a social-welfare institution. This view holds business directly responsible for correcting all the problems of the society in which it operates and for bringing all business to the aid of society. The problem with this point of view is that it disregards business's main function as a profit-making institution. It does not take into consideration that, by fulfilling its economic role, business was supplying individuals and society with a means of support. No one is helped by a company that, because it failed its primary role, is forced to close down. Jobs are lost, families are hurt, and society has to bear the burden of supporting these. Only the most extreme among the people who are dissatisfied with conventional business approaches would adopt this position. No satisfactory solution, either for business or for society, can come from a careless scrambling of the roles of business, government, and other major institutions. Business has neither the competence nor the obligation to serve as an all-purpose agent of the public. Its primary mission is economic, not social. In a free society, the establishment of social objectives is primarily the function of the political process. Despite some contrary opinion today, this will almost surely remain the consensus in our society.[3]

Part of the reason for this conflict is the changed view of society and business since Smith commented on it. The growth of the large business conglomerates upset the balance of the competition that was the basis for their views. Instead of the competition and balance of small business, a new philosophy of action arose. For example, if a manufacturer of a product was able to get control of the major resources that supplied it and to control the market in which the product was sold, then a company could literally corner the market. Men like John D. Rockefeller in the early twentieth century became heads of vast monopolies. Despite some government controls, big business continued to grow and control the market. Seeking new opportunities for profit, American business expanded abroad. Competition was the key to any big business, and the most competitive businesses were able to form great monopolies. These companies experienced tremendous growth, and the more power they attained, the more they were able to attain. These associations of companies that formed monopolies were the precursors of our modern-day multinational corporation. By these and like policies, corporations assumed vast power and influence over the hitherto free market.

Factors Causing the Development
of CSR

"Multinational corporations are enterprises which own or control production
or service facilities outside the country in which they are based. Such enterprises are not always incorporated or private: they can also be cooperatives
or state-owned entities. . . . [T]here is generally agreement in the group [of
Eminent Persons appointed to make a special study and report on the role
of multinational corporations on the international market] that the word
enterprise should be substituted for *corporation*, and a strong feeling that
the word *transnational* would better convey the notion that these firms
operate from their home bases across national borders."[4]

These multinational enterprises are made up of various companies in
different areas. In an age in which information is power, the multinationals
have tremendous communication systems and access to information that is
better than what most governments have. They control technology, finance,
capital, labor markets, and communication, which are the basic elements of
economic life. Once established, the multinationals can buy into diverse
businesses to such an extent as to almost guarantee their survival. The fall
of a company's profits in one area may mean a windfall gain in another.
Says one analyst on the size of the multinationals, future prospects for
global corporations are even more awe inspiring. Stephen Hymer estimates
that within thirty years, three hundred to four hundred MNCs [multina-
tionals] will produce 60 to 70 percent of the world's total industrial output.
If his projections are correct, we are merely at the beginning of a new
economic age to be dominated by MNCs."[5]

With the growth of business and the multinationals, come increasing expectations of the role of business, both from within and without the corporation. From within, the increasing size of the enterprises means an increasingly large constituency to be represented. These groups sometime
have conflicting goals. CSR involves the policies of a company in meeting
the demands of these constituencies. Freeman lists the following as in-
dicators of the various interests of a company:

Safety and health of employees;

Mental health;

Employment policies;

Education and training;

Retirement benefits;

Leisure (can the company, should the company guide employees in their use of leisure time?);

Civil rights including the special needs of minorities;

Treatment of women;

Welfare (dealing with employee problems outside the work place;

Employee attitudes;

Pollution;

Public safety;

Waste;

Physical environment;

Use of land;

Participation in community affairs;

Government relations;

Consumer relations;

Profits;

The company's business image.[6]

The growth of unions and government regulations began to affect the levels of expectation of businesses from without. They had to be responsible for their workers to see that they were fairly treated, and this included working conditions, hours, benefits, and the like. Minimum-wage standards were established, as well as union-wage standards. Hiring practices were examined to be sure they followed social legislation. In the last fifty years in particular, business has had to show its cooperation in the field of social responsibility for goals other than those of economic gain.

The era of unrest that occurred in the United States during the 1960s had a definite impact on the management of the corporation and on CSR. This unrest was reflected in the campus revolts, the riots in major cities, the opposition to the Vietnam War, and the questioning of the limits of the government and businesses. This tension continues today.

Despite the rising standard of living in the United States, many citizens do not share in these economic achievements. Modern communication increases their awareness of the disparity and causes a sense of powerlessness over their own lives. They often see the purveyors of goods . . . business . . . as the cause of their deprivation.[7]

CSR developed out of this period for several reasons. One was in answer to some very real and difficult problems since business had access to many resources and information to help deal with the various problems. Another was a pragmatic analysis of the situation that aided in an understanding of the relationship among business, society, and profits. CSR thus became a matter of survival. To insure the survival of the private-enterprise system meant to insure and maintain a healthy environment for both. Public confidence had to be restored to insure the system's future viability. Business cannot run without the support of the people. The corporation had to become sensitive to the broad range of public needs and desires, even if it did not fit in with immediate profitability for them. Mark Shephard, chairman of Texas Instruments, says, "but . . . [a company]. . . is permitted to operate by the societies it serves, and that privilege does not indicate the inherent right to make profit . . . [and] unless any company meets genuine needs and solves vital problems, it will not earn the profit reward."[8]

The changing levels of expectation during these times did not indicate that business had a simple decision. The process of redefining and actualizing the new role of business is an ongoing process, of which CSR is a guiding philosophy. With all the constituencies a company represents, many different plans had to be studied, analyzed, and put into action. What is important was that business was responding to the time and place in which it existed. The campus revolts of the 1960s probably resulted most permanently in eradicating in all institutions the unchallenged authority they had enjoyed in the past. The day is fading fast when "because I say so" or "because it is company policy" get any action.[9]

Public interest and intervention in this area of current concern is not a passing phenomenon but will continue to grow, tempered but not reversed by a gradually increasing awareness of the economic cost and possible inconvenience. The proliferation of major activist organizations; the impact of the conservation lobby on the Alaskan pipeline, the Florida jetport and canal, and the supersonic transport; the mushrooming numbers of consumer-oriented professionals; and expanded enforcement of antitrust laws are signs of the times. We can expect progressively tougher, more-detailed, and more rigorously enforced standards and greater pressures for accountability.[10]

Defining CSR

What is CSR? The answers are many and are not exactly the same, but each indicates that a mutual interdependence exists between society and business and therefore that business has the right, indeed the responsibility, to help solve problems in the society in which it exists. How the companies will respond, in what manner, and to what degree are the questions being debated and dealt with now. Following are several examples of corporate definitions of CSR.

1. "As the leading private-sector industrial firm in Indonesia, Caltex has a particular responsibility to participate in the improvement of the national economic and social welfare as evidenced by a wide range of public-service-oriented activities."[11]

2. CSR is "a company today must look closely at the affects of all its activities and decisions on all its relationships with all its stockholders, and it must at least try to manage change," say John Hargreaves and Jan Dauman in *Business Survival and Social Change*.[12]

3. The job of management is to create the unique corporate culture that will maximize the returns to society in the fields in which the corporation is active and that will minimize the costs to society—costs of all kinds—in achieving those returns.[13]

4. We hear much talk of the social responsibility of business, a new view of the interrelationships of corporations and society. This view holds that the community and the corporation are inevitably intertwined in our society, that they owe each other dues, that a corporation is no longer responsible and accountable merely to its stockholders but is responsible and accountable, too, to a wider set of constituencies.[14]

5. "Although we are primarily an economic institution, we recognize that we have an obligation to conduct ourselves in a way that is consistent with social goals, including those that appear inconsistent, at least in the short term, with the goals of our business. . . . Our continued economic success depends upon service to consumers, service to employees, and service to society."[15]

6. "[T]he expectations society has for the corporation have long since transcended this basic role of efficient business practice. Today the corporation is not only encouraged but also expected to be a construction participant in the betterment of society and to help solve some of the pressing problems of the times. No longer is a company judged solely on the quality of its products or the profits it generates."[16]

7. "The concept of corporate social responsibility might be defined as one of harnessing the resources of a corporation to the purposes of society."[17]

8. [C]orporate responsibilities to society lie in a sensitivity and responsiveness to the indirect impact of business operation on the society at large."[18]

9. "Chase Manhattan Bank is committed to the idea of social responsibility, which often has been defined as 'any action which in some way adds value to the society.' The basic assumption behind this concept is that there

is a thin line between charity and enlightened self-interests [and that] 'we must maintain the balance between social interests and business interests.' "[19]

10. At first, the main thrust of society's intervention in business was to ensure the proper treatment of employees and to keep business competitive. However, new expectations emerged. Many people now believe that business should contribute directly to public objectives, and some segments of society assert that the corporate system itself has to be done away with and a new system established. The prevailing notion is clearly that business has to take a greater interest and play a larger role in the society in which it exists.

11. "We once thought that the poor, the oppressed, and the handicapped were not the problem of business. This is what government was for. The same was thought to be true for law and order and justice. This same, likewise, for urban rehabilitation—and on and on through the roster of social ills. Among the many things we have learned . . . is that government alone is incapable of coping with the social ills of our time. . . . "in a highly developed society like ours, the problems are so many and so great that all stable elements of the community, including business, must cooperate to solve them.[20]

To be truly effective, CSR must be part of a corporation at the policymaking level. It is not a separate simple program added on to the company and written off at tax time. Rather, it must be taken into account in every decision made by a company. Every action made by a company must reflect a decision made by management taking into account the well-being of those who are to be affected, whether directly or indirectly. Only when this occurs will CSR be truly effective.

Many corporations have established some type of CSR program. These departments range from simple public-relations programs to full-fledged departments with an administrative vice-president. The department can examine the policies of the corporation and see how their profit-making institution can make an effective contribution to society. This ranges from choosing where to organize a high-risk program and how to fund it, to aiding minority businesses, to sponsoring art and cultural events, to hiring a janitor. Equally important is the treatment of personnel as well as policies within the company itself that do not directly affect the general public.

Codes of Conduct

The adoption of a code of conduct is being discussed in various corporate and international structures, and some representative codes have been designed. Before a company can develop a total policy of CSR, a code of conduct or principles would seem an appropriate base from which to begin.

A code of conduct is not simply defined. A very broad, overall statement of the ethics and performance of a company's policy would be difficult to formulate. However, if the code were too specific and restrictive, it would probably not be adopted at all, or if adopted, it would be so restrictive as to prevent the efficient performance of company policy.

The process of developing a code requires certain steps. One step is the discussion and labeling of the important issues a code of conduct should address, such as:

Employment practices,

Antidiscrimination clauses,

Employee training and development,

Management training and development,

Employee safety,

Reinvestment of earnings,

Local equity participation,

Balance of payments,

Profit remittances,

Degree of ownership,

Transfer pricing,

Transfer of technology,

Responsibilities of host countries,

Obligation to local labor unions,

Bribery,

Political contributions,

Information disclosure for credibility,

Resolution of investment disputes,

Environmental responsibilities,

Intercompany relations and responsible diagnosis of local quality-of-life action programs.[21]

The use of various international groups should be made in the implementation of a code of conduct. The European Economic Community,

Andean Pact, and several parts of the United Nations as well as individual multinationals have all examined the question. They have acted interdependently on the question, from within the corporation and without. This knowledge should be combined to help get a balanced view of the issue. Finally, the enforcement issue has to be established. The individual treatment was mentioned previously, but some people also feel that laws should govern the process and be enacted to ensure this.

The issue of a corporate code of conduct has elicited a variety of responses from "virtually useless" to "should be mandatory by law." Many issues need to be addressed and decided before an effective code of conduct is established.

Social Accountability and the Social Audit

With the increased pressure on business to show CSR has come the development of a system of monitoring the performance of a company and its efforts in social issues. The social audit has a dual function, operating within a company to enable management to analyze and establish social priorities and operating outside the company as a report card of corporate conduct.

Internally, the social audit functions as a review of company policy, with several dimensions. For example, the social audit identifies and examines the socially responsive programs, including the effectiveness of a program in controlling a problem or responding to a critical issue. It gives an analysis of what a program does—its functions and activities.

In October 1979, at Duke University in North Carolina, Secretary of Commerce Juanita M. Kreps told a gathering of the nation's leading business leaders that the Department of Commerce would develop a social-performance index to offer them a way of appraising the social effects of their operations. In her speech, Mrs. Kreps cited ten companies that, in her opinion, had established track records in the area of corporate social performance. "They represent a clear trend," she said but added, "they do not represent a stampede." Two of the companies mentioned—the Prudential Insurance Company and the Equitable Life Insurance Society—have been participants in an insurance-industry program to measure and make public the extent of its involvement in areas of social responsibility on a regular basis. Six years ago, one hundred chief executives representing a cross-section of the nation's life and health insurance companies gathered for two days to discuss CSR and business. They established the Clearinghouse on Corporate Social Responsibility to counsel some 450 insurance companies on issues in the area of social responsibility and to report on the activities of its members. The clearinghouse reports on six areas of activity—community projects, corporate contributions, individual involvement, social investments, equal-employment opportunities for women and minority groups, and the environment and energy conservation.[22]

A major difficulty with the social audit is that a single unified approach for all companies and agencies is not easily designed. Certain issues of paramount importance to one company will be insignificant to another. This limits the usefulness of the audit as an external process of evaluating the worth of a business's social response.

To be successful, the audit must have reliable, objective measures of performance upon which all companies can agree. They should encompass the full range of social concerns while at the same time be implemented without a major change in the corporate system. The reporting has to be in an objective, disinterested manner, factual and comparative, but not as a public-relations gimmick.

Various groups can benefit from the social audit. The most important group is the company itelf, which can make use of the audit to monitor, evaluate, and improve its policies. Government could use the audit to estimate a company's efforts toward correcting any negative influences caused by its presence. The owners and shareholders could use the audit to understand the decision-making processes of their company. Special-interest groups could use it to get a measure of concern for environmental and other issues. Workers and staff benefit from understanding the policies and ethics of the corporation in which they work. Society as a whole, from owner to consumer, would benefit from a good working relationship between itself and business—mutually supportive for mutual gain.

CSR Programs

Consumer Relations

The relationship between consumers and corporations is important. CSR in this area is equally important in continuing the long-term, as well as short-term, interests of the company by quickly and promptly satisfying consumer complaints and demands, as well as by offering them a safe product, honestly advertised at a reasonable price.

Consumer-relations boards deal with questions or complaints the consumer has about a product or company. This includes a hearing for those who request action and proper recompense if a company's policy is at fault. This compliance can be accomplished in two ways. Mattel, Inc., for example, recently withdrew hundreds of thousands of a toy product that was judged by a consumer-advocacy group to be dangerous to children. The company could have chosen legal maneuvers that may have kept the product on the shelves long enough to make a good profit, but it chose instead to address the serious social implications of the death or injury of a child's using their product. An opposite example is the Firestone-500-tire recall, which went through innumerable public agencies and hearings a process which continued long after the period had been judged unsafe. The company was eventually forced to recall and recompense all of those to whom the tire had been sold. The company had to overcome a lot of negative press that arose around this issue. The issue is not that the company was right or wrong but that the company initially tried to protect its financial investment for too long and then had to overcome additional problems caused by the resulting poor corporate image.

Community Relations/Environment

The CSR issue dealing with the environment may be divided into two areas—(1) industries that deal directly in the environmental-resource area and (2) conservation programs that any company can institute that have an indirect effect on the environment.

An example of an industry that deals directly in the environmental-resource area, and one of critical importance, is the nuclear-power industry. It has come under attack by many special-interest groups as well as by federal, state, and local governments, and CSR had become a central issue in this controversy.

The nuclear-power industry has as its most important function to supply energy. In terms of cost and effectiveness, few people doubt that nuclear power can meet our energy demands. The industry represents a benefit to all members of society, in that a constant supply of energy can be maintained, particularly during times of energy crises. The industry has one of the highest safety records of any, but accidents, while relatively few, have been highly publicized. Why then is there a controversy, and does this reflect a lack of CSR?

As noted earlier, in the relationship of business to society, any business acts with the approval of the society in which it is active. Based on this model, but without mutual cooperation, the business would not succeed. This has been questioned in the light of the rise of the multinationals, but the nuclear controversy shows what happens when an industry does not fully anticipate and meet public demands, or even demands of a small segment of the public. The reactions (such as economic boycotts, rejection of local spending, and governmental action by the special-interest groups) have been effective in preventing the construction and operation of many plants, especially in the United States. On top of this, the nuclear industry has maintained a low profile that has left its functions and aims open to questions by a doubting and uninformed public. The responsibility of business is to anticipate this and to inform the public openly as to its economics and business operations, as well as to inform the public of its activities. When this lack of information is combined with highlighted events such as the accident at Three Mile Island, public sentiment and governmental policy are turned against the industry. In this case there was a moratorium on building and permit issues as well as loss of financial backing. This shows that despite the support of tremendous amounts of money, business cannot forget its contract with society, even when the issue involves a service of which society is the intended beneficiary. Today the nuclear industry faces at best the loss of a tremendous amount of money, and at worst, it may find that it cannot exist within this society.

The other part of environment and CSR refers to the activities of any business operation in the conservation area. Some such programs are discussed in the following sections.

Water Conservation. The use and consumption of water by large factories is now being closely monitored, and new facilities have been constructed to help cleanse and reuse water efficiently. This is especially important in areas where water is scarce. Businesses have shown themselves to be concerned by establishing programs to curb water use and consumption. The compatibility between CSR and profits is demonstrated in that companies will ultimately benefit from such conservation programs. Water conservation is important to the company as well as the community the company is in.

Sewage-Treatment Facilities. Sewage-treatment facilities deal with the disposal of waste in a way that is not damaging to the environment. They represent a major expenditure in the construction of facilities and in staffing. However, the examples of many companies have shown that not only have areas been cleaned up but also that the positive feedback that comes back to a company that has such a program helps it to continue.

Use of Recycled Materials. The use of recycled materials and alternate energy resources and the establishment of energy-conservation programs, commuter networks for employees, and other programs have all helped companies, their customers, and employees, as well as the environment.

A major issue has arisen about the cost of these environmental-control projects—namely, the costs may be very high for a company, and smaller companies especially may be forced to close because they cannot afford the resources to comply with existing standards. According to Stanford Research Institute's report, multinationals have made great strides in complying with national laws (for example, in controlling pollution), but they complain that because of the costs and constraints imposed by governments the word economic progress is now in crisis.[23]

In addition to the physical environment, community-relations programs may encompass working with local residents around such mutual concerns as employment, housing, and transportation.

Corporate Foundations

Contributions are a main issue of CSR. Contributions have to do with the expenditure of money and with programs and events that do not directly involve the daily business activities of a corporation. They may be divided into two categories: (1) contributions made to political and national groups (2) contributions that fund special projects.

Determining the amount of money they can afford to contribute and the purposes the contributions will serve is a major fiscal issue for corporations.

Many corporations make contributions through a foundation established for that purpose. These contributions have little direct influence on the daily doings of a business, but they are extremely important because they reflect the attitude of the corporation towards society. They can be made in the form of outright grants to a specific program or to more general programs such as United Way.

Many nonprofit organizations are supported in major part by grants from corporations. Public television immediately stands out as an example, with companies' sponsoring parts or the complete production of programs that could never be shown without this support. Colleges and universities are also the recipients of varous scholarships established by business firms as well as by outright donations. The United Way is an important priority of most large companies' policy, with many companies' donating their time, staffs, and facilities, as well as money. Culture and the arts, from museums and historical societies to theaters and performing-art centers, also receive money. All of these programs would have difficulty remaining active without the strong and continuous support of corporate contributions.

The area of political contributions has been a controversial one. On the one hand, in keeping with a good-citizen model, corporations have been actively involved in the political arena, with donations of time, money, and services to various groups, organizations, and individuals. On the other hand, some question exists as to whether a company is also making contributions selectively to those places where they can expect later support. This issue is a delicate one and is still being examined.

Multinational Corporations

Multinational companies have been highly criticized for their actions in the international political arena. They have, as a group, been charged with manipulating national and local elections, interfering in the due processes of host countries, and bribing high officials to have decisions made in their favor. These charges are based upon the activities of a few companies, which were highlighted by the fact they were found to have actively manipulated the elections of a host government, most notably with International Telephone & Telegraph.

Multinational companies have an especially difficult time establishing a standard of conduct in this area because in many countries an individual is expected to be compensated for helping a firm. Stanford Research Institute's study of this question concludes that because of the widely differing concepts of morality from one society to another universal standards cannot be applied even by those who are deeply committed to their maintenance.[24]

Utilization of Social Workers
in CSR Programs

As of this writing, three companies are utilizing social workers as CSR officers. Chase Manhattan Bank, for instance, employs a social worker who is now a vice-president. In addition to a staff of five, the Community Development Department, as it is called, conducts a graduate internship program for four social-work students from local universities. Program activities include economic development, housing renewal, environmental issues, human-resource development, and a consumer- and personal-finance service.

Digital Equipment Corporation in Maynard, Massachusetts, employs a community-relations officer who is responsible for sensitizing the corporation to community issues and trying to anticipate a crisis before it might occur. The social worker is also involved in policy related to corporate giving.

Equitable Life Insurance Company in New York has also employed a social worker in its CSR department. This same social worker also teaches a course in a graduate school of social work entitled Corporate Social Responsibility: Social Policy and Planning with Industry and Labor.

Summary

As stated in the introduction, the purpose of this chapter was to define, as clearly as possible, what CSR is, present some of the issues, and to try to show the complexity of the subject. The need for adequate training for these positions, which will require an MBA as well as an MSW, is documented. Knowledge of economics and international business policy as well as organizational structure would be essential to the staff of the kinds of programs described. CSR as explained could provide the avenue for real social change at the highest corporate level. The chapter describes various functions of the CSR staff person. Implications for the community, both at a local as well as international level, with multinational corporations has been presented. The many facets to the subject of CSR, a fast-growing area, are pointed out so social workers may be aware of the possible options available.

Part III
Special Populations to
Be Served

7 Women, Minorities, and the Handicapped

Several populations—women, members of minority groups, and the handicapped—have long been second-class citizens of the work place, but employers are slowly adopting policies so that all workers will have an equal opportunity to work according to their skills and aspirations. Women, the handicapped, and minorities traditionally have worked in low-paying, low-status positions. One of the results of the civil disturbances of the 1960s was the government's awareness of its failure to mandate policies that would provide to certain groups opportunities in the employment area. Equally as important, the government also recognized this need in the educational field. Laws now exist to ensure that decision-making, high-pay, and executive status are not exclusive privileges of the white man. Thus, as the civil rights demonstrators once pressed for change, so now do those workers who belong to special populations when employers fail to comply with the new guarantees of employment opportunity and advancement. The lawsuit may replace the sit-in and the march as the technique of the 1980s.

Of course, lawsuits are unnecessary where fair employment practices are the rule. Many private businesses and industries have followed the lead of the federal government and established within their personnel offices so-called affirmative-action officers whose function is to implement the federal mandates against employment discrimination and to move their employees into a positive program of hiring and promoting. Thus, a new area has developed in which the skills of social workers may be particularly appropriate. Because of this new career opening for social workers, this chapter introduces students to information relevant to the subject. It describes the special populations and the existing problem of employment discrimination. It clarifies what is meant by the policy of affirmative action and explains the difference between it and employment discrimination. A description of the various executive and legislative acts that have effected employment for these populations is included, as are outlines of some of the government's programs of ensuring the integration into the work force of the three special populations. Finally, the chapter contains a discussion of the organic connection between these special populations and social workers. For years, women, the handicapped, and members of minority groups have been served by the social-work profession outside the work place. The work place may be one of the last frontiers of our country's century-long effort to reconcile the ideals of its white male forefathers with the economic needs of its special-population groups. Industrial social workers are among the best equipped to help these people obtain and meet the challenge of equality where they work.

Special Populations and Employment Discrimination

Forty percent of America's work force is female. In addition, many of these women belong to minority groups (black, Hispanic, American Indian, Asian, Alaskan natives, and Pacific Islanders). Over twenty million people, or one out of eleven Americans, have a physical or mental impairment that substantially limits one or more life activities.[1] Despite the sizable portion of the work force constituted by these three groups, they have been systematically unemployed, underemployed, underpaid, and discriminated against in recruitment, hiring, training, and employee benefits. For example, the average earnings of a full-time workingwoman went from 63 percent of the average earnings of her male counterpart in 1956 to 57 percent in 1974. Women earn less than men, and the disparity is increasing.[2] Table 7-1 shows that trends in unemployment are unfavorable to women and the minorities.

Women have long been segregated into so-called pink-collar professions. In the 1970s, two-thirds of workingwomen were in sales or clerical positions, and several of the helping professions (for example, nursing, social work, and teaching) are dominated by women. Women have neither sought nor obtained full integration in the work place. Social stereotyping by employers and women themselves is partly responsible for occupational segregation. Until the women's liberation movement of the 1970s, few women challenged the roles they usually were encouraged to assume in their families and at work—namely, housewives, secretaries, nurses, and so on.

Table 7-1
Percentage of Unemployed in Civilian Labor Force

Year	White Men	White Women	Black and Other Men	Black and Other Women
1960	5.4	5.9	10.7	9.4
1977 (January-April)	7.5	8.5	12.8	13.5
Percentage of increase between 1960 and 1977	2.1	2.6	2.1	4.1

Source: Employment, annual average (Washington, D.C.: U.S. Bureau of Labor Statistics, 1978).

The following description of the inequities within one occupational setting (administration of higher-education institutions) presents conditions that are true to some extent in every work place. Based on information from 18,000 administrators at 1,037 institutions, a study by the College and University Personnel Association for 1975-1976 shows that only a small percentage of top administrative positions are held by women and minorities:

> Employment patterns differed substantially by race and sex. White males occupied the largest portion of the administrative jobs in higher education. Both black and white women were paid only 80 percent as much as men with the same job title employed at the same institution. Minority men usually held predominantly lower-paying positions but in general were paid about the same as white males in similar positions. Men held 96 percent of the college presidencies at both white coeducational and minority institutions, 100 percent at men's colleges, and 69 percent at women's colleges. Salary differentials were more consistently related to sex than to race. The only post of those examined in the study with a sizable representation of women and minorities was the affirmative-action officer.[3]

The following survey of new laws and policies affecting the work place indicates that more progressive mechanisms for full integration presently exist than ever before.

Affirmative Action: Policy for Change

Discriminatory hiring practices have always been immoral; so was segregation; so was the disenfranchisement of men. However, specific legal measures (a constitutional amendment and a Supreme Court decision) had to enter our system of self-government before these practices could be eliminated. The laws and executive acts that have been instituted in the last two decades, which are discussed in the next section, have specifically prohibited anyone from being excluded from consideration for employment because of sex, race, or a physical handicap and have actively promoted their appointments.

Nondiscrimination requires the elimination of all existing discriminatory conditions, whether deliberate or inadvertent. Affirmative action entails additional efforts and positive steps to recruit, employ, and promote members of groups traditionally excluded. Not taxiomatic to the policy of affirmative action is the notion that inequities tolerated for years will correct themselves. Boston College, in a brochure for its personnel, defines what is involved in taking affirmative actions as follows:

As the term implies, *affirmative action* means positive action taken by an employer—not just to guarantee nondiscrimination but to begin to make up for some of the discrimination that may have taken place in the past.[4]

Employers practicing affirmative action must analyze and describe how they have utilized minorities, women, and the handicapped and develop goals and timetables for correcting any underutilization. Then employers must make necessary corrections by instituting and implementing a plan for affirmative action. The employer must demonstrate additional effort in the recruitment, hiring, and promotion of members of groups traditionally excluded, even if such exclusion cannot be traced to particular discriminatory actions on the employer's part. For example, in filling a vacant position, an employer must show evidence of advertisement and a sincere attempt to solicit applications from women and members of the minority and handicapped populations. Employers must take affirmative action because they have previously underutilized members of a special population. They often hire a member of one of these special populations even if other equally qualified applicants are available. An employer who takes affirmative action ensures that, once a member of a special population is hired, that employee receives promotions, salary increases, fringe benefits, training opportunities, and other benefits of employment comparable to those provided for white-male employees.

In order to comply with the requirements of the new measures regarding fair employment, most employers initiate some change in their present practices. The Office of Civil Rights stated this clearly in 1972:

> The premise of the affirmative-action concept of the executive order is that unless positive action is undertaken to overcome the effects of systemic institutional forms of exclusion and discrimination, a benign neutrality in employment practices will tend to perpetrate the status quo ante indefinitely.[5]

Perhaps more often than other professionals, social workers encounter the painstaking slowness of social progress. They are well equipped, however, to assist employers with taking the necessary positive step—the affirmative action. A discussion of the special populations and the new national policies concerning employment necessarily precedes, in the sections that follow, a discussion of the connection of social work to present-day employment policies.

Legislation Regarding Special Populations

Presidents Roosevelt, Truman, and Eisenhower took specific actions promoting nondiscrimination in employment in the 1940s and 1950s. The executive orders they issued, which required that any employer with federal contract monies abide by nondiscrimination policies in their employment procedures, foreshadowed the more-rigorous policies that were instituted in the 1960s and 1970s.[6] In those two decades, when the first few legislative acts that equalized employment proved difficult to enforce, precedents already existed for the executive branch of the government to act to strengthen the legislative branch on the issue of employment discrimination.

The Equal Pay Act of 1963 (Fair Labor Standards Act) and Title VII in the Civil Rights Act of 1964 were landmark actions in the cause of equal employment opportunity for all Americans. The Equal Pay Act prohibited unequal pay for men and women in identical jobs that require equal skill, effort, and responsibility and that are performed under similar working conditions. The Civil Rights Act made it illegal for an employer, employment agency, or union to discriminate on the basis of race, color, religion, and national origin.

To enforce the Civil Rights Act, President Johnson issued Executive Order 11246 in 1965. This order required specific changes in employment practices and the correction of previous inequities. Two years later, Johnson issued Executive Order 11375 that expanded the Civil Rights Act to include a ban on employment discrimination by sex.

Legally, the two orders apply to the 250,000 contractors and subcontractors that receive a large proportion of their business from the federal government. (Many construction companies, industries, research institutions, schools, colleges, and social agencies receive federal funds and are thus included in the requirements of the orders.) The breadth of the applicability of the executive orders is clearer when the fact is pointed out that those contractors employ one-third of the nation's work force, or about 30 million workers.[7] The two orders also protect an additional 4 million civilians and 2 million military personnel. To comply with the two executive orders, an employer with more than 50 employees and a government contract of $50,000 or more must develop, within 120 days after commencing a contract, a written plan for affirmative action.

An amendment to the Civil Rights Act in 1972, the Equal Employment Opportunity Act, strengthened the enforceability of Title VII. This act established the Equal Employment Opportunity Commission (EEOC), which not only can require employers to fulfill the terms of the Civil Rights Act but also take to court those who do not comply.[8]

The example set by these acts and orders has not been perfectly followed. Employers not required to do so by law have not automatically established on their own fewer discriminatory employment practices. In fact, an imperfect record exists among contractors to the federal government and within the government itself. Women and minorities continue to experience difficulty in entering the work place as equals to white men. However, the foundations for fairness now exist, and the Civil Service Reform Act of 1978 has instituted new requirements for fairness in advancement and in-service improvement for members of special populations who already have positions. The outlook for nondiscrimination and for a policy of affirmative action is neither optimistic nor bleak.

For the approximately 7.2 million handicapped members of the U.S. work force, the Rehabilitation Act of 1973 was a landmark in their struggle for equal employment opportunity.[9] Section 504 of the act provided the following:

> No otherwise qualified handicapped individual in the United States . . .
> shall solely by reason of his handicap be excluded from the participation in,
> be denied benefits of, or be subjected to discrimination under any program
> or activity receiving federal financial assistance.[10]

A qualified individual, as defined by the Labor Department, is one who is "capable of performing a particular job with reasonable accommodation to his or her handicap."[11] Reasonable accommodation includes both accessibility to a facility by the handicapped (provision of elevators and wheelchair access, for example) and a slight adjustment of job description so as not to rule out the suitability of a handicapped worker (for example, allowing a hearing-disabled worker to fill a clerical position from which telephone responsibilities have been removed is considered reasonable if the handicapped worker exchanges those responsibilities for comparable work within his or her capability).

The Rehabilitation Act not only bans systemic institutional exclusion of handicapped individuals as did Executive Order 11246, but also it ensures that almost 9 percent of the work force will no longer be made to feel as if they have little to contribute to the work place. Employers must now use, without discrimination, the skills of persons with missing limbs; impaired sight, speech, and hearing; learning disabilities; and emotional or mental illness. In 1977, the list of handicaps was expanded to include alcohol and drug abuse. Then Attorney General Griffin Bell stated

> We therefore conclude that persons suffering from alcoholism and drug ad-
> diction are included within the statutory definition of "handicapped in-
> dividuals." Thus it would seem that a person could not be refused services
> solely because he is, or has a record of being, a drug addict or alcoholic.[12]

As is true for women and minorities, the foundation for fairness in employment practices now exists for handicapped workers. However, the existence of the proper fondation has not induced every employer to immediately take affirmative action to correct the inequities of the past. As a result, many workers have sued to obtain their rights under the laws and executive orders. Descriptions of some of these lawsuits follow, along with a discussion of what implications the suits may have in the future on the policy of affirmative action. Social workers who work in businesses and industries can better serve their employers and their employee clients if they possess some background on how special populations have made use of the recent legislation.

Class-Action Suits

The additional power granted the federal government since the passage of the Civil Rights Act of 1964 to enforce that act has opened the way for women, minorities, and the handicapped to use the courts to pursue grievances. Some of the most successful enforcements have followed class-action suits—that is, suits in which one or a few individuals represent themselves and all others like themselves. One such suit was filed in 1974 by eight female and minority members of the faculty of Rutgers University on behalf of all such faculty members. As a result of this suit, the university agreed to pay more than $375,000 in compensation in retroactive payments ranging from $3,248 to $19,574.[13] After a similar suit, the University of Cincinnati was required by HHS to correct the discriminatory inequities in salaries paid to black and female employees. At that university, female professors averaging two or more years of experience had been earning $2,174 less than their male counterparts. Female associate professors with an average of 4.1 years' more experience than their male counterparts were earning $1,184 less.[14]

Class-action suits in several large companies have forced those employers to live up to the commitment to take affirmative action. In 1973, a group of sixteen female employees at the National Broadcasting Company (NBC) filed suit with the New York City Human Rights Commission on behalf of NBC's 900 female employees. As a result, NBC agreed to spend about $2 million between 1977 and 1981 to hire, promote, and train women into the mainstream of all broadcasting activities. This agreement exemplifies the kind of affirmative action that is taken so that women can begin to catch up; it guarantees that certain percentages of positions will be filled with women. Most significantly, 30 percent of the high-ranking associate directors will be women. Additionally, every time a woman is promoted, her pay will be upgraded to equal the average salary of the male employees in her new grade level who have been with NBC for five years. Formerly, women were hired at the minimum salary in each grade, whereas men started out with a salary somewhere in the middle of their grade. Thus, when a woman got a raise, her salary was still always lower than a man's in the same grade. The class-action suit against NBC represents an excellent example of the uses to which the existing laws may be put in order to significantly improve the status and conditions for a larger group.[15]

Reverse Discrimination

One recent lawsuit challenged the policy of affirmative action. The case of the *Regents of the University of California* v. *Bakke* aroused considerable public interest in the mechanisms of rectifying past inequities in educational as well as employment opportunity. Bakke, a white man, was claiming reverse discrimination. He alleged he was being denied his rights under Title VI of the Civil Rights Act of 1967, which clearly outlaws the use of race to exclude anyone from participating in a federally funded program. He sued the university, charging that a medical-school special-admissions program had discriminated against him because it had admitted minority-group applicants with grades and standardized-test scores lower than his.

In June 1978, after months of deliberation, the Supreme court ruled in favor of Bakke. In a decision heralded as a compromise, the Court ordered the University of California to admit Bakke because, in fact, its special-admissions program had illegally excluded him. However, the court did state that race may be considered as one factor in admission procedures, if not the deciding factor. Attorney General Bell called the decision a "great gain for affirmative-action programs."[16] However, many lawyers, educators, and minority-group leaders remain confused as to the full implications of the decision. The Bakke decision may prompt more claims or reverse bias, including some based on sexual discrimination, and such claims may threaten the existence of affirmative-action programs. The National Association for the Advancement of Colored People (NAACP) fears that a conservative attack in the form of court cases and new laws will do just that. Nathanial R. Jones, general counsel to the NAACP, said

> While the legal questions are being ironed out, the more-serious problem to grapple with is the overall political one stemming from the popular perception that these programs are unfair, undemocratic, reverse discrimination.[17]

Nevertheless, the Bakke decision was, as Stephen Wermiel reported in the *Boston Globe*, "a first salvo in a battle of how to deal with the lingering effects of past discrimination."[18] Since the Bakke decision, a Supreme Court ruling in another case indicates a commitment on the part of the government that seems favorably disposed to affirmative-action policy.

Brian F. Weber, a white factory worker from Louisiana, sued his employer, Kaiser Aluminum, claiming that he had been a victim of illegal reverse discrimination. Weber was turned down for an in-plant craft-training program, sponsored by his union and his employer, that was supposedly open to blacks and whites on a one-for-one basis. On 27 June, 1979, the Supreme Court ruled in a 5-to-2 vote that employers and unions that have no proven histories of discrimination may adopt racial quotas to overcome imbalances in training and promotion programs. The Court thus upheld an affirmative-action policy aimed at "conspicuous" or "manifest" racial imbalance in job categories that traditionally have been segregated. The training program established by Weber's union and his employer was a temporary affirmative-action plan. The Court ruled that the Civil Rights Act of 1964 does not forbid racial preferences in such plans.

The EEOC said the ruling could bring a relaxation of EEOC affirmative-action guidelines that require some proof of last employment discrimination before corrective programs can be required. The AFL-CIO, which had supported its affiliated union, was pleased with the outcome. The NAACP considered the ruling to be probably the most important civil rights decision in recent history. It also said that, if the Court had ruled in favor of Weber, such a ruling could have set the cause of affirmative action back by ten years.

Because the Weber case affects the work place, it is more important to more people than the Bakke decision. The Weber case reaffirmed the right of women, minority-group members, and the handicapped to expect policies of affirmative action in the work place.

Programs for Special Populations in the Federal Government

HHS has several programs for affirmative action for its employees who belong to special populations. In order to establish the kind of climate that could prevent suits such as the Weber suit from materializing, employers should initiate programs such as these. The student of industrial social work may find the following sections applicable to a variety of work places.

Program for the Employment of Handicapped Individuals

Conservative estimates place the number of handicapped persons of workforce age (16 through 64) and able to work at 7.2 million.[19] A handicapped person is defined as an individual who has physical or mental impairments that substantially limit one or more life activities, has a record of such an impairment, or is regarded as having such an impairment.[20]

The federal government has taken the position for many years that it is not only a desirable social objective but also good business to hire the handicapped and has therefore made a commitment to removing all barriers to federal government employees.[21]

The program for the employment of handicapped individuals is designed to meet the mandated objectives. This program has been a part of the Office of Equal Employment Opportunity (EEO) in HHS since October 1978. In the earlier days of this program, it was administered by the OPM. Each of the federal departments has a similar program for the employment of handicapped persons. This program's objectives are to advance presently employed handicapped persons and to get them out of the lower-paying positions. This is not to say that the handicapped are going to be promoted simply because they are handicapped. The director of this program in HHS stressed the fact that this was not a welfare effort. The handicapped have to be able to do the work required by the positions they hold. He wants to see handicapped persons placed in the higher-level positions. They are given preference in hiring through a process called excepted appointment. If they are identified as handicapped and qualified for the position they are applying for, they are not required to go through the competitive process required to secure federal employment. Standard form 256 (see figure 7-1) is used by prospective employees to identify themselves as a handicapped individual. At the present time, 6,700 employees in HHS have identified themselves as having a disability or handicap. According to the director of the program at HHS, twenty of the categories have a special emphasis placed on them due to the severity of the handicap and the number of handicapped persons.

The HHS program, as with others that involve dealing with special populations, requires a degree of sensitivity and understanding toward the type of people one becomes involved with—in this case, the handicapped. It is important to take into account the past injustices the handicapped have suffered. Many of them have been discriminated against and made to feel as if they had litle to contribute. The truth is that the handicapped have a great deal to contribute. According to the director of the program at HHS, the handicapped usually work harder than the nonhandicapped because they have fewer opportunities to work and thus use their talents more intensely than most people do.

Minorities Employment Program

The mission of the Minorities Employment Program is to expand equal opportunity for minorities. Organizationally, this program in the HHS is located in the EEO and is answerable to the Office of the Assistant Secretary for Personnel Administration at HHS. Through a reorganization of EEO, the Minorities Employment Program was formed in 1978. The department is unique in having this program in that it caters to a wide range of minorities and has yet to be formalized in other departments. The minority populations it serves are blacks, Hispanics, American Indians, Asians, Alaskan natives, and Pacific Islanders.

The technical objective of the Minorities Employment Program is to provide departmentwide leadership and direction in the development of

Self-identification of Medical Disability   Attachment 1 to FPM LTR. 290-   APPENDIX B

Last Name	Birth Date *(Mo./Yr.)*	Social Security Number	ENTER CODE HERE ⟶ ☐☐

DEFINITION OF A REPORTABLE DISABILITY: A physical or mental disability is NOT determined by a person's ability to perform his or her work but by a disability, or a history of such disability, which is likely to cause the employee to experience difficulty in obtaining, maintaining or advancing in employment. This does not apply solely to an employee's current position, but applies to the total career life cycle of that employee. *(In the case of multiple disabilities, choose the code which describes the impairment that would most likely result in such difficulties.)*

	Code
GENERAL CODES	
I do not wish to have my disability status officially recorded outside my medical records. *(Before using this code, please read the reverse side of this form, which explains the need for obtaining this information. [Note your agency may use this code if, in their judgement you have used an incorrect code.])*	01
I have no disability of the types listed in the codes below	04

SPEECH IMPAIRMENTS
Severe speech malfunction or inability to speak, hearing is normal *(Examples: defects of articulation [unclear language sounds]; stuttering; aphasia [impaired language function]; laryngectomy [removal of the "voice box"]).* ... 13

HEARING IMPAIRMENTS	Code	Total deafness in both ears, with understandable speech	16
Hard of hearing *(Total deafness in one ear or inability to hear ordinary conversation, correctable with a hearing aid)*	15	Total deafness in both ears, and unable to speak clearly	17

VISION IMPAIRMENTS		Inability to read ordinary size print, not correctable by glasses *(can read oversized print or use assisting devices such as glass or projector modifyer)*	23
Ability to read ordinary size print with glasses, but with loss of peripheral *(side)* vision *(Restriction of the visual field to the extent that mobility is affected - "Tunnel vision")*	22	Blind in one eye	24
		Blind in both eyes *(No usable vision, but may have some light perception)*	25

MISSING EXTREMITIES	Code	One leg	32	One hand or arm *and* one foot or leg	35
One hand	27	Both hands or arms	33	One hand or arm *and* both feet or legs	36
One arm	28	Both feet or legs	34	Both hands or arms *and* one foot or leg	37
One foot	29			Both hands or arms *and* both feet or legs	38

NONPARALYTIC ORTHOPEDIC IMPAIRMENTS		One or both arms	46
(Because of chronic pain, stiffness, or weakness in bones or joints, there is some loss of ability to move or use a part or parts of the body.)		One or both legs	47
		Hip or pelvis	48
One or both hands	44	Back	49
One or both feet	45	Any combination of two or more parts of the body	57

PARTIAL PARALYSIS		One leg, any part	63
(Because of a brain, nerve, or muscle problem, including palsy and cerebral palsy, there is some loss of ability to move or use a part of the body, including legs, arms, and/or trunk.)		Both hands	64
		Both legs, any part	65
		Both arms, any part	66
One hand	61	One side of body, including one arm and one leg	67
One arm, any part	62	Three or more major parts of the body *(arms and legs)*	68

COMPLETE PARALYSIS		Both arms	73
(Because of a brain, nerve, or muscle problem, including palsy and cerebral palsy, there is complete loss of ability to move or use a part of the body, including legs, arms and/or trunk.)		One leg	74
		Both legs	75
One hand	70	Lower half of body, including legs	76
Both hands	71	One side of body, including one arm and one leg	77
One arm	72	Three or more major parts of the body *(arms and legs)*	78

OTHER IMPAIRMENTS			
Heart disease with no restriction or limitation of activity *(History of heart problems with complete recovery)*	80	Mental retardation *(A chronic and lifelong condition involving a limited ability to learn, to be educated, and to be trained for useful productive employment as certified by a State Vocational Rehabilitation agency under section 213.3102(t) of scheduled A)*	90
Heart disease with restriction or limitation of activity	81		
Convulsive disorder *(e.g., epilepsy)*	82		
Blood diseases *(e.g., sickle cell disease, leukemia, hemophilia)*.	83		
Controlled diabetes with no restriction of activity	84	Mental or emotional illness *(A history of treatment for mental or emotional problems)*	91
Diabetes with limitation of activity due to complications such as retinitis, neuritis, etc.	85		
Pulmonary or respiratory disorders *(e.g., tuberculosis, emphysema, asthma, etc.)*	86	Severe distortion of limbs and/or spine *(e.g., dwarfism, kyphosis [severe distortion of back], etc.)*	92
Kidney dysfunctioning *(e.g., if dialysis [use of an artificial kidney machine] is required, etc.)*	87	Disfigurement of face, hands, or feet *(e.g., distortion of features on skin, such as those caused by burns, gunshot injuries, and birth defects [gross facial birth marks, club feet, etc.])*	93
Cancer - a history of cancer with complete recovery	88		
Cancer - undergoing surgical and/or medical treatment	89		

256-101

Standard Form 256 (1-77)
U.S. Civil Service Commission
FPM Chap. 290

Figure 7-1. Self-Identification of Medical Disability

goals and objectives for a positive, comprehensive equal employment opportunity program for minorities at all grade levels and in all occupational services in accordance with the requirements of the Civil Service Reform Act of 1978, which pertains to minority underrepresentation. Accomplishing this objective involves several different functions. The first of these is to look at the different kinds of minorities to assess their situation in terms of their representation within the agency. This is done by counting how many minorities are employed and identifying to which ethnic group they belong. Assessment of the minority population is also done by determining their status within the agency. This includes looking at where the minority person is in comparison to other employees in terms of types of positions and grade level held, which are the income determinants. A second function of this program is that of informing the minority groups about the employment opportunities within the department and getting them to apply. This involves an outreach and recruitment effort by the program. Through outreach programs, organizations, colleges, universities, and other groups that may have large minority populations are sought. The Minorities Employment Program has also tapped into skills banks and other sources than can identify potential minority job candidates. If particular types of vacancies or opportunities are available, the organizations that are a part of this established network are contacted. They, in turn, spread the word about the vacancies and opportunities and assist in the recruitment of minority persons.

The Minorities Employment Program serves agency management in addition to its recruitment responsibilities. The program's role is to keep the managers of the department constantly aware of the minority situation. One of the major issues is that minorities are being underutilized and that many who are employed are found in the lower-grade-level positions. The ongoing effort is bringing about changes in hiring practices and pushing for advancement of minorities into higher-level positions. Another important role is to help management identify resources for finding qualified minority persons.

For the minority population, the Minorities Employment Program serves an enabler role and an advocate role. The enabler role comes into focus when assisting the minority persons in gaining employment. This is done through outreach, organizational contacts, and providing information on what is available and how to get there. The Minorities Employment Program assumes the advocate role for the minority population when it has to confront management about the lack of minorities employed in the higher levels of an agency or about discrepancies in particular hiring practices.

Federal Women's Program

PL 92-261 and the Equal Employment Opportunity Act of 1972 gave OPM powers to insure that all personnel actions in goverment are free from discrimination. OPM regulations implementing PL 92-261 require that federal agencies appoint a manager for the Federal Women's Program to advise the director of EEOC on matters affecting the employment and promotion of women within the agencies. One of the requirements of PL 92-261 is that the federal agencies provide sufficient resources (for example, funds, equipment, personnel, and so on) to the Federal Women's Program to insure that the program will produce results in equal employment opportunities at the headquarters and field levels.

The goal of the Federal Women's Program is to improve employment and advancement opportunities for women. Specific priorities of the program will sometimes differ from agency to agency depending on the type of agency, the kinds of occupations it involves, the geographical location, and the available work force.

There are two perspectives from which the Federal Women's Program should operate in every agency or office. It has to work from the top down and bottom up. At the top of the hierarchy, managers who develop policy must be made aware of the patterns of discrimination that may be occurring and encouraged to develop plans for improving the situation.

The Federal Women's Program is involved in numerous functions in the interest of women, such as:

Recruiting and hiring women for agency jobs,

Placing women in jobs that offer them promotional opportunities and advancement in accordance with their qualifications and abilities,

Encouraging agencies to expand their opportunities for part-time work and to restructure jobs so that women can compete for them on an equal basis with men,

Encouraging provisions for child care for children of federal employees either in the community or within the agency,

Reviewing organizational regulations to identify any potential adverse impact on the employment of women.

One problem that is being experienced by the Federal Women's Program is that many of the staff people within various agencies are assigned to the program in a collateral-duty position. A collateral-duty position is one that involves working in another area or position in addition to the work performed for the women's program. The collateral-duty positions are not endorsed as a viable way to staff these programs because the staff people usually spend only 20 or 30 percent of their time in this effort and the remainder of the time fulfilling the duties required in the other position. For this reason, it is important that persons working in a Federal Women's Program do so without responsibilities to another part of the agency. The establishment of more part-time positions in the program is being advocated as preferable to staffing by collateral duty.

The Federal Women's Program is involved in many areas and current issues significant to the female population. It also supports activities on a community basis as well as in the federal government. It acts as the conscience of the agencies it is in by trying to insure that bias against women is eliminated in the federal workplace. In addition to this, it also provides leadership and direction for women's issues related to employment and advancement.

Women represent 30.5 percent of the total full-time federal civilian work force. On a GS scale of (GS 2-18), as of May 1977, the average grade for women was GS 5.8 as compared to GS 8.1 for men. Women with college degrees were one to three grades behind men with the same educational level. Over the past ten years, significant and important increases have occurred in the number of women who have become employed by and advanced through the federal system. However, much remains to be done.

Issues

Most companies with 3,000 employees or more, as well as universities, employ affirmative-action officers. Many employ several such officers on their staffs, and social workers should consider filling these positions.

The importance of affirmative-action programs varies; all government and private industries do not have affirmative-action programs identical to those described. Some employers regard affirmative-action officers only as a watch dog, assisting the organization by making sure it is doing the right thing and covering its flanks regarding federal regulations. In such work places, for example, when a vacancy exists, the employer may post a vacancy and solicit resumes. Often, however, the employer has predetermined his or her selection, and the advertising is merely a gesture to satisfy affirmative-action requirements. The affirmative-action officer may interpret regulations and respond to employee concerns by acting as a resource person regarding employee rights without ever soliciting employee grievances.

Because of conservatism such as this, workers in both public and private work places would benefit from more human-service professionals being employed as affirmative-action officers. The responsibilities of the affirmative-action officer activities such as coordinating, monitoring, and improving the program; assisting with the implementation of the plan that is submitted to HHS; staffing advisory councils; preparing audits and special reports; advising and counseling administrators, staff, students, teachers, and others; and, of course, serving as advocate for the special populations.

Social workers receive training in community organization, social planning, group management, and interpersonal communication as a part of their regular education. The conceptual framework of the discipline of social work and the practical internship experience that accompanies social-work training give the social worker experience that is particularly apropriate in order to carry out the typical responsibility of the affirmative-action officer. The tact, sensitivity, and initiative in human relations that social workers bring to their jobs are qualities an affirmative-action officer must also possess. As has already been stated, social workers have long served, outside the work place, the special populations the affirmative-action officer now serves in the work place. A social worker does need additional training regarding the legislation and practicalities of nondiscrimination and affirmative-action policy, but with such training, the career goal of afirmative-action officer is a realistic one for future social workers who wish to work in business, industry, or government agencies.

At present, the registry maintained by the Council on Social Work Education's industrial project indicates that only one person with an MSW is currently employed as an affirmative-action officer. She works in a large corporation in an affirmative-action program with several other affirmative-action employees from other disciplines. She leads several support groups for minority and female employees, providing them with the opportunity to share concerns and develop peer support. She helps them both to formulate and to achieve their goals. Because she is familiar with the organizational structure, she can help the employees organize, when appropriate, at the grass-roots level in order to achieve some goals by collective, persuasive action within the organizational system. She also investigates the corporation from within to identify preventable problems between the employer and the employees, thus improving the working conditions of individuals and protecting the corporation from possible litigation. She receives the support of the management of the corporation—a demonstration of their true commitment to a policy of affirmative action. The corporation is committed to eliminating or at least minimizing the influence of racist and sexist practices within itself. Their collaboration is a model for the future.

Because many employers in the United States have added affirmative-action officers to their staffs, an increase in opportunities for industrial social workers exists. Furthermore, all industrial social workers now need some knowledge of the policies of nondiscrimination and affirmative action that, since 1964, have become a permanent part of every work place.

Summary

The integration into the work place of three special populations—women, the handicapped, and members of minority groups—constitutes one of the final civil rights battles that need to be waged in this country. Affirmative-action policy connotes compensatory action for past discrimination, and at the same time it denotes positive action in the present toward hiring members of these three special populations. These policies are necessary because of the chronic underpayment and underemployment of, and discrimination against, women, the handicapped, and members of minority groups. The Civil Rights Act of 1964, two executive orders issued by President Johnson, the Equal Employment Opportunity Act of 1972, and the Rehabilitation Act of 1973 gave the government the power to ensure for all Americans equal opportunity for employment and advancement. When schools, businesses, and industries subsequently failed to treat all workers equally, several major lawsuits resulted. By its decisions in some of these suits, the Supreme Court has joined the other two branches of government in supporting policies of affirmative action. The federal government itself has instituted programs that demonstrate methods of providing affirmative action for federal employees and job applicants. Social workers employed by private businesses should promote similar methods in their work places. Some businesses may not be as progressive as the federal government at instituting affirmative-action programs. Social workers have long been allies of special populations, and they possess the training and skills that affirmative-action officers should also possess. Thus, social workers are particularly appropriate to fill positions as affirmative-action officers.

8 Americans Employed Overseas

This chapter discusses the needs of and services for Americans employed overseas as a special population. Discussion of military families overseas is not included because of the coverage in chapter 9. The author was able to observe this group of people firsthand when she lived and worked overseas from 1967-1972 in Italy and England. Subsequently visits on consulting assignments have been made annually, including trips to Iran, Iraq, Yugoslavia, Germany, Greece, Thailand, Japan, Austria, and England. She has become aware of the paucity of social services available from the employers, or the U.S. Government, to these employees and their families. Since the local services are also largely unavailable to Americans employed by U.S. firms, their plight is the more desperate. Things have in no way improved—conditions in the 1980s remain as critical as in the 1960s and 1970s.

This chapter presents firsthand experiences, knowledge, and interviews with people from other countries and offers recommendations for the provision of services for this population group.

Lack of Services

In April 1977, a conference was held in Boston by a group of multinational corporations in conjunction with the occupational physicians meeting. The conference began to pinpoint some of the growing concerns of companies regarding the high turnover of their overseas employees due to personal problems. From this meeting, a nonprofit corporation, International Occupational Program Association (IOPA), was formed from representatives of twelve multinational firms. In the summer of 1978, the author was sent by IOPA as a planning consultant to Europe and the Mideast to study the problems of overseas Americans, to explore local facilities, and then to make recommendations. She was helped by the fact that she had already been an overseas American. Having lived through moving three children (aged fourteen, eleven, and seven), a toy poodle, 12,000 pounds of furniture, and a station wagon is a very different thing from making a flying visit and talking to people who are experiencing what one has not. As she saw the effects of culture-shock, the mental and emotional anguish, the addiction problems, the misery of teenagers separated from friends, she realized that all remained as she remembered them in 1970. As glamorous as working overseas may seem, only people who have done it understand the turmoil the families experience. Only those who have felt the need will be aware of the lack of mental-health and social-service-support systems that would have helped them through the adjustments.

In preparation for this trip, many people were interviewed. The U.S. State Department offered suggestions and provided contacts. The NIMH, the NIAAA, and the National Institute of Drug Abuse, as well as the Department of Defense, provided additional assistance. Representatives from the multinational corporations, including medical directors and personnel managers, were interviewed. Organizations such as the Foreign Trade Council and AFL-CIO were involved, as well as individuals who had had overseas experience. Introductory letters were sent to U.S. embassies, chambers of commerce, unions, treatment facilities, and other appropriate people. A staff person was hired for three months to plan and coordinate the endeavor.

The trip began at the International Congress on Alcoholism and Addiction in Zurich, Switzerland. Meetings were held with a number of European representatives, and visits were made to England, Iran, Greece, Yugoslavia, and Germany.

Among the professional people interviewed during the trip were Dr. Norman Satorius, chief, director of the Mental Health Division, World Health Organization; Dr. M. Kilibarda, chief of the United Nations Division of Narcotics; Dr. Allan Sippert, director of Alcoholism Services for the Department of Health and Social Security, England; and Colonel Barlow, base commander U.S. Army Air Base, Tehran. Many meetings were held with State Department officials, who were most helpful. Interviews were also held with school officials, researchers, therapists, industrial social workers, company representatives from over one dozen of the multinational corporations employing people overseas, personnel directors from companies, and employees' wives and teenage children. AA groups, treatment facilities, and patients were also visited.

The author found that U.S. employees overseas and their families are facing significant problems of alcoholism and alcohol abuse, legal- and illegal-drug abuse, and emotional crises and that employees, wives, teenagers, and young children are experiencing pressures due to the radical lifestyle changes caused by living outside of the United States. These problems are especially evident in employees assigned to the Mideast area.

There appears to be a dichotomy between personnel directors in the United States and their counterparts in foreign countries. A director in the United States must fulfill contracted personnel requirements and literally find bodies to staff the projects. Screening is minimal, perhaps because effective screening procedures might result in a serious reduction in the number of people considered suitable for foreign work. Also companies unfortunately are not fully informing employees about the stark reality of the places to which they are going. High salaries are offered and contracts signed, and once there, employees cannot afford to come home at their own expense. Many expressed the feeling that they were trapped. As a result, U.S. industry's personnel directors in foreign countries are faced with the responsibility of working with people who do not know what to expect and who often are disappointed and unhappy with what they find. The pressure is then upon the local personnel directors to help retain these employees because it is a reflection of them when employees leave before their contracts are terminated.

Personnel directors both in the United States and abroad are handling problems for which they are unprepared and unskilled. They spoke of incidents of attempted suicides, of teenagers incarcerated in jails due to possession or sale of heroin, and of alcoholic employees—all without available treatment resources. The personnel directors are well meaning and caring people, but they understandably do not have the training for handling the emotional problems their employees are facing. Also, apparently no company of government is tracking the incidence of problems. There is no way of knowing how many addiction problems, suicide attempts, battering incidences, and depressions are occuring because no statistics are available to show the dimensions of these problems.

However, it is an accepted fact that heavy drinking and alcoholism are prevalent. A great deal of social pressure to drink exists. Entertainment is mainly done in people's homes where much drinking occurs. Alcoholism as a disease is well understood. In countries where alcohol is illegal, bootlegging is rampant. People pay high prices for liquor, or they may operate their own stills. (One medical director said that in the last two years, he had seen four executive's wives with the most seriously damaged livers he has ever seen, caused by drinking alcohol that was improperly distilled.)

Drug and pill taking is excessive among women and teenagers. Tranquilizers can be purchased over the counter in many countries. Incidences of women's taking tranquilizers were constantly mentioned as a major problem in each country visited. School officials were consistently concerned about teenage drug taking.

Lack of employment opportunities for employees' spouses (mostly wives, but some husbands) is increasingly placing a strain on marriages. This is a problem with government wives as well as multinational wives. When women find that they cannot work in a particular country, they often return to the United States. The 1978 summer issue of the *Foreign Service Journal* described this problem in an article that affirmed that an increased number of divorces occur among State Department employees.[1] Many women who do not return home become increasingly depressed and frustrated in not being able to work. Dr. Satorious, as well as State Department officials, acknowledged this to be a critical worldwide problem among overseas Americans.

Many problems exist also for children with learning difficulties and physical handicaps. School officials maintain that parents are led to believe before they leave the United States that there are special schools for such children abroad. However, school representatives stated that children often lose years from their educational development because of the lack of educational facilities. These officials recommended that dyslexic children, retarded children and children with physical handicaps not be sent to the Mideast and, if they are going to Europe, that the availability of services be explored thoroughly before bringing a child with special needs.

Treatment facilities are available in Europe, but unfortunately, unless one is fluent in the native language, they would not be appropriate for referrals. Facilities in England might be utilized from some alcoholism referrals, but in no way could they handle a large number since they are at a capacity with their own clientele. AA is also not as available as it is in the United States.

Culture Shock

Readers may wonder at the causative factors of these social and emotional aberrations that appear among overseas Americans. Perhaps the author's direct experience and/or knowledge would be useful. Excerpted here are portions of earlier papers she has authored that refer directly to the problem of alcoholism and indirectly to other problem areas. The treatment facilities (or lack of them) are similar for all the behavioral systems of social dislocation so evident in this population:

> Inadequate preparation for employees and for their family members is the beginning misstep. Overseas assignments are always thought of in terms of the employee. Families, to use the vernacular, are in State Departments terms . . . *excess baggage,* American military language . . . *dependents,* and to companies . . . *sponsored.* It is assumed the family will go wherever the husband/father is sent unless the employer decides otherwise. The state of the art, so to speak, of treating alcoholism problems overseas is at so immature a level that companies are just beginning to acknowledge the problem for the employee, much less the family.

> The seriousness of the problem, and ignorance in understanding or ameliorating it, complicates the task. The author was especially pleased that the importance of the family was realized and included in the planning. The stresses upon the family, are far greater than those experienced by the employee. He does become more vulnerable in his own job performance because of this, however. The stability of the family itself is shaken, and the strains produced for them are the other serious consequences. This

continues after the family returns and is not an experience in isolation. A company should think very seriously about its families that it sends overseas.[2]

What happens to people who are moved from their own country, most of them with spouse and children, as they try to adjust to the new culture and job situation? Culture shock is experienced in various stages by almost everyone, regardless of education and status. Because of the lack of preparation and the denial by the employer that this occurs, the troubled person feels isolated. Destructive behavior often results from the release of aggression and hostility through drinking, drug taking, crime, and other bizarre symptoms.

Everyone recognizes that a mild form of culture shock takes place in any change of social scene. However, there are qualitative differences in a move to another country.

The interesting phenomenon that accompanies culture shock overseas is the change of value structure. Being out of one's native country results in a letting down of one's usual code of conduct; this is so common that it is much discussed. What would be considered unacceptable behavior in the United States is readily seen as possible overseas, and social conditions may be so different that they require a whole new set of coping mechanisms:

When I think of Italy, not only do I think of the artistic accomplishments but also of having to carry our drinking water because of the threat of hepatitis.

We could not drink the water from the tap and had to bring purified water from a central location.

Imagine a magnificient ten-room villa with marble floors but without the convenience of closets, light fixtures, or kitchen cabinets.

For two years, we did not have a telephone.[3]

Medical facilities except for an outpatient dispensary were located two hour's driving time away. The hospital and specialists were in Germany. I was flown, Medical Air-Evac, to Germany for three days with our daughters when they needed to be seen by an ophthalmologist. Several wives went through pregnancies in Germany because of complications while husbands remained in Italy with the other children. Untold stresses resulted when medical problems combined with inadequate care. Families are flown into Germany from all the NATO countries. Medical airlifts operate weekly for civilian and military personnel.

Schools are not located at each installation. Eric, at fourteen boarded at a coed American high school two hours away in Vincenza, Italy, and when Renee was thirteen she did the same in Lakenheath, England. Civilian and military dependents attend these schools. The schools had little supervision, and because of the lack of telephones in both countries, contact was almost impossible until the weekly bus arrived home. American overseas schools are not at the level of stateside schools. There was no possibility to use the native schools. Language differences, as well as the level of math and science, would have put the American children, especially the older ones, far behind when they returned to the U.S.[4]

As a result of these differences that cause such a sense of dislocation, it is not surprising that each person experiences some difficulties. The behavioral symptoms may differ, but the cries for help are apparent in all of them:

> For example, our physicians and dentists were often known to drink heavily. Every evening the pilots engaged in the favorite sport of the officers at the Officers' Club from five to seven—throwing glasses, after finishing a drink, across the room and into the fireplace. The bartender would stand by and smile, and the club paid for the breakage. It was only when the home-company officials visited that anything was done. Drinking was so heavy that constant chauffeur service was available at the Officer's Club for both civilian and military. While we were in Italy, Americans killed thirteen Italians in auto accidents, including the local, beloved Italian parish priest (which practically resulted in a local riot against the Americans). Not one American was killed by Italians. One of the main executives from one of the companies became involved in a large illegal operation utilizing government equipment. This was tolerated by the American community with amusement.
>
> The installation in England was tiny—no recreational facilities, no medical facilities—but there were four clubs with bars.
>
> Because of the lack of facilities and the security which existed, I heard problems which wives were afraid to express to others. One pilot's wife whose husband was an alcoholic was in terror each time he took up the jet . . . she finally fled to the U.S. Another civilian wife slashed her wrists; no mental-health facilities were available. Tranquilizers flowed freely because they were the main available sedation for the women. The wives of officers and executives had cocktail parties beginning at four P.M. daily. The wives would have several martinis before their husbands returned. The men, in turn, had several at the club before coming home. The extent of the alcohol problem in the executive and officer groups cannot be minized.
>
> As we are now sending more Americans to Arab countries and Third World areas, we need to be aware of the phenomena of the overseas family. I spoke at the Second Annual Conference on Alcoholism and Drug Dependence last November in Baghdad and heard about the problems they are facing with alcohol. Their religion forbids it, but they know many people are drinking. What of Americans assigned to countries where it is illegal? The situation is similar to the one I experienced with teenagers. Drugs, at the time, were available all over Europe, especially in Holland, and American teenagers could readily get them. They all backpacked during the summer, and parents tried to instill into them the fear of drug taking in certain countries. Penalties were severe in many countries. In Turkey, hands were chopped off by authorities. Our teenagers were not provided any counseling in their schools and suffered greatly from adjustment problems.[5]

Issues

The key to implementing any recommendations depends on the commitment of a company to solve its own problems and to work cooperatively with other companies. Without a strong philosophical and financial commitment among companies, none of the following recommendations will be feasible.

The one major overall recommendation is clearly that a multinational alcohol, drug, and mental-health system be established to serve the needs of overseas employees and their families. The following are a few of many other recommendations:

A comprehensive program from screening for overseas employment to repatriation programs should be implemented.

Out-patient facilities similar to what was developed in Tehran should be duplicated wherever there is a group of 10,000 or more U.S. residents. These centers should also be able to service outlying districts of Americans.

Treatment for emergencies are badly needed, such as detoxification center and mental-health facilities for attempted suicides.

In-patient-treatment facilities are also needed for both alcoholics and the mentally ill.

Facilities should be developed in a geographical plan to include appropriate coverage by company as well as by country.

In the professional area, companies should do more to employ women and should write into their contracts that wives should be able to be employed in the host country.

Personnel directors need special training in all mental-health areas, especially alcoholism.

Medical directors and other key personnel should also receive special training, in the mental-health area.

Consideration should be given to employee's families. Counselors or social workers should be available in each overseas company that employes a large number of people (one for every 3,000 U.S. employees and family members).

Serious consideration should be given to screening wives and teenagers. Individual interviews should be held before departure to insure that families have a full understanding of the situation. Adolescent children and people with medical or special educational needs are especially vulnerable.

A coordinated plan among international companies and governmental departments will be required if these recommendations are to be successfully implemented.

The alternatives to not providing such services will be increased turn-over rates, dissatisfaction at overseas locations among employees, and a higher cost in meeting contract commitments. These costs are escalating at a rapid rate. For an individual employee who must be returned because of emotional or addiction problems, companies are reporting that the cost of replacement is approximately $100,000. In addition, companies report that some of their turnover rates in some of the countries are running over 60 percent because of high employee dissatisfaction. These costs are expected to continue to escalate because:

> There will be increasingly larger numbers of U.S. employees and their families sent to overseas assignments by our U.S. international corporations.

> There will be even more third-country nationals hired by our multinational corporations to work in countries other than their own.

> These employees and their families will have emotional and addiction problems that will need to be treated as well as prevented.

> These employees and their families will have higher rates of these problems than employees living in the United States because of the added burden of culture shock and all accompanying changes a move out of one's country brings.

Employers feel responsible for employees who are being sent to overseas locations. The multinational corporations wish to provide preventive measures as well as alleviation and support services for their employees undergoing such situations. Rather than each company developing its own program, resources, and facilities, it makes sense to cooperate and coordinate efforts.

Although this seems logical, getting companies to cooperate appears to be very difficult. Each company is concerned about sharing the extent of its problems with another. Personnel often deny that problems exist, mainly because they really are not trained to diagnose them. In addition, employees often hide family problems from the company.

Good mental-health services and alcohol/drug treatment require U.S. staffing. Of all illnesses, these necessitate good communication between the helping person and the patient.

With the added stress of the hostage situation in Iran, as well as recent shootings of U.S. embassy officials in South America, many Americans do not wish to leave the United States. For those who do, their employers have a moral responsibility to help sustain them through an experience that can be traumatizing. The results are better employees and untold savings to the company.

Summary

The mental-health needs of people employed overseas, and of their family members, present unique problems and challenges for employers. At the request of the employers, workers have uprooted their families from all familiar ties and environs; they have been thrust into cultures and value systems different from, and often opposed to their own; they have given up the familiar support systems of friends and families; and professional help for mental and emotional problems are either lacking or woefully inadequate.

Since the employer is the common denominator for all of the families, and since it stands to lose greatly from personnel problems, it behooves the employer to pay attention to the needs for services by the employees and their family members.

An awareness of the problem areas should begin at the employee-recruitment level and continue through relocation and readjustment. Since the problem is not restricted to one company or one country, it is recommended that a multinational approach be used in establishing a mental-health system to serve families overseas.

9   The Military

Almost five million Americans comprise the military establishment. This figure includes persons in uniform as well as families who are eligible for services. It does not include retired employees. The purpose of this chapter is to present the philosophical rationale for why the military is an area for employment-related social work. Then the history of practice in the armed services is discussed. The military, especially the army, provides one of the oldest examples of professional social work's functioning in the work world. Development of this practice, beginning with the American Red Cross then the army, navy, and air force, is presented. The growth of alcohol and drug programs across all the services is also discussed.

Much of the material on the recent history of military social work was gained from personal interviews since it is not yet recorded. An area in which the military has led the industrial arena is in services to employees' families. Special materials furnished to the author by the Prisoners of War Family Project and Child Abuse Program of the air force were especially helpful. One of the case studies in chapter 11, for example, concerns a child-abuse case involving a parent in the air force. The objective of this chapter is to teach the student of industrial human services.

An understanding of a special work population that encompasses millions of Americans;

The history of the social-work services to this employee group;

The variety of existing programs;

Opportunities for social-work staffing;

The issues involved with this particular employee group.

Rationale for Social-Work Services

As of 30 September 1978, 4,917,594 military personnel and dependents were in the U.S. armed forces, of whom 2,049,296 were military personnel and 2,868,298 were dependents.[1] Prior to World War II, the peacetime military was maintained by a small staff of professional men that was guided by long-established rules and traditions. Since that time, our military has grown to be made up largely of citizen soldiers with an increasing number of dependents, until today the dependents outnumber the military personnel.

Up to 1938, the military establishment was manned by volunteer soldiers and was a minor element in the U.S. way of life. Since that time the change has been dramatic. In order to protect itself in wartime and from threats of war, the United States now has a military force of millions with a financial budget of $107.6 billion a year—approximately 23 percent of the entire budget of the country.

To gain a perspective of the expanded role of today's military, consider that the Pentagon, headquarters of the Department of Defense, is the world's largest office building, with three times the floor space of the Empire State Building in New York, and it accommodates 26,000 employees.[2] As students of the industrial sector, it is important to remember that the military provides millions of Americans with a way of life. For many social workers, it represents a philosophical conflict to even consider working in or with this institution. One reason for this conflict is that many social workers have pacifist inclinations, and thus the military system itself is anathema to their beliefs. It is, however, a contention of the author that potential clients exist in this employee population and that they have an ethical responsibility to provide services to these clients. This does not mean that every social worker should be able to work in this framework, but it does call for an understanding of the real needs of this group and a compassion for its problems. In some ways they need more help since they operate in a tight bureaucratic system and are isolated and often alone, away from family or friends.

Several basic philosophical differences exist between the military institution in a democracy and the democracy itself. These differences undoubtedly affect the manner in which the insitution carries out all its functions, including social welfare. Ralph Morgan has listed them clearly:

1. The primary difference between the military and civilian environments which require a coercion-oriented social structure is that the social function of the military is performed in mobile, emergent situations which involve danger to the individual and the group. All human institutions which operate in such a milieu seem to be similarly structured—for example, police and fire departments.
2. Military organizations must base authority upon incumbency of office rather than the personal influence of the officeholder.
3. The membership must be continuously available.
4. It is hierarchically structured because this is more effective in battle than loosely structured, democratically organized armies.
5. It is a legitimate bureaucracy which traces its source of power to the federal Constitution.[3]

Because the nature of the military organization requires total discipline, there is a corresponding totality of responsibility. This is reflected in traditional statements such as "the military takes care of its own" and "an officer's responsibility is toward his men" and is evident in literature both from the military and social work:

> If the armed forces are to attract and retain a competent, dedicated nuclear group of professional personnel, and maintain military-group loyalty and morale over the long stretches of peacetime, the military must fulfill the basic obligation of any society to provide for the needs of its members in terms of currently accepted social standards.

> The social welfare of servicemen is vital to military morale. Social-welfare policies, measures, services, and structural relationships are important to morale not only as a source of some paternalistic solicitude for the individual but also because they create the kind of social institution and social relationships in which the individual can achieve his own maximum effectiveness.[4]

Social welfare is one of several instruments for social organization. Its purpose is to help society function through meeting basic human needs and assisting with adjustment to social organization. The responsibility of the military institution to provide the necessary instruments for its successful organization implies the responsibility to provide social-welfare services for its members. It may be said that, in the case of the military, the responsibility is even greater since the function of this institution requires such total commitment by its members.

History

Social-work practice in the military traces its beginnings to the Civil War period when, in 1861, the U.S. Sanitary Commission, with leaders from the field of social reform, worked in the area of returning hospitalized soldiers to active duty.[5] "It was the National Committee for Mental Hygiene, which in World War I, approached the Surgeon General's Office of the Army to describe the help which clinically trained social workers were competent to give to psychiatric casualties."[6] The result was the production of a group of trained psychiatric social workers for assignment as civilian psychiatric aides in World War I—army hospital neuropsychiatric services.[7]

The American Red Cross, founded in 1881, was the principal provider of social services until World War II, especially in the psychiatric field. However, during World War II, the social-service base was expanded when trained social workers in uniform began informally to form psychiatric teams with psychologists and psychiatrists who were also in uniform. This movement was assisted by the War Service Office of the American Association of Psychiatric Social Workers, through whose interest and influence the civilian professional body began to lay the groundwork for a more-organized social-work structure within the military establishment. "By the end of the war, the role of the psychiatric social worker in the military complex had moved beyond direct casework services to providing consultation to military training divisions, the clergy, and other military personnel."[8]

American Red Cross Services

Throughout the past ninety-nine years, the Red Cross has fulfilled its charter obligations to provide health and welfare services to the armed forces. Aid has been rendered to the sick and wounded in time of war as have voluntary relief services. It has also served as a communications medium between the people of the United States and their armed forces.

During World War I, civilian and military national leaders recognized the welfare needs of servicemen and their families. During this period, the American Red Cross provided services to men on active duty or confined to military hospitals through field directors stationed at crucial military installations in the Untied States and at strategic points overseas.

Because the need for service to families was so great, in 1917 the Red Cross began to recruit trained social workers who could organize people to serve in Red Cross chapters as both volunteers and career staff to help the families of men absent on military duty. The program that was developed then is the Service to Military Families (SMF) program of today.[9]

During the peacetime interval between World War I and the mobilization for World War II, the Red Cross maintained social-service departments in seventeen army and navy hospitals, with psychiatric social workers provided in all installations having an assigned resident neuropsychiatrist. In 1940, appeals were made to assign psychiatric social workers to the psychiatric units in naval and Marine Corps training stations. Faith in the contributions of the psychiatric social workers was evidenced by the surgeon general when, in 1942, similar requests were made for consultation services to the army. "Subsequently, Red Cross personnel were assigned to all installations having neuropsychiatric patients, including army general hospitals, naval hospitals, and later in convalescent hospitals."[10] Again, in World War II, social workers were recruited by the Red Cross to establish an effective social-welfare service.[11]

In 1976, the Red Cross merged its Service at Military Installations and Service in Military Hospitals programs into a single program, Services to the Armed Forces (SAF). The aforementioned SMF program and the Service to Veterans Administration Officers were combined under a single director.[12] The SMF program is administered and implemented through approximately 3,000 Red cross chapters in local civilian communities and in 1978 served a total of 873,860 cases including military families, veterans and their families, and civilian families. The SAF program, implemented worldwide by the national Red Cross staff, provided services to 684,119 cases in 1978.[13]

SAF

Services to members of the armed forces are provided by 670 career-staff field directors and their assistants stationed at 310 Red Cross field offices and by the 3,000 Red Cross chapters. The field offices are located on most of the larger U.S. military installations and at principal military hospitals, with 127 of the 202 domestic field offices placed overseas. As in other Red Cross programs, trained volunteers offer invaluable assistance, and more than 48,400 Red Cross volunteers served in military hospitals and on military installations in 1977.[14]

Each SAF field office may be staffed with a field director, assistant field director, and caseworker supervisor. The official position descriptions are furnished in appendix B. The casework supervisor is the only paid staff position for which a master's degree in social work or counseling is preferred. The field director and assistant field director are usually college graduates although successful work experience in social-welfare activities may be considered equivalent. Recruiting for these positions is done on college campuses, through the field offices, and through local Red Cross chapters. Clearly this is an opportunity for not only MSWs but BSWs to find work. The field director and assistant field director are program coordinators and administrators. Training in community organization would be especially relevant.

SAF provides a variety of free services to members of the armed forces. In 1978, the two most frequently provided case services were (1) assistance with communication between service personnel and their families and (2) counseling on personal and family problems.[15] There is no charge for these services.

Communications Assistance

In the field of communications and reporting, on of the missions of the American Red Cross is to provide a means of communications on family emergencies to members of the armed forces, including those assigned to ships and remote overseas locations without field-director coverage. Four offices comprise communications and reporting, of which two—the Communications Center and the Armed Forces Reporting Unit—are especially utilized in the mission.[16]

The Washington, D.C., Red Cross Chapter Communications Center, activated in 1962, provides emergency-communications service between the 3,000 Red Cross chapters including those outside the continental limits and the 202 domestic and 127 overseas SAF field offices. In fiscal year 1977, more than 739,000 messages were handled by the center. Of these, over 704,000 involved servicemen overseas.[17] In 1977, an average of over 2,000 messages were sent daily to and from overseas, with the majority concerning urgent emergency situations such as death, serious illness, marital difficulties, disasters, and crises of all varieties.[18]

The Armed Forces Reporting Unit has two foremost missions. They are (1) to act as field directors for all Department of Defense personnel who are at sea and who are covered by Red Cross field offices and (2) to maintain close ties with all military headquarters and to assist families in locating servicemen in times of emergencies. Reports of family emergencies are transmitted through the Red Cross office to the commanding officer of the ship or the isolated military units. Casualty information is cleared through the reporting unit to enable chapters to provide services to seriously ill patients and their families.[19]

Counseling

Helping the servicemember to identify and understand his or her own personal problems is the task of the field director. The director also guides the servicemember in deciding a satisfactory solution to the problem. Helping these people to adjust to separation from family and assisting in arrangement of financial allotment to the family are examples of counseling services that are frequently offered. Information given to the field director is held in strict confidence.[20]

The Red Cross SAF program is also unique in that, unlike social-work officers in the military, field directors are able to protect the confidentiality of their military clients. The Red Cross board of governors has agreed to adhere to the Privacy Act, and consequently, no Red Cross record may be part of a military file. Red Cross files are stored in locked containers, and military personnel may only gain access to a file through a subpoena by military court order.

Problems involving dependents of a servicemember are handled by the family's community Red Cross chapter unless the family resides on the installation, in which the family relies on the field director for counseling.[21]

Separation from home and family increases the likelihood of problems and makes resolutions more difficult. A wife separated from her husband is faced with having to rear children by herself and resolve difficulties that occur in everyday living. Many young military wives need advice on how to manage finances, and they rely on suggestions for copying with everday problems such as seeking jobs and making friends. In 1977, almost 2 million services were rendered by chapters and field directors concerning such problems as moving, marital discord, health, and financial management.[22]

Financial Assistance

In cases of emergency, the Red Cross assists servicemembers and their dependents with financial difficulties. Interest-free loans are available, and repayment is arranged depending on the servicemember's financial ability to pay. A grant rather than a loan is made if repayment would result in further problems to the servicemember. Financial assistance is available for problems such as emergency-leave expenses, emergency personal needs, assistance to dependents, and travel expenses—for example, when a next of kin is summoned to the bedside of a seriously ill patient.

Personal and financial services for armed-forces personnel and their dependents are available from the Red Cross, military-welfare societies, and military family-service agencies. The Red Cross, navy, army, and air force relief societies all have similar policies and procedures for providing financial assistance, and they cooperate mutually in this effort.

When initial pay is late or interrupted, the Red Cross provides financial assistance for needs such as food, rent, and other household necessities. Financial assistance totaling $12,333,913 has been provided to 6 percent of the military personnel served, with 84 percent of the assistance provided in the form of repaid loans.[23]

Controversial Areas of Help

Discharge-Review Application and Representation. A review of a less-than-honorable discharge is the right of any servicemember. The American Red Cross is committed to this and makes available free counsel to those persons who need representation. The only other organization that offers the same service is the Disabled American Veterans.[24]

The Service to Military Families and Veterans Program. This program has recently become involved with the service issues unique to women serving in the armed forces. At the end of June 1977, 117,951 women were on active military duty.[25] The 1979 Defense Appropriations Act restricts federal funding for abortions at military medical facilities and by the Civilian Health and Medical Program of the Uniformed Services (CHAMPUS). As a result, a special Department of Defense task force was established to consider the special problems of military personnel and their eligible dependents who do not meet the newly specified criteria for obtaining an abortion and who are at installations without access to acceptable civilian health-care facilities. The Red Cross is providing financial assistance to the population affected by the Defense Act.[26] In addition, the Red Cross is seeing a shift away from the traditional military family unit in that many of the families are now headed by a single, often female, parent. This produces special service needs—for example, the woman in basic training may require day-care services for her children. The Red Cross is acting increasingly as an advocate for the military woman.

The Army Social-Work Program

Social work was formally introduced into the army in 1942 when social workers inducted into service as enlisted personnel were assigned to the neuropsychiatric team in the Mental Hygiene Service at Fort Monmouth, New Jersey. In 1943, psychiatric social work became a military occupational specialty with the establishment of the position classification of social-work technician. In June 1945, the military social-work program was incorporated as part of the Surgeon General's Office, and in 1946, the first social worker was commissioned as an army officer under the classification of psychiatric social worker.[27]

Solidification of the conventional base of social-work practice in the medical and psychiatric setting occurred during the 1950s. Between 1954 and 1955, the classification of social worker was adapted and the subclassifications of psychiatrist and medical were subsequently dropped. In addition to this, the office of social-service consultant was created. The expansion of social work in the armed services came as a result of the Korean War. Areas of social-work activity included army hospitals, the Office of the Surgeon General, the Medical Field Service School, and disciplinary barracks, to mention a few. The efforts in these locations involved over 150 social-work officers as well as 65 nonmilitary professional social workers. There was also a sizable group of social-work technicians who assisted the professional staff. During the Vietnam War, military social workers served in hospital settings with mobile psychiatric teams and in combat divisions.

In less than twenty years, social work had become a vital part of the army medical system. By 1950, full-time social workers were in the surgeon general's office, and some positions requiring a doctoral degree were fully established in the Department of the Army. By January 1976, thirty-one officers had received their doctorates, and the medical and psychiatric fields were completely staffed by professional social workers.[28]

Current Trends

Of the three service branches, the army has the most extensive social-work program. In January 1979, 278 professionally trained social workers were on active duty, and even more were in army civil-service positions.[29] These figures reflect the continued expansion of army social-work activity since 1963 when social work was raised from a subsection within medicine or psychiatry to the status of a full service reporting directly to the chief of professional services.

Social work in today's army is a specialization within the Medical Service Corps with a consultant in the Office of the Surgeon General. The setting may range from mental-health clinics and hospitals to army community-service centers.[30]

Hospital Social-Work Section

Since 1963, social-work-service departments have been established in all army medical centers and in smaller army hosptials to provide casework services to patients and their families. The service is offered to both inpatients and outpatients. The team concept is applied—that is, the social worker interacts with doctors and other hospital personnel. Services provided in a military hospital are quite similar to those in a civilian hospital.[31]

Mental-Hygiene-Consultation Service

Community mental-health (CMH) services are established on most large army installations to give service that is not unlike that provided in a civilian CMH center. The CMH units operate on the team concept with army psychiatrists, psychologists, social workers, and behavioral-science specialists (paraprofessionals) as members of the team. The CMH units provide consultation to post commanders, research, psychotherapy and counseling (for individuals and groups) for active-duty personnel and their families, and education to assist the military community in promoting good mental-health practices.[32] In command consultation, a mental-health worker (a social worker) may consult with the post commander about the issue of a troubled soldier or regarding the problems of a unit that may adversely affect the mental health of its members. Examples of unit problems are a high number of AWOLs and low morale. Unit problems are usually dealt with by the CMH team.[33]

Army Corrections

Working with an offender in the army has been a traditional role for the army social worker.[34] In 1967, a new rehabilitation program, the U.S. Army Retraining Brigade (USARB) (formerly known as the Correctional Training Facility), was developed with the purpose of resocializing young men convicted of military-type offenses. The focus of this rehabilitation effort is to provide intensive training, close supervision, and correctional treatment, with the final goal being the return of the soldier to duty with improved attitude and motivation.[35]

Rehabilitation of military offenders is undertaken through the USARB, which works with all prisoners with sentences of no longer than six months who have not been discharged. A few participants seek discharges upon arrival or before completion of a program and as a result are placed in separate barracks. A module system using techniques similar to behavior modification, which offers increased privileges upon completion of a module is used for those persons who want to complete the USARB program and thus enables them to return to duty.[36]

Direct support, which includes counseling on both a group and an individual basis, advising commanders, and evaluating clients, is the major point of emphasis in the USARB social-work program. These tasks are carried out through a team of social workers assigned to each group or unit of trainees. In addition to the primary responsibility of direct support to units, the social-work branch also provides formal instruction to both trainees and officers. The social-work teams present to the trainees conferences that offer classes in drugs, alcohol, sex, military social resources, and a predischarge orientation.

The U.S. Disciplinary Barracks (USDB), located at Fort Leavenworth, Kansas, is the only maximum-security institution for army, air force, and Marine Corps prisoners. Social-work officers assigned to the USDB become part of the mental-hygiene staff that consists of social-work officers, psychiatrists, psychologists, and civilian social workers. The director of this staff is a social-work officer. The staff provides consultation and training, prisoner treatment and services, prisoner evaluations, and research. Social workers have had major responsibility in developing and supervising a number of programs for which the director of mental hygiene assumes responsibility (for example, the drug program, AA, Sickle Cell, and Guides for Better Living, among others).[37] "Other roles currently assumed by social workers in corrections are the teaching of inmate motivational courses, drug and alcohol counseling, discharge evaluations and counseling, assisting with difficulties in returning inmates successfully to duty or civilian life, staff-assistance and in-service training, and the development or introduction of new progams."[38]

Army Community Service

The Army Community Service (ACS) program, established in 1965, was the first social-welfare program within the army to provide the social-work officer with an opportunity to practice professional social work in a nonclinical setting. In 1974, sixty-five military and civilian social workers were providing services at the 180 ACS centers and points of contact worldwide.[39] Since that time the ACS has continued to expand and remains a viable program in the military communities it serves. Figure 9-1 depicts the organizational structure of the ACS.

The purpose of each ACS center is to develop an organized system for bringing together all available resources, off and on post, for the treatment of personal and family problems. ACS attempts to satisfy the need for a centrally located, responsive, and professionally based service. Social-work officers serve as professional consultants to the ACS programs and also train and supervise the volunteers who staff most of these programs.[40]

ACS is an installation-level program and is planned and developed by its staff and the commander at each post. As such, commanders and the ACS staff are allowed flexibility and can tailor the program to meet the particular community need. As a result, programs are signficiantly different. This difference is due to the commanders' various wishes, the capabilities of the ACS staffs, and the resources available to provide community services. The ACS social-work consultants feel that the wide range of these programs may be a problem because the volunteer staff may not possess the expertise required to carry out certain types of activities. At the same time it has been noted that social-welfare activities in large centers are administered poorly due to lack of expertise on the part of the director who is a line officer.[41] This is a growing concern because of the complexity of the problems of the clients and because a large number of persons needing help require a professional service. Thus, the former volunteer modality provides inadequate service, and line officers are not trained in administering human services. Here again a trained social worker could provide the necessary staff functions.

On installations that have an ACS program, an ACS Human Resource Council is established to enhance the coordination of the ACS's varied services and activities. The council consists of key command personnel such as the judge advocate, an army health nurse, and the post surgeon.[42]

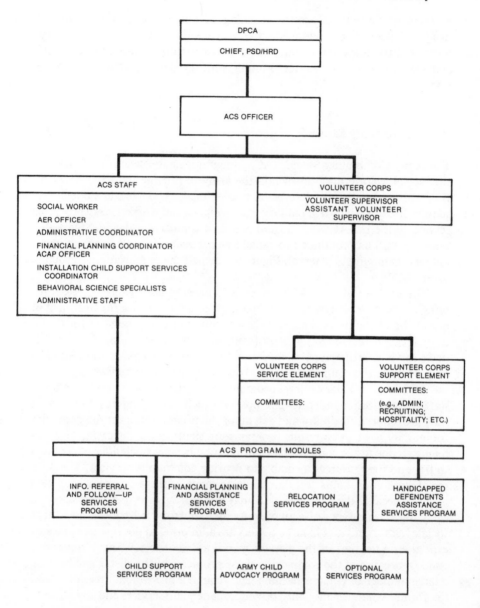

Source: Army Regulation no., 608-1, "Personal Affairs: Army Community Service Program," Headquarters, Department of the Army, Washington, D.C., 1 October 1978.

Figure 9-1. ACS Program Functional Organization Chart

As shown in figure 9-1, each ACS provides essential services that are grouped into the following program modules: (1) information, referral, and follow-up services; (2) financial planning and assistance; (3) relocation services; (4) handicapped-dependents'-assistance services; (5) army-child advocacy; (6) child-support services; and (7) family counseling. In addition, some optional services may be provided to supplement the essential programs.[43] Depending on the needs of a particular locale, the ACS centers may provide a vast array of services. A few of these are housing, community orientation program, legal assistance, and child care. In addition to the information and assistance provided, professional counseling is also available when a social worker is assigned to the facility.

A good example of an ACS program is the one at Fort Myer, Virginia. In addition to casework, the Fort Myer ACS family-counseling service has presented a weekly sex-education seminar and a marriage-enrichment seminar in conjunction with the post chaplain. It also offers a field placement for social-work graduate students attending the Catholic University School of Social Service in Washington, D.C.

ACS programs are directed by a social-work officer located in Washington, D.C. This position provides ongoing opportunities for meeting with divisions in the Department of the Army that are responsible for personnel policy. It also allows for contact with other health and welfare personnel as well as for representation on the interdepartmental Committee on Children and Youth at HHS.[44]

The Academy of Health Sciences

The Academy of Health Sciences at Fort Sam Houston, Texas, is the center for most of the army's health-care-training activities. Social workers are utilized as directors of courses designed to prepare enlisted personnel to functions as social-work specialists. Social-work personnel from the academy's behavioral-science division provide instruction in health-care administration, behavioral science, social work, and social policy. Social work has developed in several new areas and is providing training in medical family-practice residencies and at the Advanced Social Work Program in Family Studies at Walter Reed Medical Center. Some social-work personnel also are field instructors for bachelor- and master-degree-level social workers.[45]

Human Resources Development Division

The Human Resources Development Division (HRD) was added to Personnel and Administration. Combat Developments Actvity (PACDA) in 1973 and represented a new dimension of army personnel management. The goal of the HRD is "to develop a reservoir of research data and experience dealing with leadership and personnel management and to translate that research experience into practical language and positive programs for implementation within the army."[46] In order to accomplish this goal, the HRD center collects, reviews, evaluates, maintains, and disseminates social-science research and information, which is an important and useful tool in the continued development of training and education programs and personnel management.

In the mid-1970s the army conducted research in areas such as the military family, health-care delivery, substance abuse, and military corrections. Social-work officers contributed to the research effort through their assignments as full-time researchers at installations such as the Walter Reed Army Institute of Research and the Department of Defense. In most cases, social workers assigned to these positions are required to be senior-level personnel with a doctoral degree. Senior social-work officers are also assigned to offices in the Department of the Army Office of the Deputy Chief of Staff for Personnel, in the Office of the Assistant of Defense, and in most army headquarters worldwide. As researchers and consultants, these social-work officers give professional direction to the army social-work program.

CHAMPUS

The Health Resources Information (HRI) center and the Handicapped Review section of the Office for CHAMPUS are the two locations in which civilian social workers are assigned. When a request is received, HRI provides information concerning special care and treatment facilities. These requests come from ACS centers and from both government and civilian health and welfare organizations.

The Handicapped Review section's task is to process applications for the provision of services to physically and mentally handicapped persons as specified under the Civilian Medical Care Program. It is also responsible for seeing that appropriate services are maintained on a continual basis for the handicapped and, when needed, can recommend administrative and legislative action to assure a continuance and an improvement of services to meet the needs of the handicapped persons.[47]

Human Resources Directorate

One of the organizations in the army to utilize social workers most recently is the Human Resources Directorate. In the army, this function usually is considered an amalgamation of services—for example, delivery personnel in certain problem areas such as the alcohol- and drug-abuse, the race-relations/equal-opportunity specialists, the ACS group with its focus on the community social-support network, and the organizational-effectiveness staff. The major tasks of the Human Resources Directorate manager are the integration of these functions and the establishment of effective meetings with the staffs of each unit. These tasks are related primarily to equal-opportunity complaints, affirmative actions, human-relations-awareness training, and organizational effectiveness. The director, a lieutenant colonel, is a DSW, and social workers are utilized throughout the organizational managerial structure.

The Navy Social-Work Program

When compared historically with the other service branches, the U.S. Navy has traditionally placed little emphasis on the role of the social-work professional as a service provider within the military setting. Throughout World War II, the army and air force utilized the services of military psychiatric social workers; the navy, in contrast, employed only one military social worker, an officer who was assigned to the Psychiatric Department of the Medical Corps in the U.S. Naval Hospital at San Diego.[48] Spanning the World War II years until today, the U.S. Navy has primarily relied on navy physicians, chaplains, and the Red Cross to meet the social-welfare needs of its members. This is changing, however.

The navy's current social-work program is staffed and implemented by twenty-nine civilian social workers. Twenty-two are stationed with navy psychiatrists, and seven are placed at the Bethesda Naval Hospital. More appointments have been approved, which will result in the recruitment of social-service workers into the Medical Service Corps.[49] Services offered under the social-work program in the navy consist of medical social work, psychiatric social work at the navy regional medical centers, drug and alcohol rehabilitation, and support services to naval commanders and personnel.[50]

In 1973, Hunter and Plog conducted a study of a select group of navy prisoner-of-war/missing-in-action (POW/MIA) families. The results of the study indicated that an aggressive program of helping these families cope with their situation was essential, and they proposed the development of a more-adaptable, harmonious, and professionally based social-work program for these families.[51] The foundation for an organized social service department within the navy was thus established.

The Air Force Social-Work Program

Throughout World War II, the air force, then a branch of the U.S. Army, utilized the casework services of military and civilian psychiatric social workers. In 1943, it pioneered in its operation of a mental-hygiene unit at Drew Field; the unit, staffed with psychiatrists, psychologists, and social workers, provided mental-health services to the wartime personnel of the air force.[52] Four years later the air force was established as a separate service, and since that time, it has developed its own social-work program.

In 1979, there were 185 professionally trained military social workers and 25 civil-service social workers assigned to the air force social-work programs. All have secured the MSW degree and some have their doctorates. This personnel now functions in various settings including mental-hygiene clinics, hospital mental-health services, family-practice residency-training courses, alcohol- and drug-treatment programs, child-advocacy projects, the centralized correctional facility, and various staff positions.

Project CHAP

Children Have a Potential (CHAP) was established in November 1961 as an air force-wide program for handicapped children. Project CHAP lends information, guidance and financial assistance to air force families who have physically, mentally, or emotionally handicapped children. The program operates as a committee of family services and is implemented by CHAP officers, most of whom are military or civilian social workers with an MSW. The CHAP officer provides assistance to the airman and his family in the form of counseling, referral, financial aid, medical and educational services, or special consideration for assignments.[53]

Air Force Child Advocacy Program

The National Center on Child Abuse and Neglect, in its 1976 report, estimated that two thousand children a year die from parental abuse and that, if accurate reporting procedures existed, one million cases of child abuse or neglect would be reported annually.[54] In July 1973, a triservice meeting was held in Washington, D.C., with representatives of the Office of the Assistant Secretary of Defense for Health and Environment and Dr. C. Henry Kempe, University of Colorado Medical Center, a leading authority on the subject of child maltreatment and the battered-child syndrome. In January 1975, a Tri-Service Child Advocacy Working Group was formed at the direction of the three surgeons general. This working group continues to serve as a vehicle for interservice communication regarding child-advocacy programs within the Department of Defense.[55] AFR 160-38, Air Force Child Advocacy Program (AFCAP), 1975, was the first air force regulation to establish a servicewide child-abuse-and-neglect program within the

Department of Defense. This regulation gave primary attention to the social problem of child abuse and neglect within the military population eligible for care at air force medical facilities.[56]

AFCAP's mission is to "identify, prevent, and treat child abuse and to provide other necessary medical and nonmedical services for the child abuser or neglector as well as the abused or neglected child."[57] To meet this goal, a Child Advocacy Committee is established at each USAF medical facility, and education programs are designed by the committee to increase the military community's awareness of the problem of child abuse and neglect.[58] The committee is chaired by a physician who is either the hospital commander or chief of hospital services. The child-advocacy officer, the key figure in the base program, is usually a clinical social worker and also serves as a representative to the Child Advocacy Committee. The child-advocacy officers also serve as the liaison between the base, the Child Welfare agency, and the juvenile or family court. A child-advocacy-program coordinator serves at each major command, while senior clinical social workers serve as program consultants to all medical centers and regional hospitals. In 1977, at the School of Health Sciences, Sheppard Air Force Base, Texas, the third annual CHAP and child-advocacy management course was offered with training child-advocacy officers. During the course, it was planned that by the end of fiscal year 1978, all air force medical facilities that treat children would have positions for clinical social workers.[59]

Social Action Program

Since September 1971, the air force has implemented its social-action program. Each air force base worldwide is now authorized (1) a social-actions officer, (2) a noncommissioned officer, and (3) a race-relations officer. Many installations have larger staffs, and no professional training is required for these positions. The social-actions officer is to serve as a consultant to base commanders on a variety of issues such as race relations, drug abuse, alcoholism rehabilitation, and other social issues. The social-actions officer should be knowledgeable in the areas of community organization, social and behavioral structures, interpersonal relations, and the effects of situational variables on emotional stability.[60] It would seem that in order to have these qualifications, the social-actions officer would need at least a master's degree in social work or psychology. The program is mentioned in this chapter because civilian social workers are beginning to be hired in these social-action offices. These programs are a natural place for professional social work. The training provided social workers that encompasses drug- and alcohol-abuse cases, as well as equal-opportunity and race-relation matters, gives them the unique qualifications to administer and staff these programs.

Family-Practice Residency-Training Programs

The air force now has family-practice residency-training programs in four locations. Here, physicians doing their residency training in family medicine are assisted by social workers assigned to the teaching staff.

Hospital Mental-Health Services

The Joint Committee Accrediting of Hospitals (JCAH) social-service standards now require that social services be provided in all hospitals. The air force is currently assigning more social-work officers to work in air force hospitals. Many air force physicians are expressing their desires to have social workers become part of the medical professional team. Currently, medical social workers are stationed at three air force bases: Keesler, Shepphard, and Andrews. Social workers also staff mental-hygiene departments at various hospitals such as Lekenheath, England. Shepphard Air Force Base in Texas, since 1966, has provided a mental-health service that includes diagnostic psychotherapy and consultation to air force members from a wide geographical area.

Administration Posts

It is encouraging to note that social-work professionals hold important consultant-administrative positions in the air force hierarchy. Social-work officers are presently assigned to the following positions: social-work-program manager, CHAP, child-advocacy program, and alcohol- and drug-treatment program; chief social worker, Andrews Air Force Base; assistant chief, Biomedical Sciences Corps; social-action officer, Department of Defense; and the medical inspector general.

Alcoholism- and Drug-Rehabilitation Programs

Historically, the use of beverage alcohol for ceremonial or recreational purposes has been an integral element in the military environment. Soldier Sam Houston, in the major battles of the Mexican campaign, was reportedly under the influence of "demon rum." Until 1913, standard practice was for every departing naval ship to take on board more rum than water, a practice that contributed to the infamous stereotype of the drunken sailor. In World War II, air force pilots were given a two-ounce shot after combat missions to calm their nerves. In current times, the traditional wetting-down parties to celebrate a promotion and happy hours at military clubs are familiar practices to all military men and women.[61]

The use and abuse of other drugs by servicemembers is a more-recent trend in military history. It was the heroin epidemic in the Vietnam War years that alerted the armed forces to the more-widespread use of other hard drugs among military personnel and that established the need for intervention and rehabilitative efforts.

The most abused drug within the services, however, is still alcohol. In 1972, the army conducted an alcohol-research study to define the extent of problem drinking within the army. Heavy, or binge, drinkers were defined as those drinkers who consume five or more drinks a day, four or more days in a row, or who are drunk for more than one day at a time. Problem drinkers were those members having serious social consequences in their lives as a result of drinking—for example, driving while intoxicated, family and marital discord, promotions denied, and so on. Based on these definitions, the findings were that 20 percent of the officers responding to the survey were heavy drinkers and that 17 percent were problem drinkers. Among enlisted personnel, 32 percent were heavy drinkers, and 35 percent were problem drinkers.[62] The navy reported similar findings in its 1974 study, with 19 percent of the officers and 37 percent of the enlisted men classified as heavy drinkers.[63]

The enactment of three public laws between 1970 and 1974 gave impetus to the development of alcohol-abuse-control and alcoholism-treatment programs in the military services. "Specifically, Title V of PL 92-129 directed the secretary of defense to develop and maintain programs to identify, treat, and rehabilitate members of the armed forces who are drug- or alcohol-dependent persons."[64] As a result of this legislation, the army, air force, and navy developed alcohol- and drug-abuse-prevention and -rehabilitation programs to address the substance-abuse problems of their military and civilian personnel. Figure 9-2 pictures the Department of Defense organizational structure of program responsibility.

At the present time, social workers are not frequently found to be staffing the many programs for alcohol and drug education, rehabilitation, prevention, and training. Instead, they are usually found in treatment facilities under army and air force auspices. The alcohol/drug programs are growing at a rapid rate in the service and provide a wide berth of opportunity for social workers. Because of their rapid development and the innovative treatment they are providing (especially in the navy), the following sections examine the possibilities that exist for social workers in various programs.

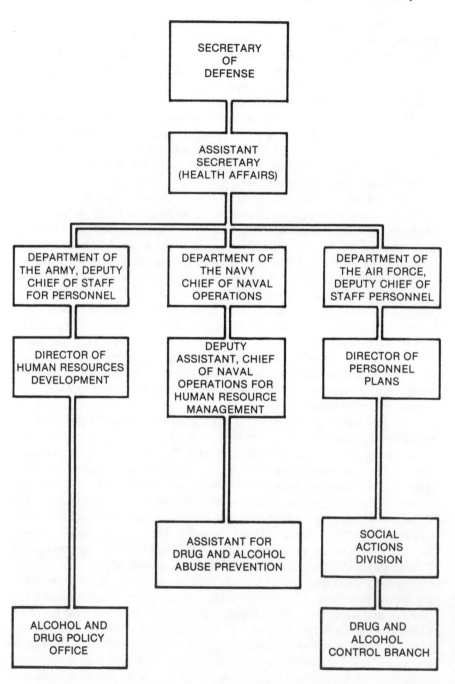

Figure 9-2. Organization Chart Showing Program Responsibility

The Army Alcohol and Drug Abuse
Prevention and Control Program (ADAPCP)

The army's drug and alcohol programs are in operation at installations throughout the world. Each program is coordinated by an alcohol- and drug-control officer who usually chairs the installation's alcohol- and drug-depency-intervention council, which coordinates the activities of the communitywide program. There is also a team of educational, clinical, and counseling personnel that staffs the program and receives support from the local medical-treatment facility.[65] These people are not social workers, but clearly the job description characterizes social-work functions.

The treatment/rehabilitation program consists of an active phase of no more than sixty days of outpatient treatment and a follow-up phase not to exceed three-hundred days. Residential treatment is provided for two to three weeks for those who require a structured alcohol/drug-free environment in a halfway house (live-in, work-in). These individuals remain with their units and receive counseling during regularly scheduled appointments at the local ADAPCP counseling center.

Soldiers who are functioning effectively on full duty at the end of the active phase are entered into the follow-up phase. They are followed up for three-hundred days while living and working with their units. During this time they receive counseling as determined appropriate by the ADAPCP staff.

In Europe, the following facilities are available: Community Drug and Alcohol Assistance Center (CDAAC), drug- and alcohol-treatment centers, and regional alcohol-treatment centers. The CDAAC provides counseling to drug and alcohol abusers and has a limited capacity to provide residential care. The drug and alcohol treatment centers are extended-care facilities that offer many therapeutic services. The individual's stay is limited to twenty-eight days, and follow-up care is provided by the CDAAC staff. The regional alcohol treatment centers provide services to older, career-oriented servicemembers, civilian employees, and their dependents. The six-week treatment plan involves medical treatment and counseling provided by trained professionals and recovering alcoholics.

Education and training are an important aspect of the army's program. Educational seminars are conducted for administrative and management personnel. The Academy of Health Sciences offers a two-week course for counselors, workshops for prevention, and teen-involvement programs for students.

As of 1978, the army was operating fourteen residential facilities and 170 nonresidential facilities. Fifty-five hospitals were available to support these activities. The only regional centers were in Europe. During fiscal year 1977, 12,460 individuals were entered into the active phase of treatment and rehabilitation. Of these, 9,857 were rehabilitated and returned to active duty. A full-time ADAPCP staff of 837 military personnel and 877 civilian personnel was utilized throughout the world to implement the army's complete program of identification, treatment and rehabilitation, education, training, and program management for both drugs and alcohol.[66]

The Navy Alcoholism Prevention Program (NAPP)

The navy has operated an extensive worldwide alcoholism program since 1971 and, as of 1977, has provided treatment and rehabilitation for over 67,000 active military personnel including navy (the majority), Marine Corps, and Coast Guard personnel. Of the 17,000 treated in calendar year 1977, approximately 700 were commissioned officers; 14,700 were enlisted; and 1,500 were in the top three ranks of the noncommissioned officers.[67]

The current NAPP programs are modeled after the original AA-type program started in 1965 at the Long Beach, California, Naval Station. The Long Beach program became the navy's first alcohol rehabilitation center (ARC) in 1971 and, later, the first alcohol rehabilitation service (ARS) when it was relocated into the new Long Beach Naval Hospital. As of October 1978, the navy had installed four ARCs, twenty-four naval-hospital-based ARSs, and fifty-four smaller local programs in facilities called counseling and assistance centers (CAAC).

The four ARCs are located at Norfolk, Virginia; Jacksonville, Florida; San Diego, California; and Pearl Harbor, Hawaii. Each is a self-contained inpatient facility with an eighty-bed capacity. The ARC program offers paraprofessional counseling, professional medical and spiritual services, and educational and administrative services to the patients. Treatment is of six weeks' duration and consists of a daily Antabuse medication regimen, group counseling, alcohol-awareness education, lectures and films, physical-training and work routines, and a thorough indoctrination into AA by enforced attendance at local and inhouse AA meetings a minimum of five nights a week. The treatment services provided at the smaller ARSs (seven of which are overseas), which are housed in or attached to naval hospitals, are similar to those in the ARCs.[68] In January 1976, the ARS staff at the Long Beach Naval Hospital included a psychiatrist, a general practitioner, three part-time psychologists, one civilian social worker, one nurse, and a staff of navy, Marine Corps, and Coast Guard counselors.[69]

The navy currently operates fifty-four CAACs designed to treat individuals at or near their place of duty. Each CAAC has the capacity to treat up to twenty individuals at a time, and nine modified CAACs were opened aboard aircraft carriers in 1977. The CAAC programs vary according to the needs of their communities and the operating environment of the locale that is served. For those CAAC alcoholism-rehabilitation programs with live-in capabilities (twenty-five CAACs have five to twenty beds), the program can include up to four weeks of in-residence therapy, followed by approximately ten weeks of follow-up treatment and counseling. For those CAACs without live-in capability, outpatient programs from six to twelve weeks' duration are conducted. All CAACs' alcohol programs stress participation in AA. The staff is comprised of four paraprofessional enlisted counselors who have been cross-trained in drug dependencies and alcoholism, with one or often two of the counselors' being recovering alcoholics trained as alcoholism-treatment specialists in the ten-week course conducted at the ARC in San Diego. The cross-trained drug counselors are trained at the Navy Drug Rehabilitation Center (NDRC) at Miramar, California. There are no professional medical or clergy personnel assigned to the CAACs.[70]

The Alcohol Training Unit (ATU) located at the Long Beach Naval Hospital ARS is the focal point of training and education for the NAPP. The navy has long recognized the importance of educating navy doctors in alcoholism and has given this training top priority. To date, over five hundred doctors have completed the two-week orientation course taught by Captain Joseph Pursch, MC, USN. In addition, several senior line officers, as well as over 350 other medical administrators, chaplains, and other health-care deliverers, have completed the Long Beach training. In 1978, similar courses were established at ARS's Great Lakes, Illinois, and Portsmouth, Virginia, locations, including a five-day course for senior line commanding officers and line admirals. The ATU also offers a ten-week, nondegree professional course to train paraprofessionals to be full-time alcoholism counselors at treatment centers.[71]

The Navy Alcohol Safety Action Program (NASAP) is modeled after the Alcohol Safety Action Project (ASAP) developed by the Department of Transportation, which was designed as a countermeasure to drunk driving. The navy's program addresses not only driving while intoxicated (DWI) offenses but also is expanded to include all alcohol-related offenses of civil law and navy regulations. Offenders are screened by counselors and receive thirty-six hours of remedial education after duty hours or are referred into a treatment program. As of March 1978, NASAP had educated 8,414 (80 percent) offenders and referred 2,040 (20 percent) into treatment for alcoholism.[72]

The navy recognizes that alcoholism creates a family dysfunction and has been providing treatment to families since 1972. All ARCs and most ARSs provide day counseling to family members and conduct couples' groups in the evenings. "Planning is currently under way to request formal budget support for family alcoholism programs in the form of providing social workers to the major treatment centers."[73]

The well-known success of the navy's alcoholism-rehabilitation program continues to be reinforced through the return of the navy member to active duty. Rehabilitation is considered successful if the member completes his or her enlistment or is discharged under honorable conditions. The navy's effectiveness rate two years following treatment is 84 percent for patients twenty-six years and older and 50 percent for the twenty-five-and-under age group.[74] The ARS at the Long Beach Naval Hospital has recently been the recipient of favorable publicity with the admissions of the former first lady, Betty Ford, and Billy Carter, brother of the former president.

The Air Force Alcohol Abuse Control Program

Since 1974, the Air Force Alcohol Abuse Control Program has been an integral part of the social-actions program, which is mandated to assist the installation commander in conducting programs for drug- and alcohol-abuse control.[75]

The air force operates ten alcohol-treatment centers with a total bed capacity of 108. All of the centers utilize individual and group psychotherapy, occupational and recreational therapy, and education to address the physical aspects of alcoholism. Eight of the centers operate twenty-eight-day treatment programs focusing on milieu therapy and attendance at AA meetings. One center employs Antabuse in its treatment program, and two offer a fourteen-day program of electro-stimulation-aversion (ESA) treatment, relaxation therapy, and a follow-up system whereby patients return to the center for reinforcement approximately sixty days following the completion of their two-week treatment. In 1977, six of the alcohol-treatment centers employed clinical social workers as program directors—three were psychologists and one was a psychiatrist.[76]

The local rehabilitation program begins with the identification of abusers via commander/supervisor referral, medical referral, or self-identification. If required, the member is detoxified in the base medical facility. Eighty-five percent of the treatment and rehabilitation in the air force is conducted locally. A rehabilitation regimen is designed for each individual by a rehabilitation committee consisting of the unit commander, immediate supervisor, an alcohol-abuse specialist, and a medical officer. This committee monitors the member's progress and determines final disposition in each case. Rehabilitation of an alcoholic at the local level is recommended. However, in the more-serious cases, the individual is referred to an alcohol-treatment center.

Upon completion of local or central rehabilitation, each member enters a period of follow-up support for up to one year. He or she usually returns to the base to be monitored and supported by the social-actions program.

The air force's drug- and alcohol-abuse-control specialists are trained in a nine-week course given at Lackland Air Force Base in Texas. In addition to this course, which is conducted solely by the air force, many advanced training programs are provided through contracts with civilian institutions. The well-known Johnson Institute provides training and practicum experience to drug/alcohol specialists, medical personnel, and chaplains. The air force also conducts a three-week social-actions staff officers' course for chiefs of social-actions programs.

Prevention and early-detection programs are an important part of the alcohol-abuse program. The air force provides alcohol-abuse education to any new entrants, at all professional military-education schools, to all persons experiencing alcohol-related problems, and to personnel upon reassignment to a new location. Early-intervention programs include the Alcohol Awareness Seminar, the Concerned Drinker Program, and a telephone-counseling/crisis-intervention program available at each base. During fiscal year 1977, 6,831 military personnel were identified as alcohol abusers.[77]

Issues

In addition to the value differences between the profession of social work and the military institution per se, which were pointed out in the beginning of this chapter, a social worker should consider several points if contemplating working in uniform or for the uniform services. A critical issue is that of confidentiality. Under military law, the only professional person in uniform to carry confidentiality is the chaplain. The physician, attorney, or other professionals do not. Although this sounds harsh, military professionals usually practice with the same integrity and manner as those in the civilian world. What is important, however, is that in reality, if there ever was a critical issue, confidentiality is not protected and under military law the professional would have to turn over names and records. What also is important about this question is that regardless of how discrete a professional in uniform may be, the client population knows about this ruling and thus the effectiveness of the relationship is affected. As a result, the client will often be found not going to the professional in uniform for assistance. Social workers contemplating working for the military would have to resolve this issue for themselves.

Another major issue in the military is the use of the nonprofessional to provide professional services. As we have seen, this is frequent in the many programs described. The responsibility for this falls on both the military and the helping professions. Because the social-work profession holds such ambivalence toward the military, little information exists in the professional literature, and little interest is shown by social workers to inform the military or to seek it out as a client. Thus the military, already an isolated community, uses its own resources and is often unaware of the latest developments. It sometimes produces programs lacking in professional expertise because it does not have the social-service knowledge available to do it. The challenge to both the social-work community and the military is to solve this dilemma.

Summary

Social workers have been employed in the military for a number of years. Their numbers have not been as extensive as they should have been because the number of problems in this commiunity is vast. Servicemembers' isolation and frequent mobility make them particularly vulnerable to social and emotional ills. The autocratic structure of the work situation and the expectations made upon families add additional stresses. More social workers, as well as people sensitive to the needs of this population, are needed.

**Part IV
Education for the Industrial
Social Worker**

10 Joint Project on Industrial Social Work

The delivery of human services at the work site is moving ahead in many directions. Whether it is toward counseling, CSR, or special populations, clearly a work force is developing in this new arena. One of the critical elements for success is an adequate and well-trained staff. Other professions also see the direction toward which this service delivery is headed. Psychology, industrial relations, educational counseling, and psychiatry, for example, are a few taking strong interest in this field of practice. Social work should be the leader in this field and accept the educational responsibility for training professionals for the expanding service.

Unfortunately, although sporadic efforts have been made by individual schools of social work, still no major thrust in this direction nor an apparent comprehension of the importance of this emerging field is evident. The schools are actually lagging behind the practice. This chapter briefly highlights what schools of social work have done thus far. It specifically discusses the activity of the Joint Project on Industrial Social Work sponsored by the Council on Social Work Education and the National Association of Social Workers (CSWE/NASW). Chapter 11 presents cases taken from practice that should, hopefully, provide learning situations for students in schools of social work.

For a field of knowledge and service to develop, it is essential that the educational and curriculum component keep abreast with practice. Unless the schools develop a theoretical base through a concerted effort, the movement toward this new field of practice may well be lost to other professionals who are less well adapted to giving the full spectrum of services social workers can offer.

CSWE/NASW Project

In 1975-1976, it became increasingly clear to the author that there were different trends in the field of industrial human-service delivery. One was involved with mental health and the more-traditional social-work approach. The other was the development of the occupational-alcoholism programs, which were rarely being developed by social workers. She pointed out to the executive director of the CSWE that there was a need to bring these groups together and to begin to conceptualize this field of practice.

On 7 May 1976, a meeting was held of approximately thirty practitioners, educators, and representatives of government, labor, and industry to discuss the topic of social work in industry. After that meeting events moved rapidly. The group was most vocal in expressing its concern that the council develop an appropriate leadership role.

The NASW had representatives there, and they also expressed an interest in the subject. Within months a joint project was formed, called CSWE/NASW Project on Social Work in Industrial Settings. The author was privileged to serve as its chairwoman for the life of the project so she can report the findings from direct involvement. Its original objectives were

To identify the particular skills and knowledge needed for responsible specialized practice in industrial settings—specific course work and field placements;

To assess the needs of the industrial community for social-work services, including identification of areas of employment and recognition by the business community of the potential role for the social worker;

To identify patterns of employment of social workers in industrial settings in order to understand their roles and tasks;

To identify knowledge skills and values relative to the world of work that should be part of the core and practice curriculum necessary for all social-work students;

To expand the recognition among social-work educators and professionals of the educational and practice potential in this field.[1]

Findings of the Project

Schools of social work have moved slowly and cautiously into the field. A survey conducted in 1977 indicated that only four graduate schools of social work had an organizationally sanctioned curriculum in industrial social work, which included both regularly available curriculum offerings and a network of industrial social-work field placements linked together as a recognized specialty for education. They were the programs at the Boston College, Columbia, Hunter, and Utah schools of social work. An additional twenty-two schools had at least one field placement in an industrial setting. The data revealed that the placements were fairly evenly distributed between direct service (case- and group work) and program development, community liaison and administration.

In order to document the current state of educational development in the field, several information resources were utilized: first the survey mentioned previously; second, a national conference—Social Work Practice in Labor and Industrial Settings; and third, interviews with faculty and students at those schools with an industrial social-work program. Each contributed to the composite picture presented. Several aspects of program development seem to be universally applicable:

1. A minimum of 2-3 years is needed to institutionalize a program within a school of social work.
2. A designated faculty member must allocate a substantial amount of time to develop an industrial social-work program, and such allocation must be strongly supported by the administrative leadership of the school.
3. The development of field placements with appropriate learning opportunities for students usually requires careful negotiation of a contract. Typically, the labor or industrial site has had no prior experience with social work, and the setting is nontraditional from a social-work perspective.
4. Students in such settings will require special supportive assistance through seminars and/or individual consultation. Role models and service requirements differ here from the more-traditional public and private agency settings.
5. Schools often must develop the capacity to provide consultant services to the field-work sites.
6. Student assignments in the industrial area generally call for a mixture of practice experience combining community and program development with direct service. When seeking employment the practitioners will need to have experience that encompasses both.
7. Students must function independently with limited supervision in complicated settings which do not offer the protection of an agency setting.
8. In most instances, an educational institution has played a leading role in expanding employment opportunities for social work practitioners—i.e., the school has developed the practice as well as the educational opportunities for a given community.
9. The faculty member responsible for a program has a dual responsibility for developing an awareness among faculty at a school of social work of the practice opportunities in industrial social work while at the same time promoting the field to the business and trade-union communities.[2]

Other Educational Issues

As shown in chapter 5, one of the fastest growing areas in the industrial setting is the EAPs. Here is a natural role for social workers who have the appropriate knowledge of alcohol and drug addiction. If schools of social work continue to teach that alcoholism is a symptom of an underlying deeper ill in the context of traditional Freudian psychotherapy, they will not be training social workers who will be accepted for EAP positions. There is enough sophistication in the EAP field to know the difference in social-work training. Training for treating alcoholism according to current theories is essential. Alcoholism treatment is most successful today when the alcoholic is confronted with his or her drinking. The continued manipulation by the alcoholic in support of drinking as well as his or her denial must be brought out in the open. Thus, abstinence becomes the model of treatment.

Then, if necessary, therapy in working with other problems is introduced. This is only done, however, after a successful period of abstinence has been achieved. Social work has not taught this approach to alcoholism even though the American Medical Association, the World Health Organization, as well as the NIAAA, advocate this approach. A few schools are beginning to alter curriculum, but it is still not unusual to find an alcoholism course in a school teaching this approach, while a psychotherapy course in the same school may be still using the older, mental-health approach.

Most of the other professions are placing Ph.D. psychology candidates and psychiatric residents in these placements so it behooves social workers to recognize the level of knowledge and practice skill required for this specialty. The recommendation made by the joint project that training for this specialty needs to be at the master's level was advocated because the experience of the committee members showed this to be essential. The practitioner and educator felt very strongly about this, and it is unwise in the author's opinion to consider undergraduate specialties in the industrial area.

A need for continuing education also exists in the industrial area. There are mature social workers who are interested in changing fields. Graduate schools, NASW, or some other vehicle should provide this opportunity for appropriate training. There is no doubt that today a regular MSW-degree training does not provide the breadth and specialization of knowledge needed to work in industry. However, for social workers with MSWs and experience, a group of appropriate courses could satisfy the requirements.

The more-difficult problem will be training faculty to teach the material. Few, if any, faculty members have had the industrial experience. For them to teach and to supervise these settings will pose major problems for the field. From the author's perspective of having directed the training program at Boston College, she would consider the lack of experienced, knowledgeable senior faculty to develop this specialty as *the* most urgent problem social-work educators must address. One solution would be to encourage faculty to take a year's leave of absence to work in a program in industry. The author's present experience is just this. On a Intergovernmental Personnel Act appointment to direct the model Employee Counseling

Program for the federal government, she obtains firsthand experience for return to the classroom.

Summary

Unless social-work educators move in the direction of developing curriculum and field placements for the industrial area, both employers and employees will lose the benefits of a profession that can serve their multifaceted needs.

Lou Ann Jorgensen, in her recent doctoral dissertation, sums it up succinctly:

> From this study it appears that many schools of social work do not see as their role the development of programs which will train practitioners to work in the area of business and industry. Yet, there appears to be a vast potential for assisting a very large segment of our population which is not now being [served].[3]

11 Case Studies

The case studies presented in this chapter represent six diverse examples of social-work practice in industry. The authors are all MSWs and were the caseworkers staffing the case. Three of the cases involve individual clients, and the other three describe groups in the industrial setting. They clearly bring out the uniqueness of the work setting for social-work practice. All cases were written by the social worker. Further discussion and evaluation by students should be encouraged. The importance of the role of the supervisor in the referral process is seen. The author hopes that these cases could be utilized by casework instructors because it is critical that students understand the role of the industrial social worker as well as the unique environment the work site provides. Social workers will also be able to learn the importance of the work supervisor to their clients and the supportive environment that work can provide.

The cases bring to life what industrial social work is all about. The author is grateful to the authors/social workers for their time and efforts. The serious nature of the cases clearly shows that industrial social work is in the mainstream of social-work practice.

A Traditional Supervisory Government Referral
Connie Donovan

This case concerns a 38-year-old white man who is employed by the U.S. government. Mr. M has been in his present position for eleven years. He has the BS degree and a rating of GS-11 ($23,000 per year). He is single (never married), the middle child of eight siblings. He was the class valedictorian in high school. His mother is deceased (cancer). His father, whom he describes as an alcoholic, is a retired newspaper printer. He has had no military service.

The agency in which Mr. M works is located in a large city in the eastern United States. The agency employs approximately 900 persons. The work force consists of military personnel, clerical/secretarial support staff, and labor-management and technical/professional staff (Mr. M's position). Most of the employees including Mr. M work in cubicles at their desks that are sectioned off by partitions. Most of the civilian personnel fill positions in technical/professional and clerical areas of service, and career opportunities for most of them are essentially limited.

The client was referred to the EAP by his supervisor, who has worked with the client as a coworker and supervisor for over eleven years. He considers himself an acquaintance of Mr. M and apparently has a sincere personal concern for him as a friend and employee. He is eager to assist Mr. M but appears to be uncomfortable in his role as supervisor of a troubled employee. Mr. M's prolonged bizarre behavior is threatening and intimidating to him.

The supervisor presented a number of reasons for the referral of Mr. M to the EAP: documented high absenteeism, problems in getting along with coworkers, inability to concentrate, restlessness on the job resulting in a frequent need to talk to other employees, frequently found sitting and staring at desk or into space for long periods of time, and threats of homicide toward other employees. In addition to the referral by the supervisor to the EPA, Mr. M was also confronted with his poor performance by a memo written by the supervisor. The supervisor was assisted in drafting such a memo by the EAP staff when he came to them for advice on handling this situation in the most appropriate fashion. The following excerpts highlight the flavor of the memo:

> The purpose of this memorandum is to bring to your attention various aspects of your behavior and job performance that are of concern to me as your supervisor.
>
> You have informed me that you are under regular care at a local community hospital. Despite this you experience fluctuating mood changes and seemingly depressive periods that affect your work and the morale of other employees. The last depressive period reached its peak when you were required to rest for over two hours in a private conference room. Shortly thereafter, you were out for eight days straight on a sick leave. Your leave balance consists of four hours sick leave and forty-three hours of annual leave, hardly appropriate for an eleven-year career employee.
>
> Your apparent depressive periods affect your work in areas of your ability to concentrate and uneasiness and restlessness in your demeanor. Frequently you get up and talk to other employees and complain of sleeplessness, meditations toward killing others, strange visions and lights that trouble you, and feelings of worthlessness. These incidents usually result in crying episodes.
>
> You complain that you are dissatisfied with your treatment at the hospital. You threaten to discontinue your medication. Associated with these periods are incidents of aggressive behavior at work and antagonism toward other employees.
>
> As a result of this, your work capabilities are not fully realized, and work projects that are normally assigned to you are assigned to others.
>
> In searching for a positive approach to this situation, I discovered the EAP. My initial contact with them has been helpful and supportive. It is a confidential service and of no cost to you. I suggest you avail yourself of this

service. I will escort you to the first visit. The social worker will evaluate your personal problems and refer you to an appropriate treatment resource. This should lead to a realistic plan to eliminate the problem observed at work.

I will monitor your performance at work for the next ninety days. If your performance does not improve, appropriate job action will be initiated. Your decision to seek or not seek treatment will be considered.

The client and the supervisor came to the initial interview at the EAP the same week the referral memo was issued to Mr. M. An intake interview was held and an evaluation made by the social worker who assumed responsibility for this case. The best referral resource for this client was determined to be the local general hospital's department of social services and psychopharmacology where Mr. M had already been receiving treatment for about ten years. The social worker at the EAP alerted the hospital's social-service department of the client's present difficulties. Treatment methodology was reevaluated, and a new plan was constructed that attempted to reconcile Mr. M's needs and the hospital's treatment recommendations and resources. The client's progress, attendance, and cooperation in treatment at the hospital was monitored by the EAP for approximately four months, and then Mr. M's relationship with the EAP was gradually terminated. The supervisor was consulted on approximately a bimonthly basis concerning Mr. M's attendance and cooperation in treatment. Suggestions were also offered to the supervisor regarding conditions that might facilitate the client's rehabilitation. The consulting relationship with the supervisor was also terminated over an eight-week period in much the same way the relationship with Mr. M was terminated.

Discussion

In discussing the situation with Mr. M, he identified several problems. He reported, for instance, that he had experienced extended periods of depression and loneliness as well as mistrust of most people. He also complained of back and neck pains and expressed concern about the difficulties he was having with the hospital social-service department. He also said that he was deeply troubled and disturbed by voices from the devil. Mr. M's previous efforts to deal with these problems have resulted in suicidal and homicidal threats and protests against the hospital by mailing back prescriptions and patient-identification cards.

The primary symptoms identified by the social worker are typical of the schizophrenic personality, resulting in disturbance in regulation and expression of affect in addition to a preoccupation with fantasy and magical thinking, autism, and ambivalence characterizing all relationships surrounding the issue of trust. Secondary symptoms were seen in the form of delusional and bizarre behavior. Efforts to deal with such problems consisted for the most part of establishing a threapeutic alliance with Mr. M and delivering concrete services to him in an attempt to foster a securer relationship. Such a service took the form of reconciling Mr. M and the treatment resource, which was the hospital social-service department.

The factors in the client's contribution to his problem are typical of the schizophrenic personality. He is unable to control and manage affect and feelings (good or bad) in appropriate and socially acceptable ways. He has difficulty in communicating and organizing his thoughts in an abstract manner. He is often preoccupied with irrelevancies concerning job tasks as opposed to grasping central issues and concepts. He is apathetic and unenthusiastic, which often leads to frustration in people who have to work with him. He has no close friends or coworkers because he does not trust people. In his own words, "It's difficult to trust people who know me, and I don't trust those who don't know me. That's my dilemma." To the client, others appear to relate to one another with warmth and intimacy while he is on the outside looking in. Mistrust and fear of closeness and dependency characterize all of his human contacts and determine also the quality of his transference with his coworkers. He has difficulty in accurately perceiving the boundaries that separate him from the outside world, and he has a wish and a fear of merging in a symbiotic union with people. The bizarre delusional behavior highlights the internal destruction within his ego as it attempts to defend against anxiety and to externalize problems—that is, he always projects his performance problems into the work environment or onto others with whom he works.

A number of significant environmental factors contributes to the pathology of Mr. M. They are evident in the work place and the family structure. Individuals at work are fearful and avoid this client as a result of the behavioral manifestations of his illness, and thus their behavior heightens his reaction. Not knowing how to deal with him, people at work call him names such as "a registered nut." The supervisor has found it difficult to give him field assignments that require his interaction with people. In his family structure, there appears to be a high incidence of parental psychopathology and subtle disorders in communication and in the relationship with the remaining parent. As a result of his family life (past and present), Mr. M has learned to protect himself by maintaining emotional distance, preferring his own autistic world to sharing experience with others. There was no evidence presented to indicate that Mr. M was experiencing community-related problems.

In terms of problem resolution, a number of significant and positive factors is present in this client's environment. The first of these is the presence of a job and a concerned supervisor who is willing to take appropriate administrative action to influence Mr. M's decision to seek treatment before the employee decompensates totally, thus avoiding possible extensive hospitalization. A second positive point is that Mr. M does have some outside interests and acquaintances on a limited basis. The third significant factor is that of contrived outside treatment.

Of equal importance, if we look at the client's environment, is the need to address the factors in the client that can lead to problem resolution. Both sets of factors are normal level of functioning. The positive factors Mr. M possesses are: he displays more paranoid tendencies than hebephrenic (hallucinatory, regressive) or catatonic tendencies, thereby increasing the likelihood that his treatment will be effective; he responds well to neuroleptic drugs when he takes them as prescribed; he displays social interests; his intellect is often intact, and he performs well in areas that are not affected by illness; he is able to develop positive transference in treatment; and he is able to introject some healthier defenses through his intellect rather than resorting to a destructive mechanism.

Prior to Mr. M's referral to the EAP, he was receiving one-half hour per month of therapy from the social-service department at the local hospital. Group therapy was offered, but the client declined. Weekly, then bimonthly and monthly sessions with the social worker at the EAP were established and continued under termination. Appropriate medication was prescribed by the hospital and was closely monitored.

Mr. M had twenty sessions with the social worker of the EAP. They gradually decreased in length and time between sessions. There were three in-person consultations with Mr. M's supervisor—one prior to the client referral, one when he accompanied the client to the EAP, and one at termination of the client from the EAP. Ten consultations took place over the phone. The social worker's role was that of mediator and arbiter between the client and the treatment resource. The social worker also evaluated the treatment plan and its appropriateness for the client and problem resolution as such problems affected his job performance. The therapeutic areas focused on by the EAP social worker were supportive casework to establish effective contact with the client to strengthen his ego, to help him in the management of his effort at work, and to assist him in day-to-day tasks (especially work tasks) that we take for granted but that cause great confusion and problems for the schizophrenic and prevention and education by the social worker for the client by discussing and isolating signs and symptoms the client must watch for and ways to cope with his illness to avoid decompensation and hospitalization. The supervisor was kept informed of Mr. M's attendance and cooperation in treatment. He was offered suggestions in dealing with this type of employee in the work force. The supervisor was advised that, when he provided directions to the employee, they should be made clear to him, but not in a condescending manner. He was also advised that people should be communicative and honest with Mr. M. In addition to this, Mr. M should be given a feeling that he has some semblance of control over his work and his environment since he may feel that he does not have control over many aspects of his life due to his medication.

The EAP strikes a delicate balance between the therapeutic interest of the clients and the management interest of the employer. Management is solely responsible for the presence of this program at the work site and will benefit from proper use of the program as in this case. The first priority, however, is to provide a service to all clients seeking assistance commensurate with the various available resources.

It is felt that, with this client, the intervention was appropriate and instrumental in reconciling the client and the treatment resource and was significant in assisting the client to resolve his personal problems that affected his work performance. It was hoped, of course, that the client would become involved in group therapy since the decision to have the hospital social-services department offer it to the client was based on the presenting therapeutic needs of the client; however, as a result of the EAP intervention, the client did not decompensate to the point of requiring hospitalization.

Finally, as a consequence of this intervention, the employer became a fully participating member agency in the EAP consortium.

The Corporate Woman as the Troubled Employee
Carvel Taylor

Ann is an employee of a large financial corporation that employs over 10,000 people. The work sites are scattered throughout the country. Ann works in the central office in a high-rise office building that holds 6,000 employees.

The corporation is a well-established business with close ties to other like enterprises. Traditionally, the business has had older men as managers and top executives. Women and minorities have held clerical or, at most, low-level supervisory jobs. Thus, clerical workers did not expect to be promoted to or to strive for management-level positions. In fact, clerical workers were not encouraged to learn more than the job they presently occupied. People who did or who wished to increase their skills were considered troublemakers. On the one hand, the work situation was comfortable, almost familylike—the boss, usually a fatherly older man, with female workers who did their clerical jobs mostly without complaint. On the other hand, initiative was not rewarded, and the talents of many people were ignored or turned aside. It is not surprising that the turnover in the clerical ranks was high, costly, and uncontrollable. People worked at these jobs long enough to learn the business, then they transferred to another, similar company with better pay and chance of advancement.

About five years ago, management changed and so did the work climate. Gone was the fatherly work environment, the familylike atmosphere, and a real revolution hit the company. Everything was reorganized, the work was refocused and redesigned in a functional work model, deadwood was cleared away, and a new group of managers trained in up-to-date management techniques was hired. As a result, many female managers were hired or promoted. There was a new emphasis on job performance, on production, and on monitoring both in quantifiable terms.

Ann was hired in the second year of the reorganization to be a manager in one of the staff-support departments. She was assigned fifteen employees, three of whom were allocated among the three supervisors. All fifteen people had worked together in the previous organization, some had been with the company for as long as twenty years, and one of the supervisors earlier had applied for Ann's job. Ann knew that this employee was still angry about Ann's being hired. Ann's manager had also been with the company for a long time was also new in his present position, having been transferred from a more-demanding position earlier. Ann had heard that he felt he had been demoted. Ann's manager had a good deal of managerial experience, but he knew nothing of the complexities of this area and had never managed a female executive before. The company grapevine believed this whole department was the worst—that is, filled with incompetent and lazy people. Ann did not know this before she accepted the job, but being astute, she found out quickly.

The EAP is designed as a broad-brush program—that is, many kinds of assistance are offered. Employees request help for legal, financial, and other environmental or emotional problems. In addition, the alcoholism and drug-abuse program is administered by the counselors. The program has consistently served about 15 percent of the employee population per year. Managers also consult with the counselors when an employee becomes upset or is unable to perform the job.

Ann first came to the EAP to get advice on managing an employee. Ann is thirty-two, an attractive, well-dressed, "new-wave," executive woman. Everything fit—the gold chains, silk blouse, suit, makeup. Ann was calm, well spoken, and confident. Her employee was an older man who was, in her words, "not able to do the job wanted for someone in his job grade." Ann had asked his supervisor to design a PERT chart that would quantify the activities of his area. The man had not been able to come up with anything acceptable. She believed that he needed vocational testing, that her employees were not well trained technically, and that this man in particular needed help. Ann explained that she had come from a company that provided more-extensive management training but did not know where to look for help for this employee here. She wondered if a transfer would be possible. The counselor met with Ann's employee on three occasions. She was correct in her assessment of his capacities. He had never heard of a PERT chart and resented reporting to a woman twenty years his junior. He was born into a culture that had a great deal of difficulty accepting women's new roles. He wanted to transfer out of the situation, not face it. Ann arranged, reluctantly, for this man's transfer because she could not understand why he did not want to learn how to do his job better.

Ann made another appointment two months later. This time she was less composed. Ann had had a series of run-ins with her manager. First, he had made a series of verbal demands for information about her area at an odd time—late in the day. When she did not have at hand what he wanted, he became angry and told her that he was disappointed in her performance. Ann was totally unprepared for these demands and had asked her manager to make his requests earlier in the day. He had ignored her requests. Ann had also heard that the manager had spoken despairingly of female managers. She believed that he was setting her up for failure. This belief was strongly reinforced by a warning letter she had received that afternoon. The letter listed a number of problems. Among them were lack of provision of information upon request, insensibility toward employees, and inability to develop and use employees' talents.

Ann was right. A warning letter was the first step to probation. She began to cry and talk about how unfair this all was. "I'm sure that he heard a lot of complaints from X before he transferred out of my unit. He wants it to seem that I don't know how to manage. I don't know what to do now. I'd like to quit."

The counselor pointed out that management on her level was tricky, with a lot of power battles fought. The counselor asked Ann if she knew of a place she could work where there were no power issues. Perhaps it would be better to learn to deal with it right now. Ann said that she had drafted a reply and pulled out the rough draft. It was an angry attack on the manager that mentioned a number of things related to his personal life. The counselor asked Ann how she knew those things about him, and she said he had asked her out for a drink after work and had told her. The counselor then asked what she thought would happen if she used this information. Ann did not understand that there was an unwritten rule that knowledge of a personal nature was *never* used. She said that she did not know this and said, "Then it's all a game." The counselor agreed that this was true and commented that Shakespeare compared life to a stage with people being actors. A game merely implies rules of behavior.

Ann had grown up in a family in which the girls expected to marry young, have children, and not take paying jobs. She never played so-called boys' games—baseball or chess—but loved playing house and dolls. Thus she had never experienced the combination of team spirit and competition that most boys have grown up with. Her former company had been oriented toward women's products and had a so-called women's orientation. In any case, Ann's position here had represented a promotion to a level at which such games are common.

Ann did not have a repertoire of behavior that allowed her to respond to the warning letter appropriately; she could only attack with the weapons at hand—the use of private information.

Being very astute, Ann could see how dangerous to them both such an approach could be. The counselor and she drafted another sort of letter that addressed the points of the warning letter and asked for clarification (the points in the warning letter being nonspecific) and a meeting to discuss each point. A copy was to be sent to the vice-president. Ann was to be calm, pleasant, and professional when the manager became angry. She and the counselor playacted all the possible reactions. This was fortunate, since the manager was furious when he saw that the vice-president had received a copy of Ann's memo. She remained calm and stated that this was normal office procedure in her former corporation. He agreed to discuss the points but remained so angry that Ann decided that the vice-president should sit in. The following day a meeting was held. Ann called the counselor who urged her to be professional and factual and to insist that the manager's complaints be clearly stated so that she could understand what was needed. The meeting worked well. The vice-president insisted that the manager reword the initial memo by deleting the judgmental remarks and agreed with her decision in transferring the supervisor. However, he did agree that she needed help in implementing her information system since her staff did not understand her orders. He reminded her that while her manager had a short fuse, he had had years of experience in getting people to do things and that she could learn much from him. They were directed to meet once a week with a prepared agenda that would satisfy them both. Neither was totally satisfied because both were used to having their way but the following week Ann said she was feeling better, less used, less paranoid. In the last session, the counselor went over the incident, and they discussed what was learned:

> Ann expected management to recognize her ability without documentation or proof of performance. Her manager expected progress reports to come without having to ask. Once these were provided early in the day, there was no nagging.

> Ann expected her manager to be reasonable and attacked him personally when he was not. She commented that she "reacted like women are expected to act—emotionally and hitting below the belt." After looking

at her behavior closely, however, she had then acted reasonably and, after initial anger, the manager has responded in a helpful way. She had not properly studied the social culture of management-level employees. She had disdained the game playing as little boys' games and had refused to see that she was handicapping herself by refusing to understand. The counselor emphasized that social rules are observed everywhere and are either acted upon openly or covertly. Better managers are open and clear about what they expect.

This male manager had never supervised a woman at Ann's level and needed reassurance that she could handle this job.

Discussion

Situations like this are quite common in the field of industrial social work. New roles and ways of communicating and behaving are opening up for all sorts of people. Yet all of us (Ann, her employee, and her manager) are locked into prior cultural and personal expectations. The manager and supervisor knew what to say to wives, daughters, aunts, mothers, grand-mothers, secretaries, cleaning ladies, and movie stars but not to a female supervisor or supervisee. Again, Ann grew up in a woman's culture where, while competition might extend to another woman, competition on a work-related issue was unknown. Women at home cooperate, usually, to get tasks done. When attacked, Ann had no weapons except to hurt the manager pro-fessionally if she could. She had no model for how to punch lightly enough not to hurt but to get the message across.

The counselor must be sure to use a short-term, problem-focused model here and not get bogged down in more past history than is necessary. These are normal, active, effective people so the problem needed to be resolved quickly before careers were threatened. They were fortunate to have a vice-president who understood them both and helped them set up a way to begin to work together. Four sessions completed the task.

Three years later, the same folks are working together. The counselor heard that things were going well for everyone. Even the supervisor that transferred was happy in his dull job that demanded no PERT charts.

Men's Divorce Group
James Agelopoulas

Industry is a microcosm of society with all of the human systems—its frailties and opportunities.

Salaried men in industry are expected to perform and function at an optimal level, but stress created by the divorce process can be interruptive and debilitating.

Fred represents one of many male employees experiencing a divorce, with all of the crucial exigencies and disruptions that eat into a person's organizational and managerial skills. Fred's search for help, which included joining with other male coworkers experiencing similar handicaps, generated an effort that was systematized into a group-counseling format, benefiting Fred and other men experiencing divorce. Fred took advantage of the company counseling service by promoting an effort that benefited his divorcing peers as well as himself.

Fred is a 41-year-old white man employed as a production manager for a large industrial firm in the northeast. He is separated and awaiting his final divorce decree. Fred went to the best private schools and took degrees from Ivy League universities, majoring in English and later receiving an MBA.

Fred considers himself a WASP since his ancestry goes back to Germany and England. His father, now retired, was a noted surgeon; his mother, unlike her middle-class husband, emerged from a lavish and wealthy background. She gladly gave up her acting career, once married, but remained socially active with her circle of friends. Fred recalls his mother as being warm and communicative but rarely at home. Fred's brother, two years his senior, is highly enterprising and commands a lucrative income. Their relationship is friendly but distant. They share the same perception of father—traditional, narrow, detached, and inclined to moralize—while mother is seen as understanding and loving but lacking maternal instincts. Fred experienced his father as rejecting. Father related to Fred in a stilted, condescending manner.

Fred married sixteen years ago. He was in a strange city, away from home, lonely, and isolated when he met Janet. Janet, a second-generation American, came from the so-called other side of the tracks, an extremely attractive woman who was impressed with Fred's well-spoken, erudite manner. Fred had no other option but to marry Janet when she informed him of her pregnancy. His moral code would not permit him to do otherwise. Fred was not seeking, nor did he feel ready for, marriage. He was lonely and flattered to be seen and to be with an attractive, vivacious woman. The marriage was clearly a mistake. He felt this almost immediately. Janet appeared nonresponsive and remote and unable to meet Fred's needs.

Fred and Janet had three children who are now aged sixteen, thirteen, and eight. The oldest and youngest are boys, and the middle child is a girl.

Fred's wife was pregnant with her second child when Fred began his graduate studies. His pecuniary circumstances and preoccupation with school left Janet feeling deprived and neglected. Although she sponsored the idea of further education, she had difficulty reconciling her circumstances. This unquestionably put a severe strain on their relationship. Janet became remote, inward, and cranky. Fred began to feel abandoned and unloved. Janet could not assume the role Fred's mother had occupied with her husband, which perplexed Fred since he expected Janet to follow his mother's role model. Fred unconsciously expected to be looked up to and served the way his mother had his father.

For some years Fred had spurned his father's domineering and nongiving behavior. It never occurred to him that his wife was experiencing similar feelings with him. He experienced Janet as demanding and uncompromising and began to question her motive for marrying him, believing she was more interested in the status he represented than him.

Fred began working at his present place of employment thirteen years ago. He came highly recommended, had an impressive background, and was assertive and well spoken. He impressed his management, was rapidly promoted to his present level, and remained there—plateaued, frustrated, unhappy, and perplexed as to why he could not receive managerial support for job upgrading. Something had gone wrong. Being somewhat introspective, he fumbled around for answers and came to the author for a career discussion. Fred concluded that his aggressiveness was threatening to his manager and that he needed to tone down his enthusiastic suggestions and phase in with his manager's style of operating.

Fred reappeared at the author's door three years later in crisis—his marriage was in deep trouble. His wife could no longer accommodate him and wanted to be free. Fred stated she would not communicate, was hostile, avoided him, and made it clear she wanted to terminate the marriage.

While Fred was able to acknowledge the marriage was unsalvageable, he was reluctant to vacate the premises. His home and children took priority. He fought hard to remain in his home; he followed legal advice and strategies and diligently held his position. The relationship with Janet became stormy and frightful. Fred experienced severe anxiety and bouts of depression. Finally, defeated, he left his home. Fred's functional apparatus faltered, but he somehow managed to hold together. Fred struggled to get his deepest feelings out. Therapy became intense and self-examination painful. His analytical abilities helped—at least he could formulate what was happening and make connections between the past and the present. He labored and fretted over his expenses. He counseled with his lawyer frequently, looking for openings to gain custody of his children. He became so preoccupied with this matter that he could not accept the futility of his efforts. His wife was perceived as an adequate mother by the court family services and was to keep the children.

Fred was stranded and hurt. He needed to think of himself—to reconstruct his life, to appreciate what was possible, and to stop pursuing self-defeating targets. Focus was tightly fastened on this theme.

He began talking to other men in the company who were experiencing separation and divorce and realized he was not alone—that what he had experienced and felt, in many ways, was common to what other men were experiencing.

Fred told the author of his encounters with other divorcing men and showed an interest in meeting with them in a formal group. Arrangements were made to gather together with Fred and other men (the author was acquainted with the majority of these men through a variety of informal and formal contacts and was able to interest them in forming a group). Here was an opportunity for Fred to draw on other men's experiences and establish new outlooks.

The group was formalized. A meeting place and time was set up, and a group task list was drawn up. The men in the group were all salaried and from lower- to middle-management positions. The age range was from thirty to forty-five. They all had well-paid positions and were beginning to fret about their managerial abilities both at work and in their private lives. Only one of the eight men held child custody. Most of them were involved in child-support payments. Those who could not afford separate residences were temporarily living with friends or relatives. Fred was living over a garage with a broken-down water heater, "stretching the dollar to its ultimate limit."

Members were looking for comradery, support, and an exchange of ideas. The majority of group members knew one another and could identify with each other around common life experiences. Being all men, salaried, in the same working environment, and experiencing similar life episodes, they rapidly fused and bonded this group into a homogeneous unit.

Fred became more buoyant and less isolated and used the group forum to ventilate his anger and hurt and to reflect on his own behavior. The group provided Fred with guidelines for appropriate and inappropriate behavior along the time-frame continuum of divorce action and concomitant life adjustments.

Fred was now involved in two treatment methods—individual and group. The individual approach was a method for exploration and identification of active but unclear feelings and a format to understand the workings of his defenses in the interpersonal and intrapersonal spheres. The group provided him with checkpoints, scope, and a feedback system.

Fred was also involved in a series of scheduled sessions with the court family services. These sessions were intended to work out existing tensions and differences between Fred and Janet and also to establish custodial rights. As expected, Fred did not receive custody and was left embittered and frustrated.

Counseling with the author focused on what was real rather than fair. Fred had to come to terms with the court's decision, to establish a sense of himself, and to begin to set in motion a life apart from his family. He gradually emerged from his monastic enclave and began to evolve a single person's life-style.

Members of the group sensed Fred's fear of rejection and isolation and encouraged him to externalize his fears. Fred's fear of rejection dated back to his relationship with his parents, particularly his father, who in Fred's eyes was critical, polemic, and autocratic.

Fred expressed a concern, shared by other group members, that management would question his effectiveness as an employee and human being. The divorce process is fraught with stress and uncertainty that can make a person such as Fred feel taxed and spent. How would such a debilitating experience affect the status and reputation of Fred and his co-group members in the eyes of management? Would their bosses understand what they were going through? What they feared the most, on one end of the spectrum, was boss-employee distance and, at the other end of the spectrum, an overconcerned, oversolicitous, and funereal, managerial attitude toward them. Neither would be acceptable to him. Members believed that an honest, open evaluation of their work by their bosses would serve as an indicator of their performance and overall functioning.

While they did not want to be treated as cripples, nor harshly, acknowledgment that they were experiencing critical life changes was paramount. A few of their bosses who had gone through divorces could easily identify with them and respond appropriately. Others were sympathetic but reluctant to approach the divorcing employee lest it be viewed as interference.

In summary, the group members were seeking an open, comfortable working relationship with their bosses, with periodic updates of their performance, along with recognition of the coexistence between lowered job effectiveness and stress.

Conversely, members needed to learn that they had the responsibility of informing their bosses that divorce-related stress at times would affect their functional apparatus and that they could request job assignments they could handle without error.

Fred found his boss responsive. He kept his manager informed of his leave schedule for court, family-service appearances, and emergency meetings with his lawyer. With managerial support, Fred was able to meet the requirements of his job. A company support system that included realistic job expectations had provided Fred with reassurance and confidence. As a result, stress was lowered and Fred's functional abilities increased.

Other group members emulated Fred's approach to his management and found their bosses cooperative and willing to issue performance reviews as an indicator of quantitative and qualitative work output. This latter point proved extremely important to members—knowing their capabilities while under peaks of stress helped them to determine their level of ego functioning.

Fred was experiencing anguishing anxiety and hurt over his children's reluctance to see him. Production demands were up and a ten-hour work day was not unusual. The pressure was intense, and Fred's mettle was being tested. Fortunately, a newly established relationship with a responsive young woman took some of the sting away from Fred's torment.

The group promoted and encouraged life additives to fill in the vacuum and imparted a conservation-of-energy approach to Fred's problem. They encouraged him to divert from feelings of rejection by building new social modalities. Members talked about the necessity of adapting to the here-an-now realities—namely, work, new and comfortable social encounters, and perspective. An awareness of one's needs, functional capabilities, and a problem-solving style in keeping with one's own individuality became a trademark of this group.

Discussion

The group has been meeting for three-and-a-half years. Three members are left from the original group. New members coming into the group are screened by the author for matching. An attempt is made to match incoming members in their life processes with the incumbent members in order to minimize retrogression and to assure the maintenance of group continuity. This has been an important feature of this group—an expectation that new members join them as rapidly as possible at the same stage of emotional and social growth at which the group is. Fred, who refers to himself as a charter member, still holds membership. Although there has been turnover in membership, group norms have been maintained. Intensity and investment has been high and participation active. The group has emerged from discussing material and legal items to self-awareness and life-style items. The group learned that each member had to travel his own course and adapt according to his traits, but a commonality existed in their emergency, phase by phase, from self-defeat and isolation to a series of new and expanding social experiences, which helped them to identify with one another and to match experiences. Social expansion and movement has been strongly supported and promoted by the group; it has a rhythm of its own that beats out a message of growth.

Members, satisfied with what was happening in the group, spoke of their divorce experiences to other men outside of the group, and knowledge of the group's existence circulated and drew in new members. Fred was active in spreading the word and offered himself as a resource to colleagues by sharing his experiences with them and encouraging membership into the group when appropriate.

The group requested that the author invite the vice-president of the personnel division and the manager of the counseling department to one of their meetings to hear about the men's group. Members were eager to share with them the importance of a group mechanism for salaried employees and to articulate what happens to men in the work world who are going through a divorce. The vice-president and manager sat with the group members, listened, agreed the problem was real, and saw a value in sensitizing and educating company heads to the perils of divorce and its affect on work life. Fred spoke eloquently at this meeting and vigorously stressed that the divorcing man did not want to be treated as an anomaly but as a healthy person going through a long passageway with many confusing twists and turns; he wanted to be looked upon as a person under stress who was challenged to his maximum capabilities within the limits of his functional capacities.

The vice-president and counseling manager responded by suggesting a plan for the distribution of educational material to personnel throughout the company on the subject of divorce and the job. Members willingly cited their divorce/job experiences and spoke out on the importance of maintaining a sense of belonging to the organization while going through the trials of a divorce. The assurance of understanding and respect for one's abilities, while under disruptive stress, they found to be integrative.

The salaried male group members expressed gratitude that they worked in a company that had a counseling resource willing to develop a format that was both supportive and useful to them. Fred, the charter member, had been the stimulus behind the development of the men's group. He worked in an organization that had had the foresight to include in its task force human specialists. The philosophy of this company extends beyond the usual benefit package. It includes a genuine interest in employees' careers and well-being.

Fred, the inspirational leader, and the other men learned that company resources could be extended beyond their usual activity level to accommodate a special need—that is, a men's divorce group. They also learned that they, as a group, could call to the attention of company heads the need for a special service for divorcing men and promote its usage companywide.

The men's divorce group became a special-interest group that was able to identify common experiences and hardships among divorcing men. The dynamic interfacing between a group of men and an industrial counselor and, later, concerned members of the company hierarchy is an exciting example of the potential for human development in an organization that sanctions an exploratory and developmental process leading to a designed human service.

The possibilities for human services for groups or individuals with a common interest and need is unlimited; men, women, hourly or salaried employees, or any groupings among varied elements of people in an employee population needing service and able to identify a problem can be the beneficiary of imaginative programming in an industrial setting.

Child Abuse in the Military
Kate A. Powell

This case study is by a clinical social worker employed in the military setting. The socal worker, working with the family, is the family-advocacy representative in the medical center, which provides for the medical care of the military personnel and their dependents. The medical center provides inpatient care, emergency medical service, and extensive outpatient services. The family-advocacy representative provides crisis-intervention services and referral for all child-abuse and spouse-abuse cases. Therapy and supportive counseling are provided during the crisis period, and referral is made if extended counseling is indicated or requested. This naval regional medical center provides medical care for a military base that includes approximately 30,000 active-duty military personnel and their dependents.

This case involves a family (the Vs) with a three-and-a-half-year-old child who was diagnosed as having a fracture of the right femur. The physician indicated that the fracture did not appear to be an accident. There were also old, healing bite marks. With this information and the vague history of the accident, there were strong indications of child abuse. The final diagnosis was a special fracture of the right femur and multiple human bites in various stages of healing, consistent with nonaccidental trauma.

Following admission to the hospital and the diagnosis, referral was made in compliance with the state laws to the Dependent Children Section of the County Department of Public Welfare and to the police department that has jurisdiction based on the established residence where the injury occurred. The child lived on the military base, therefore referral was made to the family-advocacy officer of the provost marshal's office (the military-police department).

The mother was seen soon after admission and regularly throughout the child's hospitalization. The mother visited the child regularly and provided reassurance and company during his hospital stay of nine days.

An investigation was conducted by the social worker from the Dependent Children Section and the provost marshal's office to determine whether the case would be filed in juvenile court by the district attorney. This was a traumatic experience for all involved, and the threat of a child's being removed from parental custody was an ever-present possibility.

On-going supportive services were provided for the parents, especially the mother, who visited the hospital daily while the child was hospitalized. She appeared to be extremely anxious, tense, and mildly depressed.

The public health nurse was already involved with the family because of the mother's Hansen's disease (leprosy). She knew all of the family and had established a positive supportive relationship with Mrs. V, who turned to her at this time requesting her to support her claim of being a good mother since she was feeling very insecure and vulnerable.

The social worker, along with the client, found and identified some specific problem areas that were to be worked on. Since the child only spoke a few words of English, he was not directly involved as a client. The stepfather was not motivated to participate in counseling, and his male-dominated cultural background (Somoan-American) made it difficult for him to involve himself in counseling. He left for a year-long tour of duty in Japan within six weeks after the incident. Over his wife's and the public health nurse's objections, he moved his wife and their children into the home of his mother and stepfather. This was his way to continue having control over the family while he was away. The husband is very demanding and controlling.

The family had been living in on-base housing and could have continued to live in the same house during the husband's absence. Ms. V had previously managed the home alone. The public health nurse had attempted to deal with some of the family problems in the past so she was not new to this situation.

Several factors were identified as contributing to the problem: the father's separation from the family; the family's move from their house to the mother-in-law's home; cultural factors that give the husband's parents a controlling position; the family's isolation from the community in which they had made friends, causing a lack of easy access to the military-base facilities including the medical center that they had previously had; Mrs. V's physical abuse by her husband and by her previous husband; and Mrs. V's poor relationship with her husband's family that caused her much unhappiness. They treated her as a servant and expected her to do most of the cooking and to provide more money than she could afford. She lived under constant threats such as, if she did not pay the phone bill, she could no longer use the phone.

Factors identified in the client and the environment also contributed to the problem resolution. Mrs. V turned to the hospital social worker and the public health nurse. She also received spiritual strength from her church, which was the one outlet she had for herself and her children. She showed that she had strengths, and these strengths were worked with to help her in making sufficient progress to make decisions on her own. She was able to turn to her church to help her in meeting some other needs.

Counseling appointments were coordinated with Mrs. V's clinic appointment for herself and her children. She was also seen on a drop-in basis when at the medical center.

Counseling objectives established between the social worker and the client were as follows:

Help Mrs. V improve her self-esteem and recognize her abilities as well as her rights to make decisions;

Help her in recognizing her strengths and assets;

Assist her in financial planning so she could plan for the move she desired (her expectations at one point had been unrealistic);

Prepare for her husband's return;

Help her learn how to express her feelings and to communicate with her husband and other family members;

Help her with parenting skills;

Work toward involvement with her husband;

Improve the environmental situation along with individual growth to help her to deal with her problems and to see herself as a strong person with an objecive of relief of depression.

As the weeks went by, the situation for Mrs. V and her children grew worse and the tension mounted. She was expected to do most of the cooking even though her hands were crippled from the Hansen's disease.

Seven months after the first referral, the same child was again admitted with a fractured femur. This second time, it was diagnosed as accidental but again it put a lot of pressure on the mother to have to handle the situation plus the added anxiety of living in a miserable situation. While the child was in the hospital, Mrs. V was admitted to another hospital for treatment of the Hansen's disease.

The hospital social worker wrote the husband's human-affairs officer and requested his assistance in clarifying the problems Mrs. V was experiencing in the home of the in-laws. They expected her to pay all the utility bills including the long-distance calls of about $100 per month. She was also expected to buy food and make special payments that consumed all of her income.

With supportive help from the hospital's social worker and the public health nurse, Mrs. V was able to make the decision to move to the home of her brother as the situation continued to deteriorate. The public health nurse wrote the husband encouraging his understanding in seeing his wife's needs. She has been helped in dealing with the situation and now expects her husband to assume responsibility for his instructions to his parents instead of using her as a go-between. She and the children are happier, and that should have a positive effect on her emotional health.

Discussion

There were approximately twenty sessions with the client and significant others including the public health nurse, dependency workers during two investigations for child abuse, the provost marshal and the family-advocacy officer, joint appointments with the hospital social worker and the public health nurse, and the clinical social worker or family-advocacy representative.

Mrs. V wanted her husband brought home because of the second incident, but this was not necessary. If she had not received the supportive assistance during this crisis, his military duty would probably have been interrupted. He is expected to return within several months' time In the meantime, it is felt that Mrs. V is maturing in dealing with her problems and that she has learned she can make decisions on her own.

Intervention in this case appeared effective. Six months later Mrs. V appeared more relaxed and easygoing than ever before. She reported that "things were gong really good." Correspondence with her husband was more satisfying, and they were beginning to be more open with each other. He was writing directly to his mother instead of relaying messages through his wife, which removed his wife from the middle, and the husband had to assume a more-positive role with both wife and the mother. Mrs. V had matured and appeared more self-confident in dealing with herself and her children. She was looking forward to her husband's return and to the family's move back to the base where they could be a united family.

A Female Alcoholic in the Work Place
Diane Fougere and *Karen Shaw*

Jane M is a twenty-five-year-old single woman employed in the customer-relations department of a utility company. She was referred to the EAP in April 1979 on the suggestion of her supervisor who had noticed a decline in Jane's job performance. Having smelled alcohol on Jane's breath during work hours, the supervisor suspected a drinking problem. The supervisor also felt that Jane's lack of self-confidence was affecting her contact with customers and coworkers. Jane was hesitant to respond to her supervisor's suggestion but eventually scheduled an intake appointment with the EAP caseworker.

She met with the caseworker four times before a change in the EAP staff necessitated her transfer to another caseworker. Following her fourth session with the new caseworker, Jane's office moved to another location that would require her commuting to sessions. At that time she decided that she could handle her problems on her own and discontinued treatment.

In August, the vice-president of customer relations called the EAP office because Jane's supervisor felt she had been drinking on the job that day. At this point it was decided that Jane's attendance at the EAP was no longer voluntary but mandatory if she wanted to keep her job. In addition to drinking on the job and during lunch time, Jane was becoming increasingly tense and anxious in her dealings with customers, and her absenteeism and tardiness increased as well. The referral to the EAP was considered appropriate for this agency, and Jane was assigned to a third caseworker in September with whom she has continued treatment.

Jane lives with her parents and younger brother and sister, a family of Irish Catholic descent. She has worked for seven years in the utility company and is currently earning $11,000 a year. She spends most of her workday answering phone calls from customers who call with questions and complaints. She began working at the company following high school and is now third in seniority among thirty workers.

Jane is overweight, has plain features, and dresses conservatively. She does not spend much time on her clothes or appearance—a reflection of her feelings about herself. Initially Jane gives the impression of being happy-go-lucky, an outgoing and talkative person. One can soon detect, however, the underlying anxiety and low self-esteem. Jane is anxious to please others and extremely sensitive to what people think about her.

Jane was somewhat reluctant to discuss her attitude toward being referred and the fact that she must attend sessions in order to preserve her job status. Her ambiguity and resistance were apparent when she terminated treatment during the summer, stating that she could make progress with controlled drinking on her own.

The number of changes in caseworkers meant that Jane did not have an ongoing relationship during the initial phase of her treatment. She was reluctant to verbalize her feelings but made her feelings known in subtle ways. For example, when she arrived for her first appointment with the third caseworker, she supposedly forgot and asked for the previous caseworker. Jane acknowledged some resentment about having to come to the EAP but feels that her boss is concerned and trying to help her.

Jane's statement of the problem includes overeating and excessive drinking. She began to put on weight and drink heavily following high school graduation seven years before. She states that things were great before that. She felt that her problems had worsened in the last two or three years. During that time she had become depressed over her father's increased drinking, his withdrawal from the family, and his personality changes. Jane was concerned about trying to break her negative pattern of overeating and drinking heavily.

In the past, Jane had been able to abstain from alcohol from January until April 1979. The fact that her initial referral to EAP was in April indicates that her drinking immediately became problematic. She had never sought professional help before for any of her problem areas. She had gone to a diet workshop in her attempt at weight loss and had minimal and short-term success.

Jane's caseworker diagnosed her as experiencing early-stage-alcoholism symptoms with some middle-stage signs. She was also trying to cope with her father's alcoholism. At that time her own drinking had progressed to a crucial phase. Her job had become more pressured and the drinking that had served as relief and escape was now interfering with and adding more tension to her job. The stress of her job and family situation had put pressure on her ineffective coping abilities. Jane had not been able to develop into an autonomous, self-sufficient, and responsible adult. She did not have a strong sense of personal identity and had poor self-esteem. She felt influenced and directed by those around her, especially her mother and father. She sought to please people and to let them control her and her impulses. This allowed her to reject responsibility for her own behavior. This passivity and dependence went hand in hand with her feelings of anger when needs were not satisfied.

Alcoholism is prevalent on both sides of Jane's family. Her mother's father and father's mother were both alcoholic. Jane mentioned that several aunts and uncles on both sides have drinking problems. Jane's maternal grandfather was able to attain sobriety midway through life. Her grandmother had died two years before without getting help for her alcoholism. After her death, according to Jane, her father's drinking became problematic. This information may be correct, but the family's denial has been of long standing.

Alcoholism is a complex disease, the etiology of which is still being researched. It cannot be simply understood as a personality disorder. Alcoholism may be the result of many factors including family, culture, heredity, and personality. Jane's alcoholism appears also to be part of her identification with her father and to some degree defines her role in the family system.

Jane is a passive-dependent personality and has many unfinished tasks, particularly among preoedipal issues. She has not separated from her parents, and they seem to encourage her childlike dependence on them. A connection can be seen between Jane's strong dependency needs and her anger when her needs are not satisfied. Her anger at her father's disappointing qualities, coupled with strong dependency needs, arouses considerable anxiety in Jane. She seeks relief in drinking and eating, and these are also ways of acting out. Separation is a key unresolved issue of Jane's.

Jane appears to be fixated at the oral-dependent level of development, using food and liquid as substitutes for love and security. Jane does not feel self-directed and does feel helpless under the influence of external forces. She lacks inner control for her impulses. Food and alcohol bring immediate gratification.

Jane is not a healthy person. Her obesity is a health problem that aggravates or causes her high blood pressure. Jane's mother and sister are overweight, and her father has high blood pressure. She has many somatic complaints including headaches, for which she has taken a muscle relaxant. She experiences feelings of dizziness, nausea, stomach aches, and various other aches and pains. It is difficult to determine the causes of her symptoms due to the many potentially precipitating factors such as anxiety, heavy drinking, food binges, and high blood pressure.

Jane has been able to hold a responsible job for seven years and is liked by her coworkers. There have been attempts to develop relationships outside of her family, though her drinking has interfered. She has been under much stress at work and at home. Although Jane's job is a source of frustration for her, it is also an area of satisfaction. Her supervisor refers to her as dependenable Jane—when she is not drinking—and she feels good about being a valued employee. Her supervisor likes her and she gets along well with her coworkers.

Discussion

The initial phase of treatment focused on diagnosis and education—that is, determining the extent of Jane's involvement with alcohol and the problematic nature of her drinking and teaching her the signs and symptoms of alcohol-related problems. Sustainment and ventilation were the therapist's basic techniques throughout the early sessions and continued to be employed in some form in later sessions. In addition, as sessions progressed, the therapist recognized the need to bring to Jane's attention certain realities that Jane had attempted to avoid. With confrontation, feedback, and education about alcohol/alcoholism, the therapist hoped to help Jane to see the reality of her situation as her first step toward recovery. Throughout the sessions, the therapist attempted to maintain a sensitive balance between focusing on the drinking and communicating support and the belief that Jane was capable of achieving sobriety.

While the long-term-treatment goal was the achievement and maintenance of sobriety, immediate objectives centered around Jane's satisfactory work performance. Once Jane recognized her symptoms as alcoholic, the active treatment phase would begin. This would include goals of increasing coping abilities without the use of alcohol or other drugs and finding gratification to replace the alcohol and, eventually, the overeating. The therapist recognized that Jane needed help in increasing her self-understanding and self-esteem and in learning healthy ways to express her feelings, particularly anger. Jane also needed much support and encouragement to gain sobriety and to live in a more-dependent life-style.

The treatment plan included weekly individual sessions focusing on those areas just mentioned. As treatment continued into the fourth month, several changes began to take place. The therapist began to confront Jane with the seriousness and extent of the drinking problem and initially met with resistance from Jane, who minimized and denied such a problem. As Jane began to acknowledge the problematic nature of her drinking, the therapist went one step further in pointing out Jane's lack of commitment to accepting abstinence as an alternative to her present drinking pattern. Jane slowly started to honestly examine her drinking, at which time her underlying depression and feelings of worthlessness became apparent. She admitted to the therapist her feelings of hopelessness, almost despair, and fright regarding her drinking. She abstained from alcohol for a one-week period and began to experience withdrawal symptoms such as shakiness, nervousness, nausea, and dizziness—a feeling of wanting to die. The therapist described addiction and withdrawal to Jane to help her understand what she was experiencing and that it was normal to go through withdrawal. The therapist patiently pointed out to Jane her history of binge drinking followed by abstinence, only to be followed by another drinking bout. Jane began to see the futility of looking for reasons for her excessive drinking without first stopping the drinking. She also recognized the ineffectiveness of her attempts to moderate her drinking; any drinking, she came to realize, always led to excessive drinking.

As Jane began to acknowledge the addictive nature of her drinking, she appeared to experience a sense of relief—she now knew where she stood and what she could and could not do to help herself. With the therapist's support of Jane's strengths and faith in her ability to recover from her drinking problem, Jane came to the decision that she wanted to attain sobriety. With further clarification of treatment options, Jane chose to admit herself into an inpatient alcohol program for fourteen days.

Jane is now recovering from alcoholism. She is continuing in outpatient counseling with the EAP caseworker and dealing with issues related to her recovery and to other areas of her life. She has experienced several phases of growth and recognizes that the achievement of self-understanding, self-esteem, and self-worth is an ongoing process. The prognosis for Jane is extremely good.

A Preretirement Group within an Industrial Setting
Robert Engel

It has been speculated by the counseling department of a large corporation that the preretirement group of employees might well benefit from counseling through a group experience. When it had the opportunity to have a graduate, second-year, casework student from one of the nearby schools of social work in a field placement, the department decided to attempt such a program. The following goals were established by the field-work supervisor (an MSW) and the student:

Company goals:
To identify the problems and difficulties of the retirement process as it relates to employee adjustment;

To further its efforts in developing and utilizing services to meet this identified population of employees.

Group goals:
To provide support for each group member in order to facilitate mutual assistance during the transition period from employee to retiree;

To examine the retirement process as a life situation and begin to discover avenues for exploration with respect to meeting this life situation with alternatives and options;

To provide an educational experience for group members by sharing and by learning from each other's life experiences.

Leader's goals:
To provide structure and direction so that the group stays within the retirement focus;

To facilitate exploration as to the choices that are available with respect to what to do with this new portion of life;

To help group members come to see that they must take responsibility for what they want to do and to achieve;

To help group members to verbalize the meaning work has for them and how the role change from employee to retiree will affect them;

To help the group to develop the realization that retirement does not mean death.

Upon securing the needed support from the retirement and counseling departments, a vehicle was needed to ascertain whether or not a group of this nature would appeal to preretirement-age employees within the company. With the guidance of the retirement manager, it was decided that all employees over the sixty-four-to-sixty-five-year age bracket and those sixty-five and older who were working on repeatable one-year extensions (approximately ninety-five persons—forty-two men, fifty-three women), would receive a memo on company stationary, through intercompany mail. The memo's purpose was to announce the beginning of such a group and invite those interested to make contact. Prior to the issuance of the memo it was determined that the author could not possibly conduct in-depth personal interviews with each potential group member due to pressing time constraints. This was unfortunate for it has become apparent that at least one individual session should be held with each prospective group member in order to allow for both leader and member to have an opportunity to evaluate each other and review together the purpose of the group; goals of the group; expectations and objectives of the leader; and expectations, objectives, and needs of the potential group member. Although the author could not meet with people directly, it was decided that at least a minimal exploration would occur via telephone.

Out of the ninety-five employees contacted by mail, thirty responded by telephone asking for further information as to what the group was going to be about. Five employees contacted me after groups had begun and were placed on a waiting list in the event that additional groups are developed. After an initial phone contact with the author, six people decided that they did not wish to participate in a group of this nature. Most of these people were mainly interested in obtaining financial information. A confusion that seemed to be prominent among many respondents was the belief that, despite receiving the accouncement memo, the preretirement discussion group was the same as the retirement seminar conducted by the retirement department. I clarified the purpose of the preretirement group by describing it as exploratory in nature, conducted in a supportive style, where group members have the opportunities to share and learn from one another with the focus centered on expectations and potential difficulties posed by the retirement process.

After exploratory phone contact with all potential group participants, it became clear that two preretirement groups were needed in order to keep the small-group format limited to twelve to fifteen persons. The division of group members came as a result of a practical reality that existed. The men, thirteen in number, tended to work at one of two work sites. The women, eight in number, all worked at one work site. The groups were thus formed according to sex: a men's and a women's preretirement group. The men's group was composed of five salaried employees and eight hourly employees with service to the corporation ranging from over thirty-five years to under ten years. Most male group members fell within the ten-to-fifteen-year employment mark. The women's group was composed of seven hourly employees and one salaried employee. Further breakdown points to the divergence within the hourly number were two high-level administrative assistants and five lower-level employees working within production. Length of service to the corporation also ranged from over thirty-five years to under ten years, and most female group members also fell within the ten-to-fifteen years mark. Thus, both groups were composed of highly differing employees with respect to job function, seniority, and status within the company. Many group members knew one another quite well and had worked close by one another over the years. Both groups were conducted in a confidential setting on plant sites. The men's group was fortunate in that its meeting room was located within their work area, ideal for holding group sessions. The women's group was held within a personnel conference room that was not as conducive to group meetings. For both groups, confidentiality was stressed and attendance was voluntary, but it was made clear that regular attendance by group members was essential for group development.

Men's Preretirement Group

The men's group met for a total of fourteen sessions. It was originally scheduled for fifteen sessions, but due to two canceled sessions because of poor weather, the group extended over the terminating date by just one week. Two meetings were attended by guest speakers; the sixth session was spent with the retirement manager; and the tenth session was spent with two company retirees. Attendance at group sessions was extremely high. Most test meetings were attended by at least eleven of the thirteen members. The low at any one meeting was eight members. One employee dropped out after the third session, and efforts to reach out to this employee as to what motivated him to leave were met with no reply.

The men's group was characterized by a feeling of comradery from the initial session that continued through termination. Throughout the sessions, moments were often spent reminiscing through the years of work life at the corporation. The reviewing of changes within the corporate history paralleled the individual group member's examining the history of his own life development. This going-over process seemed to be a necessary ingredient in preparing to retire. Reviewing supports the reality that the human life cycle never stands still.

The group took on the quality of a social club whose membership became well acquainted and was limited to those who joined initially. (The leader took responsibility in limiting membership to those who had joined the group prior to the first group meeting.) The steady and regular membership added to this group's ability to form close relationships rather quickly. The group's format and procedure was styled around a loose structure with a changing focus. The leader explained that his role was to be that of a facilitator of communication and to help shape the direction the group decided on taking. The group meeting began to be seen as a place where group members could come to learn from each other as plans, problems, situations, and ideas were discussed. During the initial session, the leader was active in helping the group members introduce themselves and to tell where they worked, how long they had been in the corporation, and what they thought they might get out of such a group. Most group members stressed a desire to learn about the retirement process and an apprehension about the unknown. Many were uncertain as to whether they should retire, and others were unsure of what they were going to do once retired. Each member saw the corporation as a significant part of their lives, part of their family. Many members praised the corporation's care for its employees, and many pointed to other companies that did not take into account any of their employee's concerns or interests. Most group members had grown up with the vision that age sixty-five was the magic year that marked entry into the so-called golden years. The group began to question what the golden years meant to them, what kinds of activities there were to do, what was left. Many group members knew they were going to retire, but many did not know what they were going to retire to. Uncertainty, questioning, and apprehension was a common group feeling. Group members were at various levels of preretirement planning, but all seemed intent upon discovering different bits of experience and/or information that could possibly aid them.

Understanding and accepting the changing monetary situation that comes upon retirement appeared to be a priority for all group members. The first six sessions of the group centered primarily around discussing and debating whether life would change after retirement with respect to whether or not one's financial picture changes. Social security benefits, profit-sharing accounts, pension plans, annuities, and taxation were areas the group explored and investigated. Since these were items that each group member had some prior knowledge about, they served as a means to help group members become acquainted interpersonally within the group context. They also provided the group with subject material that was not too emotionally threatening for the beginning of the group. As a feeling of trust and connectedness emerged within the group, interspersed within the talk of financial situations, the preretirees talked little about concerns and fears such as changing life-styles, interpersonal relationships, use of leisure time, and loss of identity, prestige, and productivity. The leader gently encouraged group members to explore these territories but did not push them out into the open or force them upon the group. Before this kind of interchange was to flourish, the group seemed directed toward developing a sense of security with respect to financial matters. The group requested that a list of issues and questions be kept so that they might have a record. The leader accepted this responsibility and also suggested that the group might want to have appropriate persons address it at some point in time. The leader encouraged turning uncertainties into knowledge and developing perspectives into viewing retirement instead of haphazardly falling into it.

The group took on the nature of a task group, developing questions in financial areas they felt uncertain about, with the goal of having the manager of the retirement department spend a session answering those questions. The utilization of a task approach helped group members toward feeling a sense of identity as a group and served as an opportunity for members to work together. The list of questions was distributed to all group members and the retirement manager. The sixth session was spent with the retirement manager discussing the areas of concern developed by the group. Many of the areas had been those the retirement department had covered in their seminars and individual sessions. What began to surface was the lack of exposure employees have with respect to serious preretirement planning. Lack of security and stability presented itself with repeated group uncertainties regarding the financial transition that is required upon leaving the world of work. The caring, parental quality of the corporation added to the ambivalence some group members had in separating from the corporation community. For those who had invested much energy into their work role, separating could be traumatic. The creation of substitute work roles or activities becomes confusing, complex, and at times, overwhelming. Cultural and societal pressures opposing lack of productivity became apparent, and lack of training in how to relax was observed.

The group took on a more-introspective and experiential quality after the sixth session. With a feeling of satisfaction that many of the financial questions had been dealt with completely, the group could then begin to question what retirement life would be like. Issues began to surface around how to create a new structure in one's life faced with the looseness of full-time leisure time. Group members began to appreciate the concept of preretirement-planning *rehearsing*, a term that one group member introduced into the group. Rehearsing suggests that one spends time trying out different ideas and actions while still being employed so that one will have acquired some practice in being a retiree before becoming one.

One of the group members retired during this period and became a living experiment for the group. Questions would often focus on what not going to work was like, an incredibly significant change when one considers the role work plays over a fifty-year work life. The group member who retired began to serve as a role model for the group in that he appeared to be successfully moving through the transition period although he had just begun to live as a retiree and had not fully made the switch. The concepts of filling time and choosing to retire began to be examined. Both of these seemed to be important facets for examination. The role of work was viewed in the context of its importance to giving human beings a sense of importance, self-worth, and self-esteem. These feelings about the self were seen as being terribly important to whether or not the retiree is comfortable in being a retiree. Mechanisms for maintaining a high sense of self in retirement years are difficult to come by, yet they are crucial.

The group wondered if they could spend a session talking with retirees who had been out of work for a number of years. The leader offered to explore this possibility and arranged with the retirement manager to have two past employees, both retired over five years ago, address the group. One retiree was an hourly employee who had retired with a modest reserve of money. He stressed the freedom experienced in the retirement years. One became one's own boss of time and activity for possibly the first time in one's life. The retiree stated that it was crucial to be flexible in approaching what one wants to do with free time. The other retiree was a salaried employee who had retired with a rather large reserve of money. This man stressed the importance of actively developing one's self in order to recreate structure and activity in one's life. He explained to the group that he had become extremely depressed soon after retirement as he realized that he had accumulated a large amount of money but had no real importance or work left in life. His experience was one of develping a new structure to his life, with new roles and activities to fulfill. Both retirees encouraged group members to plan and strategize for their retirement years.

Group members came away from the shared session with the two retirees sensing the importance of reevaluating their feelings about the retirement process. One finding that became clear was that one ought to develop alternatives for ways of spending the retirement years. This is easier said than done, and it seemed that many group members were not sure how they were going to go about doing this. On the one hand, banking on one plan seems risky and unnecessary. On the other hand, being assertive and developing new activities and social networks can be a difficult process after the complacency of having the work setting to fulfill this function. Communication concerning fears and uncertainties progressively improved throughout group sessions. Some retirement issues that had been guarded closely began to be verbalized, and the group responded with support, understanding, and identification. For instance, many group members began to see that the workday had created a distance between themselves and their wives. With work no longer there, they would be entering into a full-time relationship with their spouses. Planning with one's wife seemed important so as to reestablish where each other stood now that the job was gone. Many group members pointed to the fact that just because the man was retiring does not necessarily imply that the woman is retiring from her job or chores within the household. The routine that she has established while the man has been away at work is precious to her, and interruptions can create difficulties.

Group members acted to support each others' feelings of uncertainty and helped to defuse issues by presenting information, personal reflections, and alternative ways of looking at things. Retirement began to be valued as a highly personal experience that means many different things to different people. The group allowed for the free expression of a member's views upon retirement. Varying views and attitudes were presented over the course of the sessions, and group members shared responsibility for allowing an atmosphere of free talk to exist. Sharing concerns and explorations of options were looked to as a means to developing a sense of security and confidence upon the frightening moments of retirement planning. Most group members expressed the fact that retirement issues are still very much hidden and that the group served as the one place to which they could come and openly discuss their plans, situations, and concerns. Group members expressed a concern that the processes of aging and retirement living largely go unnoticed and that more information needs to be generated and shared in order to aid retiring employees.

Women's Preretirement Group

This group ran for only three sessions and was terminated by the leader after the third. There seem to have been a number of factors that could have been significant in shaping this development. Essentially, they can be summarized as an uneven balance within group composition; a setting that was not conducive to a discussion group of this nature; irregular attendance and drop out; poor weather that interrupted development of the group; loose design of group structure; and the leader's youth, sex, and relative inexperience in running groups of this nature.

The men's group was composed of varying employees with respect to hourly and salaried persons and had no significant disruption to group development, but the women's group had such divergence among its group members that it never jelled as a united group. Essentially, there were two groups within a group; one, high-level administrative support assistants and, the other, the hourly employees working within production. The meetings were held in a plant personnel conference room to accommodate for the fact that most of the women (six) scheduled to attend the group worked within this plant site. The first session was sparsely attended, with only four of the potential nine group members present. Of this four, three worked out of another location and would have preferred meeting in their own area. The first group session provided a beginning point for the women to get to know one another within a group context. The women expressed many of the same concerns and interests as the men in that they were curious about exploring different issues that emerge when one thinks about retirement. Group members seemed eager to continue meeting after the first session and were aware that additional members would be joining the next session. Due to poor weather, the group did not meet again for three weeks. When it did reconvene, the meeting had to be held in a production conference room, adding to the overall uneasiness of the group members. At this meeting, two problems evolved that seemed to present obstacles to the group's progressing. First, the group learned that one salaried woman who had appeared for the first session was not planning to continue attending. This seemed to be a blow for the three women who had originally attended in that they had appeared to respect this woman and could look to her as a role model. She had presented some enthusiastic ideas about retirement during the first session, and the decision not to participate appeared as a rejection of the other group members.

The second development was that the group took on three new members—two of whom stuck very closely together and appeared extremely timid and one who monopolized group time and was overpowering. The leader attempted to direct the group around the issues that it might like to begin discussing. The problem was that, because of the many communication difficulties posed by the extremely varied personalities in the group, a central focus could not become established. When it became obvious that this group would not be able to work together, the leader took the initiative to terminate the sessions. What became clearly apparent is that the pregroup interview must be utilized to its fullest in order to determine who will be in the group and whether or not the group experience will meet the needs of the potential group member. This group would have trouble developing because, given its composition, members had difficulty sharing with one another in a group setting. The loose structure that provides an opportunity for a group to take responsibility for its own development acted in this case to heighten the group's level of anxiety. Group members tended to deny and avoid their situations, not readily offering perspectives on how they were viewing retirement and what planning they had been doing. They looked to the leader to provide the structure of a seminar, which this group was not, and they had a difficult time in utilizing each other for support, information, and critique. The leader's youth and sex (male) also could have played a significant role in heightening the group's unwillingness to open up and share freely.

Discussion

This case presents an overview of the experience of two preretirement discussion groups run within the industrial setting. Despite the unsuccessful development of one of the groups, the concept of preretirement-planning and retirement services should incorporate the use of support groups to help bring this population of employees together. The impact of the transition from employee to retiree should not be ignored or dismissed lightly. The concept of gradual retirement needs to be developed and experimented with—that is, a mechanism could be instituted for allowing the aging employee to ease out of the work role with the security of having experimented as a retiree. Gradual retirement includes reduction of the work week (upon the employee's request), which would allow for an active rehearsing period as to what is available for the employee outside the work world. Gradual retirement was something that was mentioned by the majority of the preretirees with whom the author had contact. This concept needs further exploration, but it became clear in the groups that, without the implementation of gradual retirement, employees are forced to make the transition without experience or preparation. This leads to feelings of anxiety and depression that are often experienced in retirement years. The development of service to the preretiree and retiree is crucially needed. Preretirement discussion groups are one way of servicing this population of employees.

Summary

With only these few cases, one can see the diversity of problems that any work site presents and what a variety of methods and modes can be used to attack them. The efficacy of generic social-work training is apparent; case work, group work, and community organization tools and skills are all required.

12 Industrial Social Work in Foreign Countries

Extensive computer searches were run on subjects related to industrial social work in Europe and South America. Except for a few articles by Americans who had had brief experiences in foreign countries, little has been written in English about this field in other countries.

In 1978, the author interviewed Swiss and French social workers and was able to obtain material written in their languages by industrial social workers. A Swiss social worker, Christine Neghli, who had studied in the United States, translated several of the Swiss and German articles, and material from them is summarized in this chapter. The author is also indebted to Elise de Vries for the use of speech material that she presented to a group of social workers interested in developing the use of social workers in industry.

Granted, these materials are sparse, but they are presented as a beginning effort for allowing U.S. social workers, businesses, and government to get a glimpse of the services offered at the job sites in Europe and to note the similarities and differences with our own history and practices.

Education

According to Elise de Vries, the Netherlands (Sociale Academie, Amsterdam) has a specialization in schools of social work called "personnel social work." For this specialty, which begins in the second year—that is, sophomore year—they include a ten-week work experience as an unskilled worker and an eight-month field placement in a personnel-social-work setting. The fourth year (our senior year) "includes more-intensive study in social work, psychology, and psychiatry."[1] How typical this course of study is in other universities, and especially in other countries, the available literature does not show.

Christine Neghli, in her translation of *Social Worker in Industry* by Christina Staul, mentions that, in Germany, schools of social work provide only a basic education and very limited specialization. Students thus are seldom interested in social work in industry because they "don't want to work in a capitalistic structured company." She also sees a problem because "the goals of social work in industry have not been clearly defined."[2]

Relationship of the Social Worker to the Company

European plans for hiring social workers to serve at the job site are varied. Some firms, as in the United States, hire their own social workers; some chain stores (for example, Hema, Netherlands) have a central office that provides essential management operations, and they encourage the use of the personnel social workers in coping with internal management and supervision problems. "The division of social work was part of the personnel department, and its activities were coordinated with the other divisions by the director of personnel."[3]

In other countries, especially Switzerland, a central service is offered upon which business and industries may draw, and it is known as the SV service (Schweizer Verband Volksdienst). On its fiftieth anniversary, it published a booklet outlining its social-work standards and services. It addresses specifically workers in industry. In 1972, the SV service contracted with over eighty companies in the German part of Switzerland. The service is

> In charge of allocating and educating the social workers, of adapting the functions to changing circumstances, of formulating working contracts, and of interpreting new methods of social work. It also provides statistics about the work done. . . . Delegating the overall management of the social services to SV means for the company to delegate the responsibility to experts in the field.[4]

Strengths and weaknesses exist in each of these arrangements. European writers are concerned about the loyalty of the social worker as it is split between the company who hires the social worker and the client whom she usually serves (only recently have some men begun to be hired as social workers. SV service hired the first man in 1971). They see the role of the social worker as somewhat subverted if their first loyalty is to the company and its aim of increased productivity. However, when both the social worker and the client have the same employer, the social worker may be closely aware of the client's on-the-job problems.

The contract between the SV services and a Swiss industrial community of Horgan illustrates one kind of arrangement.

1. In this arrangement an industrial community composed of four companies contracts with the SV to provide social services for all of their 2,500 employees. The SV is notified if a worker leaves the community and SV approval is required for any new worker coming in.

2. They administer both case work services and financial aid.

3. The SV, the industries, and the social worker sustain a three-way interdependence with responsibilies and rights of each clearly delineated. For instance, the SV contracts with the social worker; the industrial employer

provides office space and work facilities; the social worker's services are given on the work site to the employees but she (seldom he) is paid by the social agency.

4. The social worker administers funds supplied by the companies. Specific amounts are allocated per client family (200 francs per year), but the social worker may request additional funds if required. An independent auditor controls the administration of these funds, adding a fourth element to the contracting parties.

5. The social worker, via the social agency, presents to the employer annual statistical reports describing the duties and activities of the year.

6. Each of the parties may break the contract but only with six months notice being given. Case reports and folders return to the SV in order to maintain confidentiality.[5]

Services to Clients

Although services vary by policy, hiring arrangements, social-work standards, and as always, the capabilities of individual social workers, nonetheless certain generalities from European literature can be made.

By and large, social services are centered on job-related problems. Individual problems that require therapy, ongoing casework services, family involvement, and problems for which other services are available are usually not served by job-site social workers.

The limits of social work in industry are described in a paper prepared by the Swiss Commission of Social Work in Industry (part of the Association Suisse des Assistants Sociaux, comparable to NASW). The paper draws our attention to the possible conflicts a social worker might encounter when the client's employer is also the social worker's employer. It points out that as the interests and needs of the company change, that is, as the productivity or solvency of company changes or the general economy shifts, so do the priorities and financial capabilities that define the social worker's functions and freedoms also change. The social worker maintains a balancing act between the needs of his client and the interests of their joint employer.

Elise de Vries describes the kind of services social workers address in a company that hires its own.

On-the-job adjustment problems: first employment experience, older worker versus young supervisor, women new to the job, general job adjustments;

Communication problems: between worker and supervisor; between management levels; among disparate groups;

Promotion problems: irrational prejudices that cause supervisors to neglect or penalize workers, motivational factors;

Listening to individual problems: both supervisors and workers often need an objective person to share their concerns or to offer concrete help

Personal problems affecting job: all workers bring their personal problems with them to the job. Problems may be financial, medical, or interpersonal, but all of them effect the workers' productivity. Services may include financial aid, case-work services, or referrals to other agencies for specific or on-going help.[6]

Examples of Typology of Cases

A few examples of the kinds of people served and the range of problems presented are offered by Yvonne Frauenfelder who has work with both the Brown Boveri Company and Kern Suisse:

BBC [Brown Boveri] has 18,000 to 19,000 employees and 5 social workers. The first social worker was hired about 40 years ago. Until a few months ago, they were responsible to the medical doctor of BBC. This is now changed and they are responsible to the personnel manager.

Goal of the social workers is to integrate profit-related goals and needs with needs and goals of the individual. They work mainly with those individuals who cannot satisfy their needs or who do not satisfy the needs of the company. Over and over again the social worker has to question the reasons for unsatisfied needs. Is something wrong with the structure of the department or with the worker?

Due to a progressing illness, a worker cannot fulfill his task any more. He is afraid he may lose his work and therefore afraid to talk to his supervisor. After three sessions with the social worker he has gained enough self-confidence to talk, together with the social worker, to his supervisor. All three together try to find a solution. For the next few months the worker stays at the same job but does not fulfill the same quantity, and after half a year he could change to an easier job within the same department.

A worker suffers from a mental illness. His character changes drastically. The social worker talks to his supervisor, his colleagues, explains his illness, and tries to make them understand why the worker starts behaving so strangely. The social worker shows them how to handle the worker.

A young woman gets transferred to another machine. She does not understand why and does not like her new job, but she is afraid to talk to the supervisor. She asks the social worker to arrange a meeting with the supervisor and to be present at this meeting. The supervisor explains the reason for the change of job and promises to find her more-suitable work as soon as possible.

A worker has difficulty with his colleagues, his work, and his family. Together with the social worker he discusses his main problem—alcoholism. The social worker meets with him on a regular basis and motivates him to join the AA.

A woman comes to the social worker and tells her that she cannot concentrate at work and that she is very impatient with her children after work. Several meetings with husband and wife show that the problem is between the couple. The talks brought man and wife together again, and the wife was able again to fulfill her task as an employee as well as a mother.

A young man got a warning to be fired because he was often absent and his work quality declined. The social worker found out that he just got a divorce and that he still suffered from this. With his agreement, she informed the supervisor, asked for a delay of the firing and helped the man to find a psychiatrist.[7]

Summary

European social workers clearly have a long history in the industrial area. The literature reflects similar issues that are experienced in U.S. practice—namely, conflict between serving the management and client simultaneously, appropriate place of social workers in the company, and so on. What is very clear, even from these few references, is that Europe has a tradition of industrial social work of at least fifty years and that much would be gained from a mutual interchange between U.S. and European industrial social workers.

Appendix A
Plan for the Office of
Employee Counseling
Services

Goals of Employee Counseling Services Program

Planning has been defined as "the ability to capture the future."[1] Over a five-year projection, the goal of the employee-counseling-services (ECS) office would be to provide comprehensive coverage of alcohol, drug, and medical/behavioral services to HHS employees. First priority would be to those problems effecting work performance.

In order to accomplish the long-range goal, three years of demonstration projects and policy development needs to occur. The first year should also be planning and mobilization for implementation.

Value Base

Human-service programs such as ECS need to clarify a value orientation from their inception. Two public laws have clearly mandated programs be implemented to help employees with alcohol and drug programs. OPM has now initiated, and HHS has followed the lead in expanding, programs to include medical/behavioral and emotional problems. By establishing the ECS office in the office of the secretary, HHS is embarking in a major breakthrough in the delivery of human services. It is placing itself squarely in the position of the humane employer who cares about the problems of its employees and sees the work place as the setting to reach troubled employees. Good-management principles, in addition, tell us that healthy employees make productive employees. This is a charting of the agency in a new arena in employee/personnel relations. Although job performance is critical, professional ethics and the Privacy Act principles will be adhered to at all times.

Mandates of the ECS Program

The mandates of the ECS program are as follows:

1. Provide leadership at the departmental level in the planning, development, and implementation of the internal alcohol- and drug-abuse programs in HHS;

Source: Dale A. Masi, "Plan for the Office of Employee Counseling Services," Office of the Secretary, Department of Health and Human Services, Washington, D.C., unpublished, November 1979.

2. Assist in expanding these programs into broad-ranged ECS programs;
3. Initiate development projects oriented toward the installation of a model ECS program in HHS;
4. Develop and implement policy and guidelines for use by departmental agencies in the establishment of programs that comply with the provision of PL 91-616 and PL 92-255;
5. Develop review criteria for assisting program effectiveness on a departmentwide basis;
6. Develop training and orientation programs for supervisory and counseling personnel;
7. Provide a clearinghouse of information on ECS programs.

The mandates for the office clearly show policy as well as programmatic responsibilities. With this as a background, two assumptions have been drawn. First, the office should develop policy that will expedite, not impede, the long-range goal. Such a policy will cut across all programs and will save each program from struggling on its own. Second, programmatically, ECS should not run programs per se. It can initiate models, encourage existing and new programs, and consult with ongoing ones.

An additional mandate was later developed by an agreement with OPM for HHS to provide the model program for federal agencies.

Method in Developing Plan

In order to develop this document, the following method was utilized by the director. She took the first six weeks of her assignment to develop the plan. In reality it is seen as a tentative document and suggestions are welcome. It is also assumed, as with all good plans, to be fluid, and it will change as new responses are received.

Because this is a planning document, intensive charting is not done for each plan/segment. A listing as well as brief explanation is furnished. An end date is given whereby that segment will be completed. Part of that end result is an individual document and/or product. In addition, appropriate experts with HHS and outside are drawn upon for the particular segment to be developed.

Policy to Be Developed[a]

Training Guidelines for Managers and Supervisors

Besides addressing suggestions as to appropriate hours and length of sessions, materials will be developed for HHS training sessions. For example,

---

[a]Note: There is no priority to the listing.

there is no film that addresses the need of the federal supervisor, but there is a need for this. Inclusion of information about the regulations as well as information about the Privacy Act and other relevant material for federal supervisors would be included. It would be hoped that the secretary as well as the ASPER (Assistant Secretary for Personnel) would participate in the film. It should be developed at HHS within its own capabilities. Other materials would also be developed, such as brochures, posters, flyers, and bibliography material.

Uniform Reporting and Evaluation System

A uniform reporting system is the key to evaluating the program. The reporting system must be comprehensive, informative, and yet succinct. The bottom line of evaluation will be the number of cases helped, followup, and how this is reflected in work performance. At present, no model-evaluation system exists in the occupational area which utilizes control groups. It is one of the major needs in the field, and HHS's taking the leadership in this area could be a major contribution to both the federal and private sectors.

Guidelines for Staffing

As we move into ECS programming, questions as to qualifications, credentials, and liability need to be explored. We need to insure that our counselors are protected while our employees receive quality service.

Develop HHS Policy on ECS

We have an HHS policy (no. 792-2) for alcohol and drugs. OPM has issued a Federal Personnel Management letter (FPM) on employee-counseling cases. HHS should review this material and develop one policy that will update the present policy as well as include the new categories.

Implementation of Privacy and Confidentiality Acts

Policy as to how records are kept, where they are kept, coding systems, kinds of forms, as well as other identifying information needs to be defined. Inclusion of training of secretaries, students, and other ancillary staff to insure confidentiality also needs delineation.

Use of Federal Facilities

The law states that, where possible, other federal facilities should be utilized for employee treatment. Public health hospitals, public health clinics, VA hospitals, to name a few possibilities, need exploring as to resource potential.

Development of Policy for Supervisory Referrals

In order to insure that the supervisor and counselor are clear in their responsibilities, referral procedures for troubled employees should be clearly delineated. Past experience has shown the average supervisor waits years before doing something about a troubled employee although the following signs were usually in the record. Initiating earlier referrals is essential for a viable ECS program. The key areas that mark problem employees are

Letters of reprimand,	Letters of warning,
No step increases,	Letters of admonishment,
Loss of annual leave,	Suspension,
Leave without pay,	Demotion,
Disability retirement,	Furlough without pay,
Overuse of sick leave,	Fitness for duty report.

Program Responsibilities

Model-Program Initiation

A variety of models that may have relevance to a number of other programs should be developed. The following is a beginning list of possible suggestions thus far:

Mini model program for Office of the Security (OS) downtown southeast complex;

A consortium with HHS, the lead agency;

Program emphasizing reaching employees with drug (both legal and illegal) problems;

Full inhouse program with counseling included;

Program emphasizing the other victims of alcoholism;

Reaching employees in areas other than regional offices;

Program for HHS American Indian employees;

Program for Puerto Rican employees;

Program for Chicanos.

It should be noted that already two unique program operations exist as models that should continue and appropriately be documented. They include a consortium with thirty-two federal agencies in Boston and Planner's Studio contract with NIAAA to implement a women's program at JFK Federal Center as well as at Textron.

Consulting and Providing Information

It is an appropriate role to provide information and assistance to other federal programs that are starting. This service will also be offered to private programs and a monthly compilation will be kept of these services.

Consulting with Managers and Supervisors

Consultation is a growing service of ECS. It is important to develop this program component. Clearly this can cross the programmatic as well as policy areas. The more this service is made available to supervisors, the more they will be willing to consider referring an employee rather than waiting too long.

Organizational Design

There are fifteen organizational units. An ECS administrator will direct each, and the units will include the following:

Ten regional offices;

Southwest complex, Washington, D.C.;

Rockville/Hyattsville;

SSA (Social Security Agency) Baltimore;

HCFA (Health Care Finance Agency) Baltimore;

NIH (National Institutes of Health) Campus.

Staffing

ECS administrators are being hired to direct each of the organizational units. They in turn will be responsible for the development of the program and will determine whether it becomes an outside contract, an inhouse counseling program, or a consortium.

The Washington office, in addition to the director, has an HHS fellow as well as full-time staff.

Appendix B
Position Descriptions:
American Red Cross

For Personnel Use Only

American Red Cross
Position Description

Date prepared _____

Position Title: ___Field Director II___ Name: _____
Service: _____SAF_____ Location: NHQ ☐ Other ☒
(Please specify) _____
Reports to: Title: _____ Name: _____

1. Summarize the overall purpose of your duties and the end result of what you do—that is, what is your primary function at the Red Cross?

   To see that all Red Cross programs and services at military installations or hospitals are carried out within established policies and guidelines.

2. List your major duties in order of importance. Emphasize *what* you do rather than *how* you do it. Begin each duty with an action verb—for example, prepare, manage, conduct, investigate, file, or record.

   a. Directs, administers, and coordinates Red Cross operations at a military installation or hospital;
   b. Supervises, evaluates, and is responsible for development of volunteer and paid staff;
   c. Maintains casework standards to assure quality service for military personnel and their families and provides direct services as needed;
   d. Interprets Red Cross programs and maintains effective working relationships with the military community, Red Cross associates, and other agencies and groups engaged in welfare and recreation activities;
   e. Carries accountability for Red Cross funds and property;
   f. Maintains files and records and submits reports as required;
   g. Develops and maintains an effective plan for after-hours coverage;
   h. Performs related duties as assigned.

215

3.   Please complete the organization chart, identifying your position.

Total number of employees supervised by you (if applicable):

Directly: _____

Indirectly: _____

4.   Give specific examples of the types of decisions you make.

a.   On your own authority. Matters related to office administration; casework; expenditures including financial assistance within policy and budgetary limitation; duty assignments and leave schedules for staff; selection, placement, and training of volunteers on installation; selection, training, and assignment of per diem workers and regular clerical staff within budgetary limitations; local training and developmental experiences for staff.

b.   Which require approval of a higher authority. Personnel actions related to promotion, reassignment, or probation of regular professional or clerical staff; staff training and developmental experiences beyond local level; staffing levels; jurisdictional coverage; discontinuance of loan-collection efforts; acquisition and disposition of nonexpendable Red Cross property.

5.   What are the minimum work experience and/or level of education necessary to perform your job? If applicable, include special skills required and/or unusual working conditions.

Graduation from an accredited four-year college or university, preferably with a major in social science, social work, personnel management, business administration, or community organization. In lieu of the college degree, successful work experience and demonstrated ability in social-welfare activities or in a closely related field may be considered equivalent. Successful experience as a FDI with overseas experience or CWS, preferably with overseas experience. Demonstrated success in administration, supervision, working with volunteers, and military-community relationships.

Prepared by: _____
(Signature)

I reviewed the information provided in this description, and I certify that it accurately describes the position.

Reviewer: _____   Date Reviewed: _____
(The Reviewer is the immediate supervisor)

For Personnel Use Only

American Red Cross
Position Description

Date prepared _____

Position Title: __Casework Supervisor__ Name: _____
Service: _____SAF_____ Location: NHQ ☐ Other ☒
                                        (Please specify) _____
Reports to: Title: _____ Name: _____

1. Summarize the overall purpose of your duties and the end result of what you do—that is, what is your primary function at the Red Cross?

   Purpose is to maintain case work standards to insure maximum quality of American Red Cross social services.

2. List your major duties in order of importance. Emphasize *what* you do rather than *how* you do it. Begin each duty with an action verb—for example, prepare, manage, conduct, investigate, file, or record.

   a. Supervises the paid and volunteer staff in their client-related functions and plans for their development in casework.
   b. Evaluates the casework services and identifies trends and developments.
   c. Confers with military medical and administrative personnel regarding clients and their needs.
   d. Assists in interpreting Red Cross services to the military, chapters, and community groups.
   e. Maintains case fields, records, and related statistical data and prepares related reports.
   f. Acts for the field director as delegated.
   g. Performs related duties as assigned.

3. Please complete the organization chart, identifying your position.

Total number of employees supervised by you (if applicable):
                                        Directly: _____
                                        Indirectly: _____

4. Give specific examples of the types of decisions you make.

    a. On your own authority. Assignment of caseload- and casework-related tasks to volunteer and paid casework staff; local training and developmental experiences for casework staff; approval of commitments made by supervisees for Red Cross services within policy; administrative approval of loans and grants made by supervisees; utilization of resources to meet clients' needs.

    b. Which require approval of a higher authority. Commitments for Red Cross services in unusual or exceptional situations; discontinuance of loan-collection efforts; personnel actions related to promotion, reassignment, or probation of casework staff; staff training and developmental experiences beyond the local level; official travel away from the installation.

5. What are the minimum work experience and/or level of education necessary to perform your job? If applicable, include special skills required and/or unusual working conditions.

Graduation from a four-year college or university with a major in social work or a related field is the minimum educational requirement with graduate training, or a master's degree, in social work or guidance and counseling preferred; successful performance in SAF or comparable experience in other Red Cross services or welfare agency, including supervisory experience; demonstrated skills in social work, administration, supervision, and training.

Prepared by: _____
(Signature)

I reviewed the information provided in this description, and I certify that it accurately describes the position.

Reviewer: _____ Date Reviewed: _____
(The Reviewer is the immediate supervisor)

Endnotes

Chapter 1

1. Shirley Hellenbrand and Roslyn Yasser, "Social Work in Industrial Social Welfare," in *Changing Roles in Social Work Practice*, ed. Francine Sobey (Philadelphia: Temple University Press, 1977), p. 149.

2. Irl Carter, "Industrial Social Work: Historical Parallels in Five Western Nations," Ph.D. dissertation, University of Iowa, 1975, pp. 45-46.

3. Ibid., p. 47.

4. Ibid.

5. Michael Howe, manager, Social Resource Center and Training, Northern States Power Company, telephone interview held on 3 August 1978.

6. Elizabeth Evans, "A Business Enterprise and Social Work," *The Compass*, January 1944, pp. 14-15.

7. Annelise Miro, "Industrial Social Work—Its Principles and Its Practices," Master's thesis, Wayne State University, 1956, p. 6.

8. Ibid., p. 9.

9. Mary Van Kleeck, "Common Goals of Labor and Social Work," *Proceedings of National Conference of Social Work*, 1934, p. 284.

10. Mary Van Kleek, "The Social Program of the Labor Movement," *Proceedings of the National Conference of Social Work*, 1937, pp. 389-390.

11. Bertha Capen Reynolds, *Social Work and Social Living* (New York: Citadel Press, 1951), pp. 53-56. For another account of the project, see Reynolds, *An Uncharted Journey* (New York: Citadel Press, 1963), pp. 243-259.

12. Reynolds, *Social Work*, pp. 56-57.

13. Reynolds, *Uncharted Journey*, p. 246.

14. Ibid., pp. 15, 339-340.

15. Civil Service Commission, Departmental Circular, (Washington, D.C.: Government Printing Office, July 10, 1942).

16. Marshall Stalley, "Employee Counseling in the Federal Service," *The Compass*, January 1944, pp. 19-24.

17. Gilbert Hudson, executive director, Hudson-Webber Foundation, telephone interview on 4 August 1978.

18. Harry Levinson, "Employee Counseling in Industry: Observations of Three Programs," in *Industrial Mental Health and Employee Counseling*, ed. Robert L. Noland (New York: Behavioral Publications, 1973), p. 141.

19. Study Group 18, "Coordination of Social Work in Industry and Other Forms of Social Work for the Family and the Individual," *Proceedings of the International Conference of Social Work*, Munich, 1956, pp. 211-212.

20. Herman Stein, "Is There a Place for Social Work in Industry?," Address at Columbia University, 1958.

21. Ibid.

22. Leo Miller, "A Counseling Program in Industry: Polaroid," *Social Thought* 3, no. 1:38.

23. Carvel Taylor, telephone interview held on 9 August 1978.

24. Marion Hackett, telephone interview held on 10 August 1978.

25. Jim Francek, telephone interview held on 8 August 1978.

26. Otto Jones, telephone interview held on 25 July 1978.

27. "Social Casework—Generic and Specific," *A Report on the Milford Conference: Studies in the Practice of Social Work*, no. 2 (New York: American Association of Social Workers, 1929), p. 3.

28. Helen Harris Perlman, "Social Casework," in *Encyclopedia of Social Work*, ed. Harry Lurie (New York: National Association of Social Workers, 1965), p. 711.

29. Walter A. Friedlander, *Introduction to Social Welfare*, 2nd ed. (Englewood Cliffs, N.J.: Prentice-Hall, 1961), p. 492.

30. Evans, "Business Enterprise," p. 15.

31. Hellenbrand and Yasser, *Social Work in Industrial Social Welfare*, p. 150.

32. Roger Baldwin, "The Challenge to Social Work of the Changing Control in Industry," *Proceedings of the National Conference of Social Work*, Toronto, 1924, pp. 373-378.

33. Leo Perlis, "Industrial Social Work—Problems and Perspectives," *NASW News*, May 1978, p. 3.

Chapter 2

1. Hyman J. Winer; Shelia H. Akabas; and John J. Sommer, *The World of Work and Social Welfare Policy* (New York: Industrial Social Welfare Center, 1971), pp. 7-10.

2. J. Miner and M. Miner, *Personnel and Industrial Relations: A Managerial Approach*, 3rd. ed. (New York: Macmillan, 1977), p. 28.

3. Dale Yoder, *Personnel Principles and Politics—Modern Manpower Management*, 2nd ed. (Englewood Cliffs: N.J.: Prentice-Hall, 1959), p. 32.

4. Walter Friedlander, *Introduction to Social Welfare*, 3rd. ed. (Englewood Cliffs, N.J.: Prentice-Hall, 1968), p. 128.

5. William Glueck, *A Diagnostic Approach* (Dallas: Business Publications, 1974), p. 452.

6. Miner and Miner, *Personnel and Industrial Relations*, p. 111.

7. U.S. Department of Labor, Manpower Administration, *Comparison of State Unemployment Insurance Laws*, January 1978.

8. Commonwealth of Massachusetts, Division of Employment Security, *Unemployment Insurance—Suitable Work Requirement*, Form P-2551, Rev. 2-77.

9. Commonwealth of Massachusetts, Division of Employment Security, *Unemployment Compensation for Federal Employees in Massachusetts*, Form P-3537, Rev. 1-77.

10. U.S. Department of Labor, *Comparison of State Unemployment Laws*.

11. U.S. Department of Labor, Employment Standards Administration, *State Workers' Compensation Laws Compared with the Nineteen Essential Recommendations of the National Commission on State Workers' Compensation Laws*, (February 1978).

12. Paul Feeney, "A First: Pension for Stress," *Boston Globe*, 25 July 1979.

13. Miner and Miner, *Personnel and Industrial Relations,* p. 109.

14. U.S. Department of Health, Education, and Welfare, Social Security Administration, Your Social Security, HEW Publ. no. (SSA) 78-10035, February 1978.

15. HEW, *Higher Social Security*, HEW Publ. no. (SSA) 78-10324.

16. Glueck, *Diagnostic Approach*, p. 489.

17. Ibid., p. 490.

18. Ibid., p. 494.

19. Miner and Miner, *Personnel and Industrial Relations*, p. 533.

20. Mildred Arrill, "The Role of Community Agencies and Their Relationships to HMOs," in *Social Components of Health Maintenance Organizations (Institutes on Health and Health Care Delivery: National Conference on Social Welfare; New York: Columbia University Press, June 1975),* p. 30.

21. Congressional Quarterly Almanac 24 (1973):499-508.

22. Glueck, *Diagnostic Approach*, p. 463.

Chapter 3

1. Shelia Akabas, "Labor, Social Policy and Human Services," *The Encyclopedia of Social Work* (Washington, D.C.: National Association of Social Workers, 1977), p. 738.

2. Samuel Gompers, "The Philosophy of Trade Unionism," in *Unions, Management and the Public*, ed. E. Wight Bakke and Clark Kerr (New York: Harcourt Brace, 1948), pp. 30-31.

3. Robin O'Keefe, "Meeting the Needs of Working Woman," *Labor-Management Alcoholism Journal* November/December 1980, p. 129.

4. Leo Perlis, "De-Ciphering Workers," *The New York Times*, 14 July 1977.

5. George Meany, *Basic Principles*, Foundation of the AFL-CIO Community Services Program, AFL-CIO Community Services Committee pamphlet.

6. Perlis, "The AFL-CIO Community Services Program: What It Is and What It Does," *U.S. Labor Bulletin*, July 1978, pp. 3-4.

7. Ibid., p. 5.

8. John McManus, "The Labor Agency—Designed, Developed and Operated by the Consumer-Contributor" (Paper presented at the 21st annual program meeting of the Council of Social Workers in Education, Chicago, 3 March 1975), p. 1.

9. Perlis, interview with author, Washington, D.C., October 1980.

10. McManus, "The Labor Agency," p. 5.

11. Ibid., p. 1.

12. Perlis, *The Human Contract in the Workplace* (AFL-CIO Department of Community Services Council on Social Work Education pamphlet, April 1976, no. 76-810-38), p. 2.

13. Perlis, "The Human Contract in the Workplace" (Central Rehabilitation Council of New York City, September 1978), p. 3.

14. Perlis, interview with author, October 1980.

15. Perlis, "The Nature of Meaningful Work" (Paper presented on ethics and economics, University of Delaware, Newark, 10 November 1977), p. 6.

16. Carl Schramm, "Development of Comprehensive Language on Alcoholism in Collective Bargaining Agreements" (Reprint from the *Journal of Studies on Alcohol* 38, no. 7 (July 1977):1405.

17. *A Joint Union-Management Approach to Alcoholism Recovery Programs* (Pamphlet printed by the National Council on Alcoholism, September 1975), p. 2.

18. Adopted, Thirteenth Constitutional Convention of the AFL-CIO (Washington, D.C., November 1979).

19. Statement by the AFL-CIO Executive Council on Human Services in the Workplace, Bal Harbour, Florida, 25 February 1980.

20. Terry Cook, "Unions Deliver Services," UAW (Paper for course social work in industry, Boston College, Chestnut Hill, Mass., March 1979), pp. 3-6.

21. Cook, "Unions Deliver Services," pp. 6-7.

22. Shelia Akabas, John Sommer, Hyman Weiner, *Mental Health Care and the World of Work* (New York: Association Press, 1973), p. 7.

23. Roger N. Baldwin, "The Challenge to Social Work of the Changing Control in Industry," *Proceedings of the National Conference of Social Work 51st Annual Session*, Toronto, 1924, p. 377.

24. Annelise Miro, "Industrial Social Work, Its Principles and Its Practices," Master's thesis, Wayne State University, 1956, pp. 18-19.

25. Bertha Capen Reynolds, *Social Work and Social Living* (New York: Citadel Press, 1951), pp. 53-56.

26. Reynolds, *Social Work and Social Living*, pp. 54-55.

27. Perlis, "Industrial Social Work—Problems and Prospects," *National Association of Social Workers News* 23, no. 5 (May 1978):8.

28. Ruth Antoniades, *Conference on Social Work Practice in Labor and Industrial Settings*, no. 78-405-19 (New York: 7 June 1978), p. 1.

29. Perlis, p. 8.

Chapter 4

1. Herbert Pardes, M.D., director, National Institute of Mental Health, Speech delivered to the General Mills American Family Forum, 13 May 1980, Washington, D.C.

2. Beatrice M. Rosen; Ben Z. Locke; Irving D. Goldberg; and Haroutun M. Babigian, "Identifying Emotional Disturbance in Persons Seen in Industrial Dispensaries," in *Industrial Mental Health and Employee Counseling*, ed. Robert L. Noland (New York: Behavioral Publications, 1973), pp. 57-58.

3. Alan McLean, M.D., "Occupational Mental Health: Review of an Emerging Art," in *Industrial Mental Health and Employee Counseling*, ed. Robert L. Noland (New York: Behavioral Publications, 1973), pp. 125-126.

4. Dale A. Masi, "Social Services and the World of Work," *Social Thought* 3, no. 1 (1977):3.

5. Hyman Weiner; Sheila Akabas; and John J. Sommer, *Mental Health Care in the World of Work* (New York: Association Press, 1973), p. 65.

6. Ibid., p. 9.

7. Ronald W. Conley; Margaret Conwell; and Mildred B. Arrill, "An Approach to Measuring the Cost of Mental Illness," in *Industrial Mental Health and Employee Counseling*, ed. Robert L. Noland (New York: Behavioral Publications, 173), p. 71.

8. Rosen et al., "Identifying Emotional Disturbance," pp. 57-58.

9. Gerald Gordon, "Industrial Psychiatry—Five-Year Plant Experience," in *Industrial Mental Health and Employee Counseling*, ed. Robert L. Noland (New York: Behavioral Publications, 1973), pp. 150-152.

10. Bertram Brown, "Obstacles to Treatment for Blue-Collar Workers, New Dimensions in Mental Health" (Report from the director, National Institute of Mental Health, June 1976), p. 3.

11. Ibid., p. 4.

12. Interview with Carvel Taylor, July 1978.

13. Brown, "Obstacles to Treatment," p. 8.

14. Weiner; Akabas; and Sommer, *Mental Health Care*, p. 128.

15. Conley, Conwell, and Arrill, "An Approach to Measuring the Cost of Mental Illness," p. 71.

16. Ibid., p. 77.

17. Robert McMurray, "Mental Illness: Society's and Industry's Six-Billion Dollar Burden," in *Industrial Mental Health and Employee Counseling*, ed. Robert L. Noland (New York: Behavioral Publications, 1973), p. 9.

18. Ibid., p. 14.

19. Weiner; Akabas; and Sommer, *Mental Health Care*, p. 143.

20. Michael J. Austin and Erwin Jackson, "Occupational Mental Health and the Human Services: A Review," *Health and Social Work*, February 1977, p. 93.

21. McLean, "Occupational Mental Health," p. 130.

22. Bradley Googins, "Industrial Social Work," in *Social Work Practice*, eds. Bernard Ross and S. Khinduka (Washington, D.C.: National Association of Social Workers, 1976), p. 203.

23. Ibid., p. 202.

24. Weiner; Akabas; and Sommer, *Mental Health Care*, p. 24.

25. Ibid., p. 74.

26. Ibid., p. 24.

27. Ibid., p. 59.

28. Glen Roderick, "Modes of Intervention, Industrial Social Work: Pre-Treatment/Intervention Model Enters Business World," SASS [Alumni School of Applied Social Sciences], (Summer 1977), p. 1.

29. Weiner, Akabas, and Sommer, *Mental Health Care*, p. 61.

30. Donald Norfolk, "Executive Stress," *Engineering Today*, March 1978, p. 19.

31. Ibid.

32. Beric Wright, *Executive Ease and Disease* (London: Pan Books, 1975), p. 23.

33. Michael Roddy, "Overcoming Stress on the Job," *Business Magazine*, 15 May 1977, p. F-3.

34. Ena Naunton, "Factory Stress: Feeding Machines," Knight News Service. Unavailable date.

35. Rolf E. Rogers, "Executive Stress," *Human Resource Management*, Fall 1975, p. 24.

36. Thomas Holmes and Richard Rahe, "The Social Readjustment Rating Scale," *Journal of Psychosomatic Research* 2 (1967):213-218.

37. Wright, *Executive Ease and Disease*, pp. 37-67.

38. Ellen Goodman, "Working Their Hearts Out," *Washington Post*, 23 April 1980, p. A-19.

39. Wright, *Executive Ease and Disease*, p. 131.

40. Pam Proctor, "How to Survive Today's Stressful Jobs," *Parade*, 17 June 1979, p. 4.

41. Sarah Clarkson, "Policeman Gets Retirement on Psychological Disability," *Newton Graphic*, 26 July 1979, p. 1.

42. General Mills Family Forum material.

43. Leonard Moss, Speech to the General Mills Family Forum, Washington, D.C., 13 May 1980.

44. Ibid.

45. Mike Casey, "Federal News," *Washington Post*, 26 September 1980, p. 2.

46. Alan Campbell, director, Office of Personnel Management, "Policy Statement and Definition of Sexual Harassment," Washington, D.C.,12 December 1979.

47. Alice Coudroglou and Lynn Almer, "Retirement: Opportunity or Dilemma," *Proceedings of a Conference on Retirement*, Tempe, Arizona, January 1979, pp. 1-5.

48. John Pelligrino, director, Employee Personal Services, Mead Packaging, Panel discussion at General Mills Family Forum, 13 May 1980.

49. Coudroglou and Almer, "Retirement: Opportunity or Dilemma," p. 7.

50. Robert Engel, "A Pre-Retirement Group with an Industrial Setting," unpublished paper, p. 1.

51. Ibid., p. 2.

52. Ibid., pp. 2-5.

53. Coudroglou and Almer, "Retirement: Opportunity or Dilemma," p. 24.

54. Interview with William Pitochelli, Director Occupational Health, Office of Personnel Management, Boston, June 1980.

55. Leo Miller, "A Counseling Program in Industry: Polaroid," *Social Thought* 3, no. 1 (Winter 1977):37.

56. Andrew Weisman, "A Social Service Strategy in Industry," *Social Work* 20, no. 5 (September 1975):401.

57. Beatrice W. Smirnow, Employee Mental Wellness Programs, Background Paper for 1-2 December 1978 Conference, "Industrial Programming for Mental Wellness: A Case Study Approach," p. 10.

58. Ibid., p. 47.

59. Sheila Akabas, Paul A. Kurzman, and Nancy S. Kolben, "Labor and Industrial Settings: Sites for Social Work Practice," (New York: Silberman Fund, June 1978), p. 40.

60. Ibid., p. 74.

61. Austin and Jackson, "Occupational Mental Health," p. 94.

Chapter 5

1. Public Law 91-616, 31 December 1970, p. 2.

2. Patricia Thomas, "Alcoholism Gets a Treatment from Business," *Business Insurance* 21 (December 1971):15-18.

3. Stanford Research Institute, March 1976. Report no. 572, *Occupational Alcoholism Programs in United States Companies*.

4. Thomas, "Alcoholism Gets a Treatment," pp. 15-18.

5. R. Smart, "Employed Alcoholics Treated Voluntarily and under Constructive Coercion: A Follow-Up Study," *Quarterly Journal of Alcohol Studies* 358 (1974):196-209.

6. Paul Roman, *The Current Status of Occupational Alcoholism Programs: Review and Documentation* (New Orleans: Tulane University, March 1978), p. 3.

7. "Health Maintenance Organizations," Study financed by the National Institute on Alcohol Abuse and Alcoholism, Washington, D.C., 1978. U.S. Department of Health, Education, and Welfare.

8. B. Hayward; W. Schlinger; and J. Hallan, *Occupational Programming: A Review of the Literature* (Raleigh, N.C.: Human Ecology Institute, May 1975), p. 5.

9. Roman, "Executives and Problem Drinking," in *Proceedings of the Third National Conference of the National Institute of Alcohol Abuse and Alcoholism*, ed. M. Shafety (Washington, D.C.: U.S. Government Printing Office, 1973).

10. Roman, *1976 Executive Caravan Survey Occupational Alcoholism Programming in Major American Corporations*, (New Orleans: Tulane University, March 1977).

11. Roman, *Current Status of Occupational Alcoholism Programs*, p. 13.

12. Ibid.

13. Leo Perlis, as quoted in Carol Schromon, *Alcoholism and Its Treatment in Industry* (Baltimore, Md.: Johns Hopkins University Press, 1977), pp. 71-72.

14. Dale Masi, "The Employed Woman Alcoholic: Her Problem, Solutions and Outreach Strategies," *Labor-Management Journal on Alcoholism*, March/June 1977. p. 43.

Chapter 6

1. J. Irwin Miller, "Future of the Multinationals: An Overview," *Top Management Report on the Management of International Corporate Citizenship, International Management and Development Institute*, hereafter *TMR Citizenship*, September 1976, p. 8.

2. Exxon Background Series, "Social Responsibility," Exxon Background Series No. 4 (March 3, 1973), p. 5.

3. Ibid.

4. Group of Eminent Persons, United Nations, "The Impact of Multinational Corporations on Development and on International Relations," e/5500/Rev./ST/ESA/6, New York, 1974, p. 25.

5. Walter L. Owensby, "Multinational Corporations in Less Developed Countries: Impact and Accountability," in the Social Accountability of the Corporation, Institute on the Church in Urban-Industrial Society Occasional Paper, no. 6, January 1975, p. 9.

6. Orville I. Freeman, "Analyzing Corporate Impact," *TMR Citizenship*, September 1976 figure 1, p. 13.

7. Exxon, "Social Responsibility," p. 3.

8. Mark Shephard, Jr., "Setting Goals and Objectives," *TMR Citizenship*, September 1976, p. 19.

9. Prudential Insurance Company of America, Public Affairs Department, "Prudential Social Report," Newark, N.J., 1976, p. 5.

10. Exxon, "Social Responsibility," p. 15.

11. Stanford Research Institute (SRI) International, "International Business Issues Perspectives," no. 32 (Menlo Park, Calif.: Stanford Research Institute, 1977):21.

12. Editor's Foreword in *TMR Citizenship*, September 1976, p. 1.

13. Shephard, "Setting Goals and Objectives," pp. 19-20.

14. Frank Cassell, "The Social Cost of Doing Business" in the Social Accountability of the Corporation, ICUIS Occasional Paper, no. 6, January 1975, p. 3.

15. General Mills, Statement of Corporate Social Responsibility, (Minneapolis, Minn.) p. 3.

16. Corporate Responsibility at Wells Fargo, Wells Fargo & Company, San Francisco, p. 2. *No date.*

17. Exxon Corporation, "Multinational Enterprises," New York, 1974, p. 48 (pamphlet).

18. Exxon, "Multinational Enterprises," pp. 4-5.

19. Shelia Akabas, Paul Kurzman, and Nancy Kolben, eds. *Labor and Industrial Setting: Sites for Social Work Practice* (New York: Silberman Fund, June 1978), p. 44.

20. Prudential, "Prudential Social Report," p. 4.

21. Stanford Research Institute International, *International Business Principals—Company Codes*, no. 25, Menlo Park, Calif.: Stanford Research Institute, 1976:11.

22. Barbara Gamarekian, "Washington and Business: A Social Index for Companies?," *The New York Times*, 29 December 1977.

23. Stanford Research Institute International, article, p. 18.

24. Ibid., p. 33.

Chapter 7

1. "Nondiscrimination on the Basis of Handicap," *Federal Register* 42, no. 85, 4 May 1977, p. 22676.

2. Louise Kapp Howe, *Pink-Collar Workers: Inside the World of Women's Work* (New York: Avon Books, 1978), pp. 26-32.

3. "Study Shows Few Women and Minorities in Higher Education Administration," *Affirmative Action Newsletter*, Boston College, October 1977, p. 3.

4. Boston College Affirmative Action Office, "Affirmative Action and You," Chestnut Hill, Mass., OUD 7/73 AM 175/705.

5. U.S. Department of Health, Education, and Welfare, Office of Civil Rights, "Higher Education Guidelines, Executive Order 11246," October 1972, p. 3.

6. "Major Legislation, Executive Orders, and Other Regulations Requiring EO/Affirmative Action Activity in Employment and Education: A Historical Overview, *Affirmative Action Newsletter,* Boston College, January 1978, p. 2.

7. HEW, Office of the Secretary, Office of Civil Rights, "A Survey of the Executive Order 11246 as Amended," 1975-567-603, Washington, D.C., U.S. Government Printing Office, October 1972.

8. "Major Legislation, Executive Orders and Other Regulations," p. 2.

9. Office of Personnel Management, *Handbook of Selective Placement of Persons with Physical and Mental Handicaps in Federal Civil Service Employment*, Document 125-11-3 (Washington, D.C., March 1979).

10. "Nondiscrimination on the Basis of Handicap," *Federal Register* 42, no. 85, 4 May 1977, p. 22676.

11. "Rights of Alcoholics under Federal Law," Advisory memorandum from the Ad Hoc Forum on Occupational Alcoholism convened by the Occupational Branch of NIAAA, Fall 1976, p. 3.

12. Ibid., p. 4.

13. Sara Ann Foster, "Sexual Discrimination in Salaries against Women Faculty Members: One School of Social Work's Experience," Ohio State University, presented at CSWE Annual Meeting Philadelphia, Penn., 1976, p. 3.

14. Ibid.

15. Mary Scott Welch, "How Women Just Like You Are Getting Better Jobs," *Redbook*, September 1977, p. 178.

16. Cheryl Fields, "In Bakke's Victory, No Death Knell for Affirmative Action," *Chronical of Higher Education* 16, no 17:12.

17. Lorenzo Middleton, "NAACP Calls for Campaign to Preserve Affirmative Action," *Chronical of Higher Education* 16, no. 21:5.

18. Office of Personnel Management, *Handbook of Selective Placement*.

19. Stephen Wermiel, "Three Months After Bakke—A Minimal Impact on Civil Rights," *Boston Globe*, October 15, 1978, p. 73.

20. Comptroller General of the United States, "Employment Opportunities in the Federal Government for the Physically Handicapped," (Report to Congress, Washington, D.C., 16 September 1974).

21. Interview with the director of the Program for Employment of Handicapped Individuals, Department of Health and Human Services, Summer 1980.

22. Ibid.

Chapter 8

1. "The Superfluous Spouses: Excess Baggage," *Foreign Service Journal*, April 1975, pp. 21-22.

2. Dale A. Masi, "Family Perspectives in Being Assigned Overseas" (Paper presented at the International Conference on Alcoholism in Multi-National Corporations, Boston, April 1977), p. 1.

3. Ibid., p. 2.

4. Dale A. Masi, *Exploring Italian Social Work: Columbus in Reverse*, National Institute of Mental Health, Rockville, Md., 1972, p. viii.

5. Masi, "Family Perspectives," pp. 5-6.

6. Ibid., pp. 7-8.

Chapter 9

1. American Statistical Index, "Military-3544-1.2" *Selected Manpower Statistics* (Washington, D.C.: Office of the Secretary of Defense 1978), p. 63.

2. *World Almanac* (New York: Newspaper Enterprise Association, 1976), p. 666.

3. Ralph W. Morgan, "Clinical Social Work in the U.S. Army, 1947-1959" (Ph.D. dissertation, Catholic University of America, 1961), p. 1.

4. William S. Rooney, *Army Emergency Relief as a Social Welfare Program* (Cleveland, Ohio: Western Reserve University, 1956), pp. 5-6.

5. Joseph J. Bevilacqua and Paul Darnauer, *Encyclopedia of Social Work,* vol. 2, 17th issue (New York: National Association of Social Workers, 1977), p. 927.

6. Elizabeth Ross, "Early Efforts of the War Service Office," in *Adventure in Mental Health,* 1951, p. 176.

7. Ibid., p. 176.

8. Martin Nacman, "Social Workers in Mental Health Services," *Encyclopedia of Social Work,* vol. 1, 16th issue (New York: 1971), National Association of Social Workers, p. 824.

9. American National Red Cross, *Red Cross Pamphlet #2* (Washington, D.C.: 1978), p. 13.

10. Imogene Young, "American Red Cross Psychiatric Social Work," in *Adventure in Mental Health* (1951) 228-230.

11. *Red Cross Pamphlet No. 3,* p. 15.

12. *Red Cross Pamphlet No. 2,* pp. 2-3.

13. *Red Cross Pamphlet No. 4,* p. 6.

14. *Red Cross Pamphlet No. 2,* p. 10.

15. *Red Cross Pamphlet No. 4,* p. 6.

16. *Red Cross Pamphlet No. 5,* p. 1.

17. Ibid., p. 2.

18. *Red Cross Pamphlet No. 2,* pp. 4-5.

19. *Red Cross Pamphlet No. 1,* p. 8.

20. Ibid., p. 3.

21. Ibid.

22. *Red Cross Pamphlet No. 2,* pp. 4-5.

23. Ibid., p. 5.

24. *Red Cross Pamphlet No. 6,* p. 1.

25. *Red Cross Pamphlet No. 2,* p. 3.

26. *Red Cross Pamphlet No. 7,* p. 4.

27. Bevilacqua and Darnauer, *Encyclopedia of Social Work,* pp. 927-929.

28. Ibid.

29. Interview with social-work consultant, Walter Reed Hospital, January 1979.

30. U.S. Government Printing Office, *Social Work Officers in the Medical Service Corps,* Army pamphlet (1975), p. 1.

31. Ralph Morgan, "The Army Social Work Program" (Report prepared for Office of the Surgeon General, Department of Army, Washington, D.C., 1970).

32. Morgan, "Army Social Work Program," p. 2.

33. John Kisel and Michael Doolittle, "Specialty Seminar: MHCS and Command Consultation Programs," *Current Trends in Army Social Work,* pp. 154-155.

34. Bevilacqua and Darnauer, *Enclyclopedia of Social Work,* p. 930.

35. Edgard J. Habeck, "Army Corrections," *Current Trends in Army Social Work,* 1968, p. 31.

36. James B. Rosenfield, "Corrections Seminars," *Current Trends in Army Social Work,* 1968, p. 151.

37. Habeck, "Army Corrections" p. 33.

38. Rosenfield, "Corrections Seminars," p. 150.

39. Raymond Marsh, "Overview of the Army Community Service Program," *Current Trends in Army Social Work,* 1974, p. 26.

40. Bevilacqua and Darnauer, *Encyclopedia of Social Work,* pp. 929-930.

41. Marsh, "Army Community Service Program," pp. 26-27.

42. U.S. Department of the Army, "Personal Affairs: Army Community Service Program," Army Regulation no. 608-1, Washington, D.C., 1978.

43. Ibid., chapter 2, p. 1.

44. Bevilacqua and Darnauer, *Encyclopedia of Social Work,* p. 930.

45. Ibid.

46. James M. Timmons, "Human Resources," *Current Trends in Army Social Work,* 1977, p. 127.

47. Morgan, "Army Social Work Program," p. 4.

48. Elizabeth Ross, "The Navy Story," *Adventure in Mental Health,* p. 226; and Daniel Prosser, "Navy," *Adventure in Mental Health,* (New York 1951), p. 140.

49. Vice Admiral John Parentzen, "Surgeon General of Navy," *U.S. Navy Medicine,* 1979, p. 3.

50. Bevilacqua and Darnauer, *Encyclopedia of Social Work,* p. 928.

51. Hamilton I. McCubbin; Edna J. Hunter; and Philip J. Metris, "Family Adaptation to the Prisoner of War and Missing in Action Experience: An Overview," *Current Trends in Army Social Work,* 1973, pp. 76-85.

52. Alfred Kahn, "Mental Hygiene Unit in the Air Force," *Adventure in Mental Health,* 1951, pp. 24 and 28.

53. Bevilacqua and Darnauer, *Encyclopedia of Social work,* p. 928.

54. Stuart S. Myers, "Child Advocacy Program: A Brief History and Status Report," *Medical Service Digest* 28, no. 4 (1977):3.

55. Myers, "Child Advocacy Program," p. 4.

56. Richard Macartson, "An Exploratory and Descriptive Study of the Implementation of Air Force Policy Regarding Child Abuse/Neglect" (D.S.W. dissertation, University of Utah, 1978), p. 6.

57. Ibid., p. 15. See also USAF Regulation 160-38, paragraph 1e, p. 2.

58. Hartson, "Exploratory and Descriptive Study," p. 10. See also 160-38, paragraph 8(f), p. 4.

59. Myers, "Child Advocacy Program," USAF Regulation p. 7.

60. Dale A. Masi, "Model for Mental Health Services in the United States Air Force," (Community Organization Case Study, University of Utah School of Social Work, Salt Lake City, 1975).

61. Harold E. Allen, "The Army Alcohol and Drug Abuse Prevention and Control Program," *Current Trends in Social Work,* 1975, pp. 15-16.

62. Ibid., p. 16.

63. Joseph A. Pursch, "From Quonset Hut to Naval Hospital: The Story of an Alcoholism Rehabilitation Service," *Journal of Studies on Alcohol* 37, no. 11 (1976):1656.

64. Stuart M. Brownell, "The Navy Alcoholism Prevention Program Worldwide," *Alcoholism: Clinical and Experimental Research* 2, no. 4 (1978):362.

65. "Department of Defense Alcohol Abuse Control Program," Summary of Department of Defense Directives and Tri-service Alcohol Programs, February 1979, pp. 5-8.

66. Ibid., pp. 6-8.

67. Brownell, "Navy Alcoholism Prevention Program," p. 363.

68. Ibid., p. 362.

69. Pursch, "Quonset Hut to Naval Hospital," p. 1658.

70. Brownell, "Navy Alcoholism Prevention Program," p. 363.

71. Ibid., pp. 362-363.

72. Ibid., p. 365.

73. Ibid., 364.

74. Ibid., p. 363.

75. Dept. of Defense Alcohol Abuse Control Program, pp. 7-8.

76. Myers, "Child Advocacy Program," pp. 12-13.

77. "Department of Defense Alcohol Abuse Control Program," pp. 5-8.

Chapter 10

1. Advisory Committee to CSWE/NASW Project on Social Work in Industrial Settings, "Review of Specific Goals," 19 September 1977, p. 1-2, N.Y., N.Y.

2. Nancy Kolben, director, "Graduate Education for Social Work Practice in Labor and Industrial Settings: An Interim Report" (Prepared for CSWE/NASW Project on Social Work in Industrial Settings).

3. Lou Ann Jorgenson, "Social Work in Business and Industry," (Ph.D. dissertation, University of Utah, 1979), pp. 135-136.

Chapter 12

1. Elise de Vries, "Personnel Social Work in the Netherlands." Speech delivered to a group of representatives from private industry and government, 26 March 1970, p. 1.

2. Christina Stahl, Social Worker in Industry, Blätter der Wohlfahrtr Pflege, 124 (Stuttgart, Germany: July 1977), p. 147.

3. de Vries, "Personnel Social Work," pp. 3-4.

4. M. Gumfler, "Social Work in Industry—A Model of Social Work in Industry When the Social Worker is not Directly Hired by the Company," Schweizer Verband Volksdienst, Switzerland, 1942.

5. Translation by Christine Neghli of a contract between SV services (Schweizer Verband Volksdienst) and the Industrial Community of Horgan, Switzerland.

6. de Vries, "Personnel Social Work," pp. 5-6.

7. Interview with Yvonne Frauenfelder, former social worker with Brown Boveri, Switzerland, August 1978.

Appendix A

1. Richard Bolan, "Theory of Social Review," *Urban and Social Change Review*, February 1977.

Index

Index

About the Author

Dale A. Masi is the director of the Office of Employee Counseling Services, Department of Health and Human Services. She is also a professor at the School of Social Work and Community Planning and an adjunct professor at the College of Business and Management at the University of Maryland. She has been a consultant to the White House and to many organizations, including the National Institutes of Alcohol, Drug Abuse, and Mental Health; the Bechtel Corporation; and the Stanford Research Institute.

In addition to administering the model Employee Counseling Services for the federal government, she has developed employee-assistance programs with the New England Telephone Company; J.F.K. Federal Building, Boston, Massachusetts; a consortium of nineteen small companies with the Chamber of Commerce at Taunton/Brockton, Massachusetts; Hanscom Air Force Base; and Boston College. She has been sent by a group of multinationals to study problems of overseas employees and treatment the Chamber of Commerce at Taunton/Brockton, Massachusetts; Hanscom Air Force Base; and Boston College. She has been sent by a group of multinationals to study problems of overseas employees and treatment facilities.

Date Due

MAY 3 1 '86			

BRODART, INC.   Cat. No. 23 233   Printed in U.S.A.